FINGAL COUNTY

D1334389

940.54 2591

WE GAVE OUR TODAY

By the same author:

Operation Barras: The SAS Rescue Mission, Sierra Leone 2000

WE GAVE OUR TODAY

BURMA 1941–45

WILLIAM FOWLER

Weidenfeld & Nicolson
LONDON

First published in Great Britain in 2009
by Weidenfeld & Nicolson

1 3 5 7 9 10 8 6 4 2

© William Fowler 2009

All rights reserved. No part of this publication may be
reproduced, stored in a retrieval system, or transmitted,
in any form or by any means, electronic, mechanical,
photocopying, recording or otherwise, without the prior
permission of both the copyright owner and the above publisher.

The right of William Fowler to be identified as the
author of this work has been asserted in accordance
with the Copyright, Designs and Patents Act 1988.

A CIP catalogue record for this book
is available from the British Library.

ISBN 978 0 297 85337 4

Typeset at The Spartan Press Ltd,
Lymington, Hants

Printed and bound in the UK by
CPI Mackays, Chatham ME5 8TD

The Orion Publishing Group's policy is to use papers
that are natural, renewable and recyclable products and
made from wood grown in sustainable forests. The logging
and manufacturing processes are expected to conform to
the environmental regulations of the country of origin.

Weidenfeld & Nicolson

The Orion Publishing Group Ltd
Orion House
5 Upper Saint Martin's Lane
London WC2H 9EA

An Hachette UK company

www.orionbooks.co.uk

CONTENTS

MAP SECTION

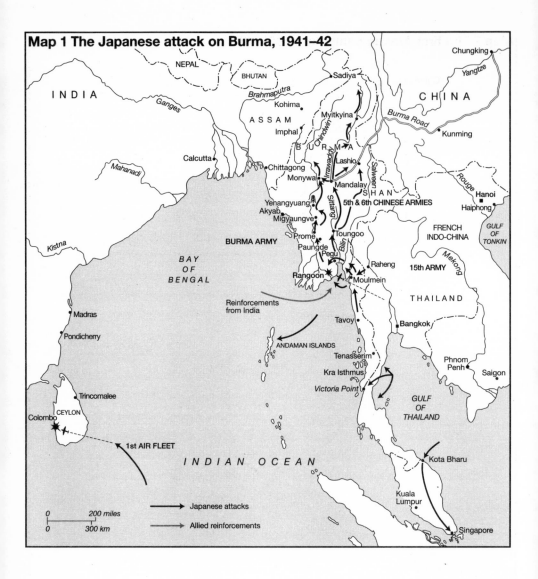

Map 1 The Japanese attack on Burma, 1941–42

NEPAL

BHUTAN

INDIA

Ganges

Brahmaputra

ASSAM

Kohima

Imphal

Mahanadi

Calcutta

Chittagong

Monywa

B U R M A

Sadiya

Myitkyina

Burma Road

CHINA

Chungking

Yangtze

Kunming

Kistna

BAY
OF
BENGAL

BURMA ARMY

Yenangyuang

Akyab

Migyaungye

Prome

Paungde

Lashio

Irrawaddy

Mandalay

Sittang

Salween

SHAN

5th & 6th CHINESE ARMIES

Chindwin

Toungoo

Bilin

Pegu

Rangoon

Raheng

Moulmein

15th ARMY

Rouge

Hanoi

Haiphong

FRENCH
INDO-CHINA

GULF
OF
TONKIN

THAILAND

Bangkok

Mekong

Madras

Pondicherry

Reinforcements
from India

ANDAMAN ISLANDS

Tavoy

Tenasserim

Kra Isthmus

Victoria Point

Phnom
Penh

Saigon

GULF
OF
THAILAND

Trincomalee

Colombo   CEYLON

1st AIR FLEET

I N D I A N   O C E A N

Kota Bharu

Kuala
Lumpur

Singapore

0	200 miles
0	300 km

→ Japanese attacks

→ Allied reinforcements

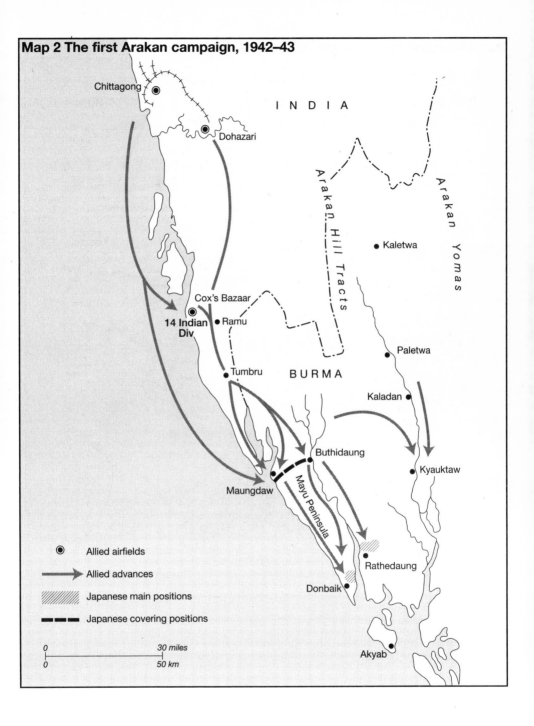

Map 2 The first Arakan campaign, 1942–43

Chittagong

Dohazari

I N D I A

Arakan Hill Tracts

Arakan Yomas

Kaletwa

Cox's Bazaar

14 Indian Div • Ramu

Tumbru

B U R M A

Paletwa

Kaladan

Buthidaung

Maungdaw

Mayu Peninsula

Kyauktaw

Rathedaung

Donbaik

Akyab

◉ Allied airfields

→ Allied advances

▨ Japanese main positions

▬ ▬ Japanese covering positions

0   30 miles
0   50 km

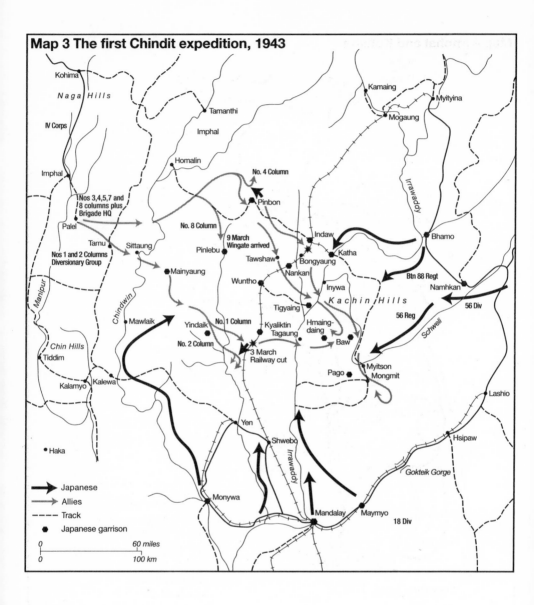

Map 3 The first Chindit expedition, 1943

Kohima

Naga Hills

Tamanthi

IV Corps

Imphal

Homalin

Imphal

No. 4 Column

Kamaing

Myityina

Mogaung

Nos 3,4,5,7 and
8 columns plus
Brigade HQ

Palel

Tamu

Sittaung

No. 8 Column

Pinbon

Indaw

Bhamo

Nos 1 and 2 Columns
Diversionary Group

Mainyaung

Pinlebu

9 March
Wingate arrived

Tawshaw

Katha

Btn 88 Regt

Irrawaddy

Chindwin

Mawlaik

Wuntho

Bongyaung

Nankan

Inywa

Kachin Hills

Namhkan

56 Div

Manipur

Yindaik

No. 1 Column

Kyaliktin
Tagaung

Tigyaing

Hmaing-
daing

56 Reg

Schweli

No. 2 Column

3 March
Railway cut

Baw

Chin Hills

Tiddim

Pago

Myitson
Mongmit

Lashio

Kalamyo

Kalewa

Yen

Shwebo

Hsipaw

Haka

Irrawaddy

Gokteik Gorge

Monywa

Mandalay

Maymyo

18 Div

→ Japanese
→ Allies
--- Track
● Japanese garrison

0   60 miles
0   100 km

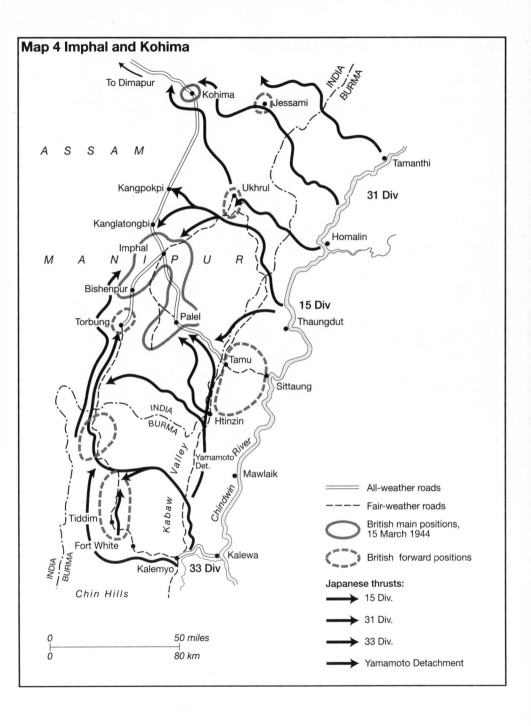

Map 4 Imphal and Kohima

To Dimapur

Kohima

Jessami

INDIA
BURMA

A S S A M

Tamanthi

Kangpokpi

Ukhrul

31 Div

Kanglatongbi

Homalin

Imphal

M A N I P U R

Bishenpur

15 Div

Torbung

Palel

Thaungdut

Tamu

Sittaung

INDIA
BURMA

Htinzin

Kabaw Valley

Yamamoto
Det.

Chindwin River

Mawlaik

Tiddim

Fort White

Kalewa

Kalemyo

33 Div

INDIA
BURMA

Chin Hills

	All-weather roads
	Fair-weather roads
	British main positions, 15 March 1944
	British forward positions

Japanese thrusts:

→ 15 Div.

→ 31 Div.

→ 33 Div.

→ Yamamoto Detachment

0   50 miles

0   80 km

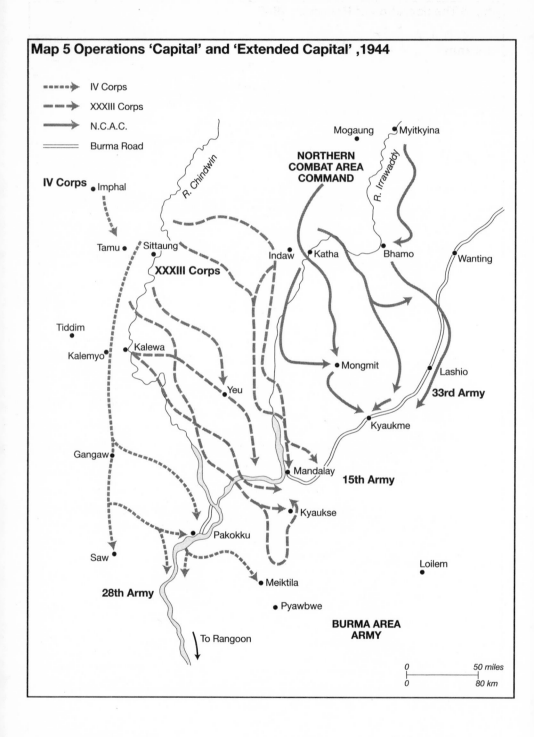

Map 5 Operations 'Capital' and 'Extended Capital', 1944

- ·······▶ IV Corps
- ----▶ XXXIII Corps
- ──▶ N.C.A.C.
- ═══ Burma Road

IV Corps

Imphal

R. Chindwin

Mogaung

Myitkyina

NORTHERN COMBAT AREA COMMAND

R. Irrawaddy

Tamu

Sittaung

Indaw

Katha

Bhamo

Wanting

XXXIII Corps

Tiddim

Kalemyo

Kalewa

Yeu

Mongmit

Lashio

33rd Army

Gangaw

Mandalay

15th Army

Kyaukme

Kyaukse

Saw

Pakokku

Loilem

28th Army

Meiktila

Pyawbwe

BURMA AREA ARMY

To Rangoon

| 0 | 50 miles |
| 0 | 80 km |

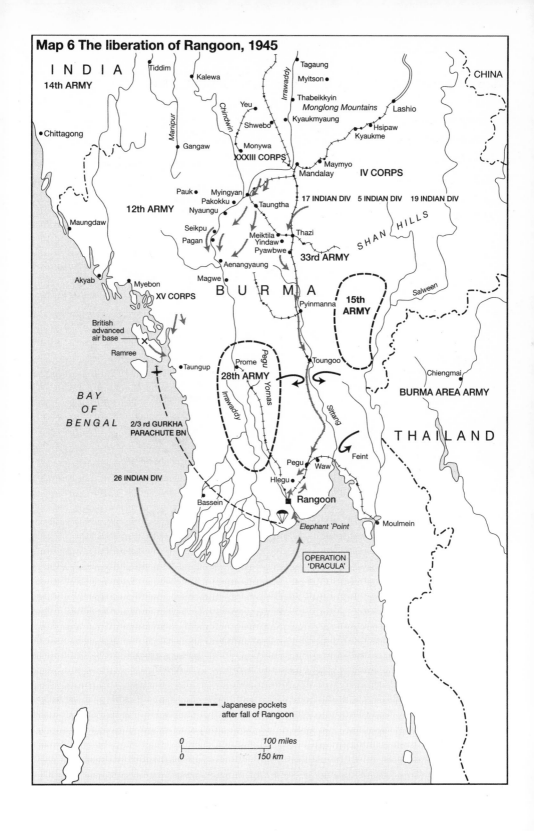

Map 6 The liberation of Rangoon, 1945

A simple stone monolith, similar to a Naga tribal grave marker, serves as the memorial for 2 Infantry Division and the Commonwealth War Graves cemetery at Kohima. Rose bushes and indigenous grasses soften the neat lines of white headstones in this cemetery on the eastern border of India. The monolith stands on a 15-foot dressed stone pedestal, with a small cross carved at the top and a bronze panel inset below.

The panel bears the inscription:

> When You Go Home,
> Tell Them Of Us And Say,
> For Their Tomorrow,
> We Gave Our Today

The words are attributed to John Maxwell Edmonds, an English classical scholar, who composed them as an epitaph for the dead of World War I. His inspiration was the Greek lyric poet Simonides of Ceos who, following the Battle of Thermopylae in 480 BC, wrote:

> Go tell the Spartans, thou that passes by,
> That faithful to their precepts here we lie.

After the fighting at Kohima Edmonds's words were chosen for the memorial at the suggestion of another classicist Major John Etty-Leal, an officer in the headquarters of 2 Infantry Division.

The haunting words commemorate the Allied soldiers who died fighting the Japanese Fifteenth Army in March 1944 and have now become a traditional part of the services and ceremonies that remember the cost and sacrifice of war.

FOREWORD

The British Army in Burma was such a multi-national force that to call them 'British' is perhaps misleading. Englishmen fought alongside not only Welshmen, Scots and Irishmen, but New Zealanders, Australians, Canadians and South Africans. From the Far East came Chinese, Kachins and Karens who fought side by side with Ghurkas and Indian sepoys. There were soldiers from both East Africa – Uganda, Kenya and the Sudan – and West Africa – Nigeria, the Gold Coast and Sierra Leone.

Together, these men took part in the longest campaign of the Second World War: the desperate fight to push the Japanese out of Burma. They were nicknamed the 'Forgotten Army' because they often felt they were last in the queue for supplies and weapons. But then Britain was busy fighting a bitter war in her own back yard; it was therefore inevitable that the war against Japan would take second place.

From the spring of 1942 this huge melting pot of different nationalities was commanded by the charismatic General William Slim, affectionately known as 'Uncle Bill'. Slim was respected by both his peers and those who served under him, for not only did he get results, but he was also scrupulous about looking after his men.

By the time he arrived in Burma he was much needed. The British had suffered a whole string of defeats at the hands of the Japanese, as had the Americans. Within a few months Japan had conquered most of Southeast Asia, and were even threatening the jewel in the British imperial crown itself: India.

That Slim and his Fourteenth Army were able to turn this grim situation around is a testament to the tenacity and skill of his men and commanders alike. When Slim wrote his memoirs after the war the title he chose was *Defeat into Victory*, which aptly describes the painful and remarkable process the Allies underwent. In *We Gave Our Today*, William Fowler captures the disastrous retreat to the borders of India, the remarkable stand at Kohima and Imphal, and then the turnaround and the retaking of Mandalay and Rangoon.

His fascinating account is enhanced with some of the most eccentric and brilliant characters of the war. Orde Wingate was a commander who seemed to rejoice in his ability to make enemies amongst his own superiors, and yet he has since been hailed as one of the most inspired tacticians of the war. His American counterpart, Frank Merrill was another pioneer of jungle warfare, who refused to leave his men until he had suffered both a heart attack and a bout of malaria. He in turn served under 'Vinegar' Joe Stilwell, a general who had a profound hatred for the Japanese.

Serving under these characters were the likes of the courageous Lieutenant George Cairns of the South Staffordshire Regiment, who led an attack against a Japanese position despite having already had his arm hacked off with a samurai sword. Or Lance Corporal John Harman, who twice charged down Japanese machine-gun positions armed with no more than a bayonet.

It is through the stories of such men that William Fowler brings this conflict to life. He writes with intelligence and compassion about the dilemmas faced by both generals and ordinary soldiers alike, and he has an acute eye for the telling detail. It is also interesting to see how the battles looked from the Japanese point of view. This book is a fitting tribute to the men who fought and died in this most unforgiving of theatres. If at the time they were considered the 'Forgotten Army', it is books like *We Gave Our Today* that ensure they will always be remembered.

MAX ARTHUR
2009

PREFACE

To be a schoolboy in the early 1960s was to be taught by remarkable men, many of whom had served with distinction in World War II.

Some were eccentric, many gifted, some scarred by their experiences, while some, like the survivors of the Japanese prisoner of war camps, seemed blessed with quiet wisdom and extraordinary patience. All of them brought a breadth of vision to the education of the stroppy generation of the 1960s that was tempered by experience of a wider and much tougher world.

We were very lucky to have been taught by them.

Holiday jobs brought further contact with veterans. Perhaps reluctant to talk to friends or family they seemed happy to share their experiences with a young, informed and attentive companion working with them for a month or two in the summer.

Among the recollections of those days and subsequent encounters, five men stand out.

In a discussion at school about economics, a former Japanese prisoner of war recalled that when they 'went into the bag' at Singapore amongst the kit that more cerebral soldiers packed were copies of the complete works of Shakespeare or the Bible. As the months dragged painfully into years these books ceased to have spiritual and intellectual solace to their owners and took on a new value in PoW camps. The Japanese supplied coarse tobacco for smokers who were prepared to barter food and other valuable commodities for paper to make cigarettes. The pages from the Bible and Shakespeare printed on fine quality paper were perfect for roll-ups.

With a smile he recalled the internal debates that tortured the book owners – what should go first, the minor prophets from the Old

Testament or Shakespeare's lesser known sonnets? By 1945 even some of the most uplifting and inspiring texts had turned to ash.

Another schoolmaster, who as a colonel in his early twenties commanded a Royal Engineer field squadron, described the work needed to span bridges demolished by the retreating Japanese in Burma. The first task was to clear the wreckage with explosives so that there was no risk of girders and rubble clogging with vegetation and becoming a dam in the heavy monsoon rains.

A young infantry officer arrived as a demolition was about to be fired. The colonel recalled the visitor's attitude: 'We front-line soldiers know a thing or two about explosions.' His disdain verged on contempt, when moments before the demolition was due to be fired, he remained upright, while they wisely took cover. So there was quiet satisfaction as they watched the plunger descend and the blast from the explosion slam the young officer backwards into the jungle scrub.

He was unharmed but his dignity was not.

Another memory came from a conversation one comfortable Christmas evening on the Scottish island of Mull. Our host had joined the army under age and was soon promoted and commissioned, commanding a platoon in a Highland regiment. In 1944 in the hot months before the monsoon, as the Fourteenth Army pursued the Japanese Burma Area Army south towards Mandalay, small front-line actions were often fought to gain access to wells and waterholes. The Japanese would leave behind one or two of their number carefully camouflaged with orders to shoot the first Allied soldier who dashed forward to replenish his comrades' water bottles. The approach to these water sources therefore became a tense game of cat and mouse.

The platoon had reached the edge of the jungle clearing by a water source and the officer carefully began to scan the surrounding vegetation with his binoculars. Suddenly he became aware of a frenzy of activity at ground level. As he focussed he realised that it was a mortal struggle between a cobra and a mongoose. Immediately he returned to the world of his childhood and the story of Rikki-Tikki-Tavi, the heroic mongoose in Rudyard Kipling's *The Jungle Book*.

'I was fascinated. The war went completely out of my mind and I watched until the mongoose delivered the fatal bite and then it was back to business.'

A summer work mate and Fourteenth Army veteran, who also recalled the dash to a well or water source, had fought in France, been evacuated at Dunkirk in 1940 and then posted to Burma.

However even here front-line soldiering could have its small pleasures. 'If we found that there was an Indian unit next to us we would do ration swaps. They would make chapattis, the traditional flat circular bread that were delicious. I would come back with a big pile for the boys and we would sit down and eat them spread with tinned army jam.'

And finally there was one of the giants of the Burma campaign and later an influential authority on counter insurgency and special forces – Brigadier Mike Calvert. He came into our office as a consultant on a publishing project in the mid 1970s. It was hard to reconcile this modest and at times terribly shy man with the 'Mad Mike' of Chindit fame. He took over a desk, worked diligently on checking copy, was delighted to sign my copy of *Prisoners of Hope*, and when the project ended, slipped away as quietly as he had arrived.

These were some of the men, all of them heroes, who by a combination of skill and good fortune returned home to enjoy their tomorrows – remembering friends and comrades who between 1941 and 1945 gave their today.

It was an honour to have met them.

Years later as I researched this book my respect increased. Burma was, and remains an incredibly tough place in which to live, let alone to fight a resourceful and determined enemy and one who was not afraid to die. Many of the young men of the Fourteenth Army were thousands of miles from home and faced the prospect of a war that might possibly end in the 1950s. As the wireless and newspapers reported Allied operations in Europe in detail it was with grim humour that they called themselves 'The Forgotten Army'.

This is their story.

THE MAN

The famous Fourteenth Army, under the masterly command of General
Slim, fought valiantly, overcame all obstacles, and achieved the
seemingly impossible
Winston S. Churchill, *The Second World War*, Vol. VI

'He has a hell of a face'
Churchill on General 'Bill' Slim

Leadership in war is both complex and very simple. The background, experience and circumstances that produce great leaders can sometimes be difficult to comprehend. Men blest with the advantages of birth and education can fail when put to the test, while others who have come from humble origins rise to the challenge and triumph.

What successful leaders achieve can be presented as a simple geometric model, a right-angled graph that delineates the two objectives of the Goal and the Group. Ideally a leader directs his operations so that he bisects the angle, giving equal weight to both the personnel under command (the Group) and the mission with which they have been tasked (the Goal).

A slightly more complex model is made up of three circles interlocked within a triangle – the Goal, the Group and the Individual. Here the interests and ability of a subordinate are not swamped by the demands of the commander, nor does the group suffer because of being given an impossible mission – the individual and group work together in harmony and the mission is achieved.

Some successful military commanders won their victories by browbeating and threatening subordinates and achieving their goal at a cruel cost in human life. The Soviet commanders in World War II may have defeated the German armies on the Eastern Front and beaten the Allies in the race for Berlin, however they achieved this by expending the lives of their soldiers with a cruel profligacy.

Between June 1941 and May 1945 of the approximately 30 million men and women who served in the Soviet armed forces 11 million were listed as killed and missing and many of the approximately 6 million who were captured never returned home from the slave camps of Nazi Germany. Soviet commanders like Marshal Georgi Zhukov may have seen the lives of the men under their command as expendable, but remarkably the tough front-line soldiers or *frontoviks* felt a real affection for him – because he delivered victories.

In Western Europe and the Mediterranean the British and American Allies produced successful military commanders who achieved less costly victories by using the weight of tactical air power and artillery. However while they achieved their goal at a relatively low cost to the armies under their command often their vanity and ambition meant that many were not interested in the individual. Many British and American commanders, notably Patton and Montgomery, were hostile and their personal ambition put Allied harmony and consequently the prosecution of the war in jeopardy.

It is against this background that General William Slim who commanded the Fourteenth Army in Burma, Britain's longest campaign in World War II, stands out as a truly remarkable military leader. While he was respected by his peers he was held in real affection by the soldiers under his command.

One such soldier, Patrick Davis, a Subaltern with 3 Gurkhas, remembered that this was universal.

'General Bill Slim . . . was a man known by repute to everyone. His rise had been rapid since 1939 . . . This did not worry us. He had earned his promotion in the only way an infantryman respects: he won battles. We trusted him not to embroil us in a major botchery. We accepted the possibility of death, and the certainty of danger, discomfort, fatigue and hunger, provided that our fighting was constructive and with a reasonable chance of success. Moreover Slim had been weaned with the 6th Gurkhas, so we had an extra reason for liking him.'[1]

The Fourteenth Army was the largest Commonwealth army in

World War II. By late 1944 it was composed of nearly a million men. At different periods of the war four corps (IV, XV, XXXIII and XXXIV) were under command. A total of thirteen divisions – 5, 7, 17, 19, 20, 23, 25 and 26 Indian Divisions, 11 East African Division, 81 and 82 West African Divisions, and 2 and 36 British Divisions – passed through its ranks at various times in the war.

Slim was able to work well with superiors, subordinates and soldiers from three continents and different backgrounds. His time in the British and British Indian Army had given him the skill to communicate in the language of the soldiers. After the war was over, veterans of all nationalities and ranks would recall with pride and affection that in Burma they served 'with' Bill Slim and not 'under' him. He in turn, when addressing the soldiers under his command, would tell them not that 'I' or even 'we' have won a victory or defeated the enemy, the word he chose was always 'you'.

This was the Group with which Slim achieved his Goal to defeat the Japanese in Burma. He did so with far fewer resources than those that were available to generals in Europe and with a real care for the lives of the men under his command.

An adjective for Slim not commonly used to describe generals or even senior officers was chosen by Lt Colonel James Lunt.

'He was extraordinarily *simpatico*. I was then a very young officer, just 23, and Slim would sit down beside you with a mug of tea and just chat. The thing I loved about him was he was so down-to-earth. He'd say, "You know, Jimmy, we haven't got a snowball's hope in hell of beating those buggers – but the point we must make to everyone is that we musn't give up. Because once we give up, they will just corral us like cattle. We've got to fight . . . and maybe, who knows, we may suddenly find their weak spot or something of that nature, that will give us the opportunity, because we've still got a lot of fight left in us." That was what endeared me to Slim.

'He was a very extraordinary man – hadn't been to Eton or Harrow. He'd served in the Indian Army – a poor man's army compared with the British Army. But he was called "Uncle Bill" and it sums him up, really.'[2]

Australian journalist Roy McKie would say of Slim, 'He understood men. He spoke their language as he moved among them, from forward positions to training bases. He had the richest of common-sense, a dour soldier's humour and a simple earthy wisdom. Wherever he moved he lifted morale. He was the finest of Englishmen.'[3]

It is a measure of his man management skills that he could win the respect and trust of the peppery American Anglophobe General 'Vinegar Joe' Stilwell who presented him with an American M1 Carbine that became Slim's personal weapon. At the other end of the spectrum he could also work with his superior, the urbane but mercurial Vice Admiral Lord Louis Mountbatten the Supreme Allied Commander South East Asia Command (SEAC).

Mountbatten would say of Slim after the war that 'he was the finest general that the Second World War produced'.

Field Marshal Sir Claude Auchinleck, 'The Auk' to the soldiers he commanded in North Africa and later Commander-in-Chief India, was less sweeping but much more perceptive in his analysis of Slim's character.

'One of Slim's chief characteristics was his quite outstanding determination and inability to admit defeat or the possibility of it: also his exceptional ability to gain and retain the confidence of those under him and with him, without any resort to *panache*. Success did not inflate him nor misfortune depress him.'

William Joseph Slim was above all a soldiers' soldier. His square jaw and stocky build have led some to characterise him as 'tough' – if this means a man prepared to take difficult decisions under terrible pressure, then that is correct. If 'tough' means an uncaring or insensitive man, nothing could be further from the truth.

He was a man who had come from humble origins. He was born on August 6, 1891, in Bristol, England, the son of John Slim, an iron merchant. Work took the family to Birmingham at the turn of the century where between 1903 and 1910 William attended St Philip's School and King Edward's School, Birmingham, his favourite subject being English literature.

From 1910 to 1914 he was employed as an elementary school teacher and as a clerk at Steward & Loyds, a firm of metal tube makers, and in the first move in his military career joined Birmingham University Officers' Training Corps, in 1912.

Life in industry in Birmingham left a lasting memory. 'I am against the legal minimum wallah every time,' he would say and in an interview with Colonel Frank Owen for *Phoenix* the South East Asia Command magazine that appeared in 1945,[4] Slim recalled how he had seen 'Men who were fathers of families cringing before a deputy-assistant-under-manager who had the power to throw them out of their jobs without any other reason than their own ill-temper or personal dislike. That, at any rate, can't happen in the Army. You don't have to cringe in the Army, though it's true some incorrigible cringers do. In the Army you don't have to go out to dinner with a man if you can't stand the sight of him.'

Before World War I he had joined a Territorial Army Battalion of the Royal Warwickshire Regiment as a Private. In August 1914 at the outbreak of war his Territorial Army battalion had been assembled for its two week training camp. Like the rest of the Territorial Army (a volunteer militia similar to the US National Guard), the battalion was immediately embodied into the Regular Army, and Slim was promoted to Lance Corporal. In his interview with Owen he recalled the only demotion he ever suffered in his military career.

'It was a sweltering, dusty day and the regiment plodded on its 20-mile route march down an endless Yorkshire lane. At that time British troops still marched in fours, so that Lance Corporal Slim, as he swung along by the side of his men, made the fifth in the file, which brought him very close to the roadside. There were cottages there and an old lady stood at the garden gate.

'I can see her yet, she was a beautiful old lady with her hair neatly parted in the middle and wearing a black print dress. In her hand she held a beautiful jug and on the top of that jug was a beautiful foam, indicating that it contained beer. She was offering it to the soldier boys.'

Lance Corporal Slim took one pace to the side and grasped the jug. As he did so, the column was brought to a halt by a bellowed command. The Colonel riding on horseback at its head, had glanced back. Slim was marched up and 'busted' back to Private on the spot. As he demoted him the Colonel bellowed, 'Had we been in France you would have been shot.'

Slim confided to Owen, 'I thought he was a damned old fool – and he was. I lost my stripe, but he lost his army.'

Soon after the outbreak of war he was commissioned with the rank of temporary Second Lieutenant, and fought at Gallipoli, where he was seriously wounded in 1915. It was here that he had his first encounter with Gurkha soldiers – men with whom he felt a natural bond and whom he would later command.[5]

The injuries he had suffered in Gallipoli were severe enough to have him medically discharged. However after recuperating in Britain, he managed to contrive not only to remain in the Army but also to be commissioned into the West India Regiment. He served in Mesopotamia in 1916, where he was awarded the Military Cross and during fighting for Baghdad was wounded again and evacuated to India.

He worked as a staff officer at Army Headquarters, India, from 1917 to 1920, with the rank of temporary Captain in 1917 and temporary Major in 1918. In the language of the class-ridden army of the early twentieth century, these wartime promotions made Slim a 'temporary gentleman'.

Now with the war over he seriously wondered if he should resign his commission and take a better paid job. The only place it was said that an officer could get by on his pay was in the British Indian Army so, in 1919, he transferred to the Indian Army with the rank of Captain.

He joined 1/6 Gurkha Rifles, who were stationed at Abbottabad in 1920 to 1922, and then Malakand on the North West Frontier between 1922 to 1925, where for three years he served as Adjutant.

In 1926 he married Aileen Robertson and they had a son and a daughter.

Slim was a student at the Staff College, at Quetta from 1926 to 1927 passing out top. He returned to Army Headquarters, India, as a staff officer, from 1929 to 1933, and was promoted to the rank of Major in 1933.

He was the Indian Army instructor at the Staff College, Camberley, Britain from 1934 to 1936, a student at the Imperial Defence College in 1937, and a student at the Senior Officers' School, Belgaum in

1938. Life on a Major's pay in Britain was difficult and, in what would now be seen as a very twenty-first-century move, the man, who as a boy had enjoyed English Literature at school, supplemented his Army pay by writing thrillers under the pen name 'Anthony Mills'.

He was promoted to Lt Colonel in 1938 and took command of 2/7 Gurkha Rifles, stationed at Shillong in Assam. Promotion to Colonel came a year later. He returned to the Senior Officers' School, Belgaum, as Commandant with the local rank of Brigadier in 1939.

As with so many military careers the outbreak of war in 1939 led to new challenges and responsibilities. In 1940 Slim was given command of the Tenth Indian Infantry Brigade (Inf Bde), part of the Sudan Defence Force under General Sir William Platt that had been ordered to block a threatened invasion of British-administered Sudan by Italian troops based in Eritrea.

This would be Slim's first action in World War II and it could have been the end of his career – there would indeed be repercussions two years later in Burma in his dealings with Lt General Noel Irwin.

On July 4, 1940 men of the Italian Northern Army under General Frusci crossed the border into southern Sudan and captured the border villages of Kassala and Gallabat. Slim and his brigade (10 Essex, 4/10 Baluchis and 3/18 Garhwal Rifles) were ordered to retake the fort at Gallabat. The Italian garrison at the fort and neighbouring town of Metemma was formidable. It consisted of a colonial battalion reinforced by an extra company with two more stationed in the dry *khor*. They also had the support of two machine-gun companies of Blackshirts, a platoon armed with captured British Boyes anti-tank rifles, a mortar company, a detachment of artillery and a small *banda* – a group of Italian-commanded irregulars.

In support of his brigade Slim had a regiment of field guns, six Mk III (A 13) cruisers and six Mk VI light tanks and a mixed force of bombers and fighters.

Slim's plan was to move his artillery as close as possible to the fort using the cover of the tall elephant grass. Following as heavy a bombardment by air and artillery as was possible the Garhwalis would take the fort with tanks in support, the Essex would pass through them to seize Metemma while the third battalion would secure the flanks.

At dawn on November 6 the air and artillery support worked well and the tanks crushed the wire and thorn scrub obstacles allowing the Indian troops to fight their way into Gallabat against stiff opposition.

As the Essex moved forward the plan started to unravel. The tank commander reported that five of his Mk IIIs and four of his Mk VIs had lost tracks – either to mines or thrown on rocks. It would take four hours for spares to arrive. The second phase of the attack would therefore have to be delayed.

The RAF – whose fighters were inferior to the Italian fighters – had been ordered to operate en masse to compensate for this. Instead two aircraft appeared and were shot down and this was repeated until all the Gladiator fighters had been shot down or crash landed and the brigade had no air cover.

Now the Essex and Garhwal Rifles were bunched on Gallabat hill in an area about 50 yards square with ground so hard that it was only possible to dig a very shallow shell scrape. Under sustained air attack the rear companies of the Essex panicked, seized some vehicles and drove off shouting that the Italians had recaptured the fort and they had been ordered to withdraw. One group encountered Slim to whom they shouted that both their colonel and the brigadier were dead and that they were the sole survivors of the battalion.

At this point Italian bombers hit the truck carrying the spares for the tanks, having already hit an ammunition truck. Under intense bombing Slim's troops held the fort for 36 hours but on the night of November 6–7 he pulled them back to the safety of the surrounding hills. Though the Italians never re-occupied the fort it could be counted as an Italian victory.[6]

Slim took responsibility for the failings at Gallabat, but as part of the rebuilding process for the Essex he sacked their commanding officer.

Slim could be tough when he knew that it was necessary. Recalling a critical point in the retreat in Burma when he came across a unit in a jungle clearing who were clearly in a bad way he said, 'I took one look at them and thought "My God, they're worse than I supposed" then I saw why. I walked round the corner of that clearing and I saw officers making themselves a bivouac. They were just as exhausted as their men, but that isn't my point. Officers are there to lead. I tell you, therefore, as officers, that you will neither eat, nor drink, nor sleep, nor smoke, nor even sit down until you have personally seen that your men have done those things. If you will do this for them, they will follow you to the end of the world. And, if you do not, I will break you.'

He would say at the close of the campaign in Burma that 'the fighting capacity of every unit is based upon the faith of soldiers in their leaders; that discipline begins with the officer and spreads downward from him to the soldier; that genuine comradeship in arms is achieved when all ranks do more than is required of them. "There are no bad soldiers, only bad officers," is what Napoleon said, and though that great man uttered some foolish phrases, this is not one.'[7]

Writing less than a year after the campaign in Burma Lt Colonel Frank Owen would say of the general, 'Slim proves his beliefs by example. The well-being of his troops is his permanent priority. Probably the central pillar in this rock-like character is a loathing of humbug.'[8]

Slim's views on courage are a key part of current British Army doctrine that identifies physical and moral courage. Part of the latter is the strength to identify weakness or failure in oneself or the troops under command and being prepared to admit to it and resolve it. This was something Slim believed the Japanese lacked.

'The fundamental fault of their generalship,' he explained, 'was a lack of moral, as distinct from physical courage. They were not prepared to admit that they had made a mistake, that their plans had misfired and needed recasting . . . Rather than confess that, they passed on to their subordinates, unchanged, the orders they had themselves received, well knowing that with the resources available the tasks demanded were impossible.'[9]

Soon after the action at Gallabat in East Africa, Slim was again wounded when Italian aircraft strafed his vehicle. While recovering from these injuries, he was promoted in May 1941 to the temporary rank of Major General (later Lt General) and given command of 10 Indian Division in Iraq and Syria.

The previous divisional commander Major General W. A. K. Fraser had asked to be relieved of his command because he knew that he no longer had the confidence of his subordinate commanders.

General Sir Claude Auchinleck, Commander-in-Chief (C-in-C) India cabled General Wavell C-in-C Middle East recommending Slim, then a Brigadier on the General Staff, be promoted as Fraser's replacement.

In a letter to Lord Linlithgow the Viceroy of India, Auchinleck wrote, 'I have every reason to expect that Slim's energy, determination and force of character generally will prove equal to the task.'[10]

The division was in training for North Africa but Slim enjoyed the challenge of the command. In *Defeat into Victory* he recalled, 'A division . . . is the smallest formation that is a complete orchestra of war and the largest in which every man can know you.'

Of the division's operations in the Middle East he wrote, 'We had scrambled through the skirmishes of the Iraq rebellion, been blooded, but not too deeply against the French in Syria, and enjoyed unrestrainedly the *opéra bouffe* of the invasion of Persia. We had bought our beer in Haifa and drunk it on the shores of the Caspian.'[11]

The campaign had been triggered by a coup in Iraq on April 1, 1941 by Rashid Ali, a pro-Axis politician who overthrew the regent who reigned in the name of King Feisal II. Iraqi troops attacked the RAF base at Habbiniyah near Baghdad, one of the two that the British had retained after the termination of their mandate in 1930. The 10 Indian Division was among the reinforcements shipped to Basra to help quell the rebellion. An armistice was concluded on May 31 and the regent reinstated.

Following the operations in Iraq, British and Free French forces invaded the French mandate of Syria since the French High Commissioner in Syria had declared loyalty to the pro-Axis French government at Vichy in June 1940.

The German successes in Russia, and the drive towards the Caucasus made the oilfields of Iran a likely objective so to secure these vital supplies 8 and 10 Indian Divisions now invaded Iran.

Slim's division forced the Pai Tak Pass and advanced through Kermanshah to Hamadan linking up with Soviet troops who had attacked from the north. The Allied invasion began on August 25 and was over in three days when the Shah ordered his troops to cease fire and abdicated in favour of his son.

It was during the operations in Iraq that 5 Field Company of Bengal

Sappers under Major G. Loch and Captain (later Lt General) J. S. Dhillon built a unique Boat Bridge across the Shatt-al-Arab waterway. Using Mohaillas, a local working boat, they constructed the bridge in two sections, one of 970 feet and the other of 830. Construction took a week and when the bridge opened on August 14, 1941 it was recognised as the longest boat bridge in the world.

Three years later the Bengal Sappers would set new records in bridge construction at Kalewa on the Chindwin in Burma.

In March 1942, Wavell, now C-in-C India, requested that Slim be posted from Iran to take command, in a rapidly deteriorating operational situation, of the British-Indian First Burma Corps.

For Slim this change of command was unwelcome and he initially thought that orders to fly to India was a discreet way of breaking bad news.

' "Am I sacked?" I asked.

' "No, you've got another job."

' "But I don't want another job. I want to stay with my division."

' "A good soldier goes where he's sent and does what he's told!"

'And the telephone rang off in my ear.'[12]

CHAPTER 1

RISING SUN

1905 to December 1941

'The toughest war machine in the world'
Colonel 'Banzai' Simpson, British Defence Attaché, Tokyo on the
Imperial Japanese Army

At 07.55 hours local time on December 7, 1941 at the US Pacific Fleet base at Pearl Harbor, Oahu, Hawaii the course of World War II suddenly lurched in a new and terrifying direction.

On that quiet Sunday morning the first of two waves of 423 Imperial Japanese Navy fighters, dive bombers and torpedo bombers took off from the aircraft carriers *Agaki, Hiryu, Shokaku, Soryu* and *Zuikaku*. They were the cutting edge of Plan Z, the attack on the US Navy Pacific Fleet that was intended to neutralise American control of the Western Pacific and give the Japanese time and freedom to realise their imperial dreams.

The first wave of aircraft swung in from the west over the island and the second from the east. By 09.45 hours it was all over. Thick columns of black smoke rose from the wrecked installations, the water was slick with fuel oil and wreckage, and secondary explosions continued to rock the harbour and airfields. As the casualties were collected the death toll mounted. It would reach more than 2,400 US servicemen killed.

For the loss of 29 aircraft, the Japanese had sunk five American battleships, damaged three others, sunk three cruisers and three destroyers, and destroyed 188 US Navy and Army Air Force aircraft on the airfields. They had achieved complete surprise and an overwhelming victory. However they had failed to sink three US carriers that were at sea and did not launch a third wave to destroy the fuel storage tanks on the island.

Mitsuo Fuchida who commanded the aircraft operating from the *Agaki* recalled the death of the battleship *Arizona*. 'As the first squadron followed us again into a bombing run, there was a huge explosion close to our objective. A deep red flame burst into the sky, followed by soaring dark smoke. Then white smoke, to a height of what looked like 3,000 feet. That must be the magazine! A shock like an earthquake went right through our formation and my aircraft shuddered with the force of it. It was the *Arizona* going up.'[13] Aboard the battleship 1,200 men died.

A day later the United States, Great Britain, Australia, New Zealand, the Netherlands, the Free French, Yugoslavia, several South American countries and China declared war on Japan.

So began the war in the Far East and Imperial Japan's drive to create an area of influence that embraced the Philippines, French Indo China, the Dutch East Indies, Malaya and Singapore with all their rich natural resources. This was 'The Greater East Asia Co-Prosperity Sphere' as Japanese Foreign Minister Matsuoka Yōsuke had named the policy in August 1940. Ultra nationalist Japanese had long been advocating what they called the 'Southern Advance', as they saw it, to liberate these colonial empires.

In fact Japan had been expanding her empire even before World War I. In 1905 Korea had become a protectorate of Japan and was annexed in 1910 when the king was forced to abdicate. The rice and raw materials from the peninsula would help to feed and fuel Japan's growing population and industrial programme.

As one of the Allies in World War I Japan had been ceded a mandate by the League of Nations for the German colonial empire in the Pacific. This consisted of the Marshall, Caroline and Mariana groups of islands. As part of the mandate Japan was required to improve the conditions of the population of the islands and prepare them for self-government. In reality, because the League exercised no real supervision over the conduct of the mandated powers, Japan was free to build up and fortify bases on the islands that occupied a strategic position east of the Philippine Islands.

The next move to widen its empire came with the establishment of the puppet regime of Manchukuo in Manchuria. This area had been coming under Japanese influence following the Russo-Japanese war of 1904 to 1905. In 1907 a garrison was established by international agreement to protect the Southern Manchurian Railway and in 1919 it was given independent status as the *Kantogun* or the Kwantung Army. Though only one division with support troops including military police the Kwantung Army would become the driving force behind Japanese nationalist expansion. Highly politicised, it attracted ambitious young officers including Hideki Tojo who would later be Japan's ultra nationalist Prime Minister. With its headquarters at Mukden from 1928 the Kwantung Army was almost beyond the control of the Tokyo government. Seeing Manchuria as a source of essential raw materials and an area into which Japan could send its growing population as colonists, the officers of the Kwantung Army became concerned when the Chinese warlord in Manchuria Chang Tso-lin began making overtures to the Chinese Nationalist leader Chiang Kai-shek. Japanese officers assassinated the warlord in 1928 and three years later engineered what became known as the *Manshu jihen* or Mukden Incident. An explosion on the Southern Manchurian Railway outside Mukden was blamed on Chinese troops and even though Tokyo attempted to halt the operation the Kwantung Army moved to occupy Manchuria. With no authorisation from central government it even brought reinforcements from the Japanese colony of Korea and by early 1932 had secured the three eastern provinces of Manchuria. In March of that year a puppet state called Manchukuo was established and a year later Jehol province was added.

Eight hundred thousand colonists moved from Japan to this new territory and enjoyed a new and very comfortable life.

Japan's next move was to make powerful new allies when in November 1936 it signed the 'Anti-Comintern Pact', a treaty with Fascist Italy and Nazi Germany binding them to combat the 'Comintern, the Soviet-controlled system of international Communism. The Nazis' convoluted theories of Aryan racism made the treaty acceptable when Reich Propaganda Minister Dr Josef Göbbels asserted that 'the blood of Japan contains virtues close to the pure Nordic'. However three years later Japan withdrew from the pact after the Russo-German Non-aggression Pact had been signed. This was not the first pact that Japan abrogated. As far back as 1933 she had withdrawn from the League of Nations and a year later the Washington and London Naval Treaties – which attempted to restrict the weight and armament of major warships. In great secrecy Japan would eventually build two huge 64,170-ton *Yamato* Class battleships the *Yamato* and *Musashi*, the largest and most heavily protected battleships in the world.

China was the next land Japanese nationalists planned to invade.

Even before they went to war, China was a country riven by conflict. Communist forces under their charismatic leader Mao Tse-tung battled with Nationalist troops the Kuomintang led by Chiang Kai-shek. In addition to this local warlords controlled areas that they were determined to defend.

On July 7, 1937 open war broke out between China and Japan following a clash at night between Japanese forces under the future Lt General Tomoyuki Yamashita and Chinese troops at Wanping near the Marco Polo Bridge at Lukouchiao near Peking. Attempts were made to resolve the situation but more crises followed engineered by the Japanese. The offensive launched from Manchuria took Japanese forces into northern China and by the end of the year they had occupied an area that included Mongolia and the cities of Peking and Tientsin.

On August 13 after an incident near the treaty port of Shanghai fighting broke out on a new front. In Shanghai, Tientsin, Canton, Hankow and other treaty ports, Europeans, Americans and Japanese enjoyed special privileges through a series of agreements imposed by force on the Chinese in the nineteenth century. The Japanese presence in these ports also gave them a foothold in China and with the out-break of war the ability to prevent imports of munitions. It took heavy fighting for the Japanese to capture Shanghai though Japanese losses were estimated at 40,000 and those of the Chinese civilian and military were around 300,000. The Chinese Nationalist government withdrew inland to Nanking but that city fell to the Central China Expeditionary Forces on December 13. What followed came to be now known as The Rape of Nanking as Japanese soldiers embarked on days of killing, rapine, pillage and looting. However this was not a collapse of discipline but a policy of calculated terror and brutality to cow the Chinese.

The savagery of the war in China would later spill over into fighting with British, Dutch and American forces. In the summer of 1941 in the Yangtze Valley near Chungking a senior Lieutenant confronted Tominaga Shōzō with a group of candidate officers with 'a trial of courage' that would qualify them as leaders.

In front of the regimental commander, Shōzō and the group were ordered to behead bound and blindfolded Chinese prisoners.

'I didn't want to disgrace myself. I bowed to the regimental commander and stepped forward. Contrary to my expectations, my feet firmly met the ground. One thin, worn-out prisoner was at the edge of the pit blindfolded. I unsheathed my sword, a gift from my brother-in-law. Wet it down as the lieutenant had demonstrated, and stood behind the man. The prisoner didn't move. He kept his head lowered. Perhaps he was resigned to his fate. I was tense, thinking I couldn't afford to fail. I took a deep breath and recovered my composure. I steadied myself, holding the sword at a point above my right shoulder, and swung down with one breath. The head flew away from the body and tumbled down, spouting blood. The air reeked from all that blood. I washed the blood off the blade then wiped it with the paper provided. Fat stuck to it and wouldn't come off. I noticed when I sheathed it that my sword was slightly bent.'[14]

After he had killed the prisoner Shōzō said that he felt that he had gained strength and respect. One candidate slashed at a prisoner's head by mistake and the man ran around with his blindfold hanging off, screaming with blood pouring from his face. The candidate failed again and Shōzō recalled that when it was finally over, 'Everyone got covered in blood when we butchered him.'

For private soldiers this murderous rite of passage would be less ritualised. Where other armies used straw-filled canvas dummies for bayonet practice Japanese soldiers used the 20-inch Type 30 sword bayonets mounted on their Arisaka rifles against bound Chinese and Allied prisoners.

By the end of 1938 these armies, which combined medieval barbarity with twentieth-century technology, had seized large swathes of eastern China and the area around Canton and the coast inland from the British colony of Hong Kong.

The war in Europe that broke out a year later would not have an immediate impact on Japan's territorial ambitions. The Japanese gloried in Germany's military triumphs and in 1939 swastika flags appeared on the streets of Tokyo. It was the fall of France in June 1940 that would give Japanese nationalists the opportunity to realise greater territorial ambitions.

In July Tokyo demanded that supplies should no longer be sent to China via the Burma Road, a land link that was connected to the Burmese capital and port of Rangoon. The 600-mile-long road ran through very rugged mountainous country. The sections from Kunming to the Burmese border were built by 200,000 Chinese labourers between 1937 and 1938 during the second Sino-Japanese War. Supplies for China would be landed at Rangoon and shipped by rail to Lashio, the start of the road in Burma.

In 1940 with the Battle of Britain raging in the skies over southern England London was in no position to challenge the Japanese demand and now China was isolated. A similar demand was made of the French to close the road and rail link from the port of Haiphong in the French colony of Indo China to Yunnan.

The Vichy government in unoccupied France had directed Vice Admiral Jean Decoux to negotiate with the Japanese. It took about a year for the Japanese, using a mixture of threats and crude diplomacy, to achieve their aim. Nominally still under the control of Decoux, Indo China was now garrisoned by 35,000 Japanese troops with aircraft operating from French airfields. The Japanese Fifteenth Army held the territory around Haiphong and Hanoi in the north and had its HQ in Saigon. Without a fight the country had entered the Greater East Asia Co-Prosperity Sphere supplying Japan with rice, coal and rubber. To the west the kingdom of Siam was ruled by the pro-Japanese C-in-C and Prime Minister, Field Marshal Pibul Songgram who had renamed the country Thailand.

On October 18, 1940 with support from the United States, Britain reopened the Burma Road. On July 26, 1941 concerned at Japan's war in China and remorseless expansionism, the United States froze all

Japanese assets and imposed an embargo on oil exports to Japan. Britain and the Netherlands followed suit on August 5. To the Japanese this was seen as a conspiracy by the Americans, British, Chinese and the Dutch – the ABCD countries – to strangle Japan and thwart her legitimate plans for South East Asia.

A month after the embargo was imposed, P-40 Curtiss Warhawk fighters of the American Volunteer Group (AVG), better known as The Flying Tigers, began operating from a British airfield at Toungoo in Burma. The germ of the idea for the force made up of volunteers from the US Navy, Marine Corps and Army Air Force had begun back in 1937 with a conversation with a retired US Army Air Force (USAAF) Captain Claire Chennault and the wife of the Chinese Nationalist leader Chiang Kai-shek. The role of the fighter group would be to protect the Burma Road. Mme Chiang Kai-shek promised a bounty to pilots with confirmed kills and the men enjoyed very good rates of pay.

By November 1941, when the AVG pilots were trained and most of the P-40s had arrived in Asia, they were assigned to three squadrons: 1 Squadron 'Adam & Eves'; 2 Squadron 'Panda Bears' and 3 Squadron 'Hell's Angels'. To cover the Burma Road two squadrons were based at Kunming in China and the third at Mingaladon near Rangoon. At the time of Pearl Harbor the AVG had 82 pilots and 79 aircraft in country, though not all were combat-ready. After the fall of Rangoon, the AVG was redeployed to bases in northern Burma and finally in China.

In the course of their operations the AVG was officially credited with 297 enemy aircraft destroyed, including 229 in the air. However recorded Japanese losses were 115 enemy aircraft in the air and on the ground. Thirteen AVG pilots were killed in action, captured, or posted missing in action and ten killed in accidents.

At the outset of the AVG operations Chiang Kai-shek assured the British that if Burma was attacked the AVG could be employed in the defence of that country – it was a promise that would have significant consequences.

On October 17 the failure of negotiations with the United States over Japan's expansion into China led to the fall of the government headed by Prince Fuminaro Konoye. He was succeeded by General Hideki Tojo – the same man who had been a political activist in Manchuria. To informed observers Tojo's appointment by the Emperor was a sure sign that Japan would become involved in a wider war. In fact attack orders were issued on November 20, with the proviso that operations were not to begin until the outcome of diplomatic negotiations had been reported.

On November 27 Japan rejected the US demand for outright withdrawal from China, but opted to continue talking.

To the youthful Nogi Harumichi, a member of the clandestine Patriotic Students' Alliance, Japan at last had the strong leader that it had been craving. 'Japanese youth at that time adored Hitler and Mussolini and yearned for the emergence of a Japanese politician with the same qualities. We wanted decisive action.'[15]

However there were others who did not share Nogi Harumichi's enthusiasm for Japan's increasing belligerence. On November 30 there were still members of the government who questioned the wisdom of war with the United States, but under Tojo's forceful leadership they were overruled and the decision to attack was made.

Long before the attack on Pearl Harbor the Japanese had been amassing intelligence about their land and air objectives. They were in a unique position to call on the loyalty of a Japanese Diaspora that before the war had seen men scattered across the Pacific and even to the US West Coast in search of work. It would be exploited by Japanese military and foreign office intelligence agencies in a variety of ways. This ranged from gathering information on troop strengths and dispositions, the layout of depots and docks to what today would be described as 'psychological preparation of the battlefield'.

This was the work of the *tokumu kikan* or Special Service Organisations that included professionals like doctors, dentists, journalists and businessmen who were in confidential contact with nationalist leaders. The most notorious of the Kikan was the Minamu that organised the Burma Independence Army and the F commanded by Major Fujiwara Iwaichi that fostered the Indian Independence League before the war and sent operatives to foment dissent and gather intelligence before the outbreak of war. 'F' had been chosen as its title since it was the family name of the commanding officer, but could also be interpreted as standing for 'Freedom' and 'Friendship'. Though Japanese operations caused the Allies concern Japanese commanders in the field often did not value the intelligence with which they were provided. When Fujiwara was posted to the Fifteenth Army in northern Burma he had the frustrating experience of seeing its commander Lt General Mutaguchi dismiss his collated intelligence in favour of the abstract idea of *seisho* or 'spirit' to guarantee victory for the Fifteenth Army.

As the United States began to recover from the shock of the attack on the Pacific Fleet, Japan launched the theatre-wide offensive that they had been planning as far back as November 6.

As part of these operations 20,000 men under Lt General Sano Tadayoshi commanding the Japanese 38 Division part of Twenty-third Army crossed the Sham Chun River from China at 08.00 hours on December 8 and attacked the British colony of Hong Kong. They had excellent intelligence from agents who had been operating in the colony including a colonel who had worked as a barber at the Peninsula Hotel.

The outcome of the battle was a foregone conclusion. Major General Christopher Maltby had two British, two new Canadian and two Indian infantry battalions in his garrison supported by 28 guns of the Hong Kong and Singapore Royal Artillery. In addition he had the keen but older men of the Hong Kong Volunteer Defence Corps – some were veterans of World War I and even the Boer War. Maltby also had seven obsolescent aircraft, one destroyer, eight MTBs and four gunboats. His aircraft were quickly destroyed when Japanese bombers hit Kai Tak airfield.

By the evening of December 9 Japanese forces had reached the 11-mile-long Gin Drinkers' Line in the New Territories that stretched from Gin Drinkers' Bay to Port Shelter. Overnight Colonel Teihichi Doi's 228 Regiment captured the Shing Mun Redoubt and this unhinged the defensive position, forcing Maltby to withdraw to Hong Kong Island. This was completed by December 13.

Heavy bombardment from the land and air damaged the destroyer and two MTBs. The Japanese attempted to cross the 500-yard-wide

Lei U Mun Strait on December 15 but were repulsed. However three nights later they landed in strength between North Point and Aldrich Bay and began pushing south across the island.

On December 19 in fighting around Mount Hill, Warrant Officer Class II John Osborn of 1 Winnipeg Grenadiers, Canadian Infantry Corps would win Canada's first Victoria Cross of World War II. He had helped organise resistance but would die when he covered a Japanese grenade with his body to save the lives of soldiers in a trench. Led by men like Osborn the resistance was still tough and on December 20 Sano was forced to halt to reorganise. The Governor, Sir Mark Young had a radio link out of the colony to the British Embassy in Chungking and on December 23 the *Daily Telegraph* reported that he had signalled that he would resist until he was captured. At Churchill's urging, over five days, the governor had rejected three offers from the Japanese to surrender 'on grounds of humanity'.

By December 24 the surviving defenders were exhausted. With the loss of the reservoirs water was running out and ammunition was also low. On Christmas Day a cease-fire was arranged and at 19.05 hours Sir Mark Young formally surrendered. In a 15-minute ceremony at the Peninsula Hotel lit only by candles he told Lt General Takashi Sakai commanding the Twenty-third Army, 'I am here to become a prisoner by ordering the entire British forces to cease all resistance.'

The garrison had suffered 4,400 casualties while the Japanese admitted 2,754. The final days of the campaign and the immediate aftermath were marked by Japanese atrocities committed notably by 229 Regiment commanded by Colonel Ryozaburo Tanaka. Among their crimes were binding and bayoneting captured gunners from an anti-aircraft battery and bayoneting male and female staff and even the bed-bound patients in a medical station. Tanaka would reach the rank of Major General, survive the war and be tried in Hong Kong as a war criminal. He was found guilty and sentenced to 20-years imprisonment.

Hong Kong stands out as a heroic, tragic but ultimately doomed defence. Britain and the United States had greater confidence in the ability of their bases in Malaya and the Philippines to withstand Japanese attacks.

Almost hours after the attack on Pearl Harbor the Imperial Japanese Army had launched a blitzkrieg across the mainland and island groups of South East Asia. Like Germany's blitzkrieg in Europe the Japanese offensive operations had been carefully planned. However whereas in 1940, Britain and France did not underestimate their enemy, in London, New Delhi and Singapore, British staff officers expressed a low opinion of Japanese military competence and equipment. General Sir Frank Messervy, who from 1942 would command with distinction 7 Indian Division in Burma, remembered a Colonel Simpson of the Royal Scots who among senior officers in the War Office was known derisively as 'Banzai Simpson'. Simpson who had been the military attaché in Tokyo for several years asserted that the Japanese Army was 'the toughest war machine in the world'. The given thought however was that the Japanese would be no match for a modern European army. Recalling the way in which Simpson had been ridiculed Messervy added, 'At the same time the War Office showed another dangerous tendency, one even more strong in American military thought. It was the tendency to underestimate the human factor and look to machine power to win wars.'[16] Worse still the war in North Africa had creamed off the best British and Indian troops and those that remained in India and Asia had until recently been employed as Imperial policemen.

In *Battle Tales from Burma* John Randle, who served with distinction with the Baluch regiment in Burma, explains that 'In 1941 the old Imperial Indian Army was going through an enormous and, in hind-sight, somewhat imprudent expansion. Regiments which in 1939 con-sisted of five regular battalions were doubling (and then, after Japan entered the war, redoubling). Pre-war regular battalions were heavily milked of experienced VCO (Viceroy's Commissioned Officers), Non-Commissioned Officers (NCOs) and senior sepoys; then as soon as newly raised battalions were knitted together, they too were milked to meet the demands of the new wave of expansion, and to replace casualties from the heavy fighting in east Africa and the West-ern Desert.'

On the night of Monday December 8 Imperial Japanese Navy bombers attacked Singapore killing 200 civilians. Despite this there was a feeling of confidence bolstered by the presence at the base of the formidable Force Z composed of the 14-inch battleship HMS *Prince of Wales* and 15-inch battle cruiser HMS *Repulse* and four destroyers HMS *Electra, Express, Tenedos* and HMAS *Vampire*.

The Government and Headquarters in Singapore did not know that the first act of aggression in the war in the Pacific had actually taken place a few hours before the attack on Pearl Harbor and much closer to home. On the morning of December 7 as the invasion fleet was approaching the east coast of Malaya, to ensure the security Japanese aircraft operating from Indo China shot down an RAF Catalina flying boat.

Reports of landings around 01.00 hours on December 8 by two divisions of the Japanese Twenty-fifth Army, at Kota Bharu in Malaya and five at Singora and Patani in Thailand produced quick action. The landing at Kota Bharu was opposed with small arms fire by men of 2/10 Baluch, 3/17 Dogras and 1/13 Frontier Force Rifles and 21 Mountain Battery of 8 Indian Brigade (Bde). The situation looked promising for the British when at 02.00 hours RAF Hudson bombers flew in and hit three troop transports including the *Awajisan Maru*, the vessel on which the headquarters staff of 18 Division under Major General Hiroshi Takumi were embarked. The bomb killed 50 men and started a fire.

Takumi's division was an interesting formation with a high proportion of coal miners from Kyushu – tough quarrelsome men kept in line by harsh discipline. It also contained detachments from the Imperial Guards Division, an élite formation of taller soldiers groomed in ceremonial duties. The last time the Imperial Guards had been in action was in 1905 in the Russo-Japanese War.

Further offshore 56-year-old Lt General Tomoyuki Yamashita commanding Twenty-fifth Army was uncertain how the landings were developing. A landing craft returning to Takumi's HQ brought a signal from Colonel Nasu that read '01.30 hours. Succeeded in landing but there are many obstacles. Send second wave.'

By now the fire had taken hold on the *Awajisan Maru* and so Takumi transferred his HQ to a launch and ordered the coxswain to head for the shore. It was the first example of aggressive leadership, flexibility and the ability to take and maintain the initiative that would give the Japanese a psychological edge over their adversaries in Malaya.

Takumi gives a vivid account of the landing. 'Many officers and men were killed or wounded, many jumped into the water before the craft had beached and swam ashore. The enemy positions were about 100 yards from the water, and we could see that their posts were wired in. Their guns were pointing directly at us . . . There was utmost confusion all along the beach, but the commander realised that if they remained where they were, they would be killed to a man, so the order was "go on". The officers rushed inland and the men followed. Then the troops began to get round to the back of the enemy positions and dig away the sand under the barbed wire.'

The Dogras had fought well and inflicted heavy casualties on the Japanese, but at 03.45 hours two of their central positions either side of the Kulla Pa'amat had been taken. At 16.00 hours following rumours that the Japanese had broken through, the RAF evacuated Kota Bharu airfield. Three hours later Brigadier Key commanding 8 Indian Infantry Bde was told that more transports had been seen offshore and received permission to withdraw his troops. The Japanese had suffered 850 casualties but gained a lodgement ashore.

On the ground the Japanese were actually outnumbered. The British command had 88,600 men but Yamashita considered that the 60,000 men of three divisions the 5, 18 and Imperial Guards were sufficient for the task even though he could have landed a fourth division.

However the Japanese were supported by 158 Imperial Japanese Navy (IJN) aircraft and 459 aircraft of the Imperial Japanese Army Air Force (IJAAF) III Air Division. Offshore were the guns of Vice Admiral Ozawa's Malaya Force, a battle cruiser, ten destroyers and five submarines. The Twenty-fifth Army also had medium and light tanks, armoured cars and two regiments of heavy field artillery as well as divisional artillery.

The Japanese Type 94 Tankette and Types 95 and 97 tanks deployed in Malaya and Burma were obsolete by the standards of 1942. All the tanks were powered by reliable air-cooled diesel engines, but armour was thin and armament light. However in some cases they were up against raw Indian troops who had never seen a tank before and so these defects were not an issue.

The British had only 158 obsolescent aircraft, artillery and anti-tank guns, but no tanks. The command structure consisted of C-in-C Far East, the 63-year-old Air Chief Marshal Sir Robert Brooke-Popham with General Arthur Percival GOC Malaya as his land forces commander.

The ground forces consisted of Lt General Lewis 'Piggy' Heath's III Corps made up of 9 and 11 Indian Divisions and 28 Independent Infantry Bde that were tasked with the defence of northern Malaya. The 8 Australian Division commanded by the abrasive Major General Henry Gordon Bennett defended Johore. At 52, when he returned to the active list in 1939, Bennett was the youngest Major General in the Australian Army. He had enjoyed a highly distinguished career in World War I, fighting at Gallipoli and on the Western Front where he had been decorated for gallantry. However Bennett was a man who made enemies easily and his actions at the end of the campaign would make him more.

Percival had two infantry brigades in Singapore with a third in reserve. There were tensions in the command even before the invasion. Heath had been Percival's superior officer before the latter was appointed GOC Malaya and now found it difficult to serve under him.

Though there seemed to be a decent number of British and Commonwealth forces available to Percival, numbers can be misleading. While the Japanese Twenty-fifth Army were seasoned veterans of the war in China, some of the Indian formations had received only basic training and this had been directed towards mobile vehicle mounted operations in the open deserts of North Africa.

In Japan, in the last months of 1940 when the 'Southerners' had won the day, a 38-year-old Colonel, Masanobu Tsuji, received orders to establish the innocuous-sounding Taiwan Army Research Station. His mission was to study the logistic and tactical challenges of an invasion and operations in Malaya.

Masanobu Tsuji remains a colourful and mysterious figure. He served with the Japanese Expeditionary Force in northern China, the Kwantung Army, in Malaya, the Dutch East Indies, Guadalcanal, the

Philippines and Thailand. He was self-opinionated and arrogant and his numerous and varied postings were not because he was a valuable intelligence asset, but rather a difficult subordinate. At the end of the war he escaped to China, served as an adviser to Chiang Kai-shek and four years later returned to Japan. He was last heard of in North Vietnam in 1961 and declared dead in 1968.

Perhaps the most significant conclusion this young officer drew at the Taiwan Army Research Station was the importance of rivers in the Malay Peninsula. The Kelantan and Pathang in the east and Perkas, Slim and Muar in the west would, along with other watercourses, be used by the British to anchor a defence against an attack from the north towards Singapore. Tsuji further refined his analysis by identifying 250 key bridges. He proposed that each infantry division should have an attached engineer regiment and that these troops should practise bridge repair operations in Formosa. It was a shrewd move that would pay off.

At a lower level the study also included clothing, hygiene, disease prevention, and logistics. The drawback for Tsuji was that the vegetation on Taiwan did not resemble that of Malaya so jungle warfare tactics only evolved when the Imperial Guards Division entered southern Indo China, but even so Tsuji added 'there was no malignant, swampy jungle as there is in Malaya'.[17]

To British soldiers between 1941 and 1942 the Japanese, who had before been disparaged as cartoon-like Orientals with poor eyesight and buck teeth, were now seen as soldiers born to the tropics for whom the jungle held no terrors. In reality the average Japanese soldier was either a rural peasant or labourer some of whom lived in the chilly northern regions of Japan.

British training for jungle warfare before 1941 was constrained by the idea that the jungle was a natural obstacle – this made the men of 2 Argyll and Sutherland Highlanders remarkable since they had embarked on a programme of jungle warfare training that had earned them the nickname 'The Jungle Beasts'. If the jungle was an obstacle for British staff officers, roads and railways were the route through it and consequently bridges the obvious choke points.

In the autumn of 1941 the Colonel of the Argyll and Sutherland

Highlanders Ian MacA. Stewart had remarked to his commanding officer, 'I do hope, Sir, we are not getting too strong in Malaya, because if so the Japanese may never attempt a landing.' Only weeks later as the British and Commonwealth troops would withdraw down the Malayan Peninsula his tone would change when he asserted that 'in close and mountain country one Japanese soldier is as good as three British or Indian soldiers'.[18]

Corporal Frank Pierce of 2 West Yorkshires, 7 Indian Division who served in Burma recalled being told, ' "The little yellow bastards shouldn't give you chaps too much trouble, they're only little runts." That caused a big laugh after our first fight, for all the dead Japs we picked up were over 6 feet tall! It so happened we were up against the Japanese Imperial Guards!'[19]

Japanese training for Malaya came in part from the 70-page pamphlet the title of which has been translated as either *Read this Alone – and the War can be Won* or *You can Win the War Just Reading This*. Despite its rather grandiloquent title the 400,000 copies issued to men on board the troop ships en route to Malaya included a lot of good sense, advice and guidance. Divided into 18 headings the manual was written in colloquial Japanese. In *The Oxford Companion to Australian Military History*, John Coates describes it 'as good a primer for troops about to embark on complex operations as can be found in any language'.

Among the advice and guidance it identified an enemy that would eventually prove the nemesis of the Japanese in Burma. 'Since ancient times far more have died through disease than have been killed in battle. In tropical areas, as in Japan, the majority of diseases enter through the mouth, but in South Asia you must take precautions also against mosquitoes and snakes. To fall in a hail of bullets is to meet a hero's death, but there is no glory in dying of disease . . . or carelessness. And a further point you would do well to consider is that native women are almost all infected with venereal disease . . .'

Prophylactic advice was sound – to use insect repellent, drink anti-malarial medicines and burn joss sticks to keep mosquitoes away. However amongst advice that could not have come from a British training manual was the bizarre exhortation that if a dangerous snake was killed the soldier should eat the liver raw and the meat cooked, since this would help to strengthen him. However by late 1944 the starving, malaria-racked soldiers of the Japanese Burmese Area Army would be so desperate that they were not only eating snakes, vermin and grass – some were even eating each other. It was the butchered remains of their comrades that would lead some Japanese to believe that the jungle was inhabited by demons.

Before they were confronted by these horrors, in the years from December 1941 to 1943 the aggressive tactics and military philosophy of the Japanese would serve them well in Malaya and other theatres.

All arms had been trained to operate and fight at night with complete confidence. The Japanese infantry night attack, always accompanied by terrifying screaming and shouting was disorientating and demoralising to inexperienced troops. Night could also be used to locate the automatic weapons around which a defensive position was based. Patrols or single soldiers would approach Allied positions and shout out challenges or attempt to imitate the tortured cries for help of wounded Allied soldiers. Jittery soldiers would open fire in the direction of these voices and sometimes large amounts of small arms ammunition would be expended needlessly into the dark.

Later in the war Slim would give his soldiers in the Fourteenth Army a simple slogan for facing these voices and shots from the dark: 'The answer to noise is silence.'

In some respects Japanese tactics drew on an outmoded European model favoured by the French and Germans in 1914. In place of the slogan *'l'attaque toujours l'attaque'* and the French ideal of *élan* the Japanese substituted the more mystical *seishin* or 'strength of will'. This spiritual essence, it was believed, would allow them to defeat technologically and numerically superior forces.

Lt Ken Cooper with the Border Regiment saw this 'spirit' in action in fighting close to the Irrawaddy in 1945.

'Banzai! Banzai!' the screams were distinct and struck terror into my heart . . .

A tall Japanese officer ran across the street twenty or thirty yards away. He reappeared with a bunch of ragged-looking yellow men behind him. They came straight at us, apparently oblivious

31

of the furious blizzard of steel which was screaming about them.

They were just running straight into it – unconcerned, uncaring – as though each man were an inviolate demi-god – running into the flailing cones of bullets and mortar-bomb explosions like fiends, confident of passing unscathed. And somehow, because the sight had so much of its own unique and uncanny terror, for a moment I experienced a wired shock of total panic. I almost believed that these figures were indeed more than human, and that they could advance unhurt – fantastic beings to whom bullets and shells were harmless, who would come on and on until they reached us at the bunker.

And then they were not there any more . . .

But back in 1941 the Japanese belief in their invincibility looked as if it might carry the day.

Following the landings at Singora in Thailand on December 8, 1941 the Japanese III Air Group had quickly established itself and began air attacks in northern Malaya. The under-strength squadrons of obsolescent RAF fighters and bombers were either shot down in air combat or often caught on the ground. By the evening the operational strength of the RAF in northern Malaya had shrunk from 110 aircraft to 50.

Among the Japanese pilots who dominated the skies was the legendary Lt Colonel Kato, commander of a Sentai (squadron) of modern Nakajima Ki-43-Ia Hayabusa fighters. Kato's squadron was employed in ground attack missions as well as air combat in Malaya and later in Burma. He was eventually killed in air combat in Burma in 1942 but with seven Testimonial of Gallantry awards he had earned the honorific title amongst his fellow pilots of 'God of Air Battles'.

When 62 Squadron RAF, a Blenheim Bomber squadron based at Butterworth, was bombed and machine gunned, only one aircraft was left intact: Squadron Leader Arthur Scarf took off alone to attack Japanese aircraft at Singora airfield. Under attack from AA fire and fighters he pressed his attack on aircraft and installations at Singora and though now wounded, flew the badly damaged bomber back to Alor Star. He died from his wounds and was awarded a posthumous

VC. After this heroic attack the surviving RAF squadrons withdrew to Singapore.

Both the British and the Japanese had realised that the airfields and ports at Singora and Patani in southern Thailand were critical to the defence of the Kra Peninsula and northern Malaya. In an operation that was reminiscent of Plan D, the Anglo-French deployment into Belgium in May 1940 that followed the German attacks, the British had drafted Operation Matador, a plan that would send 11 Indian Division north to take and hold Patani and Singora.

However it was felt that the neutrality of Thailand, like that of Belgium in 1940, could only be infringed following an enemy attack. Moreover it was calculated that to be effective Matador required that the British have 24-hours warning of a Japanese attack.

Another similarity with the debacle in France in 1940 would become evident as the campaign in Malaya developed. The excellent roads built by the British colonial administration, particularly along the west coast, would allow the Japanese, once they had pushed the British off balance, to maintain the momentum of their attack.

The decision by General Percival to defend as far north as possible in the Malayan peninsula was predicated on the idea that this would allow reinforcements sailing from Australia and India to arrive in time to reinforce and defend the naval base of Singapore. Percival and his staff failed to realise that they would be up against an agile and aggressive enemy who would keep them off balance and take and hold the initiative.

On December 8 Brooke-Popham finally ordered Percival to launch a limited version of Matador. The Indian 11 Division pushed into Thailand to take The Ledge, a prominent feature that if held would delay the Japanese advance from Singora and Patani.

CHAPTER 2

DISASTER AND DEFEAT
December 10, 1941 to February 15, 1942

'No question of surrender be entertained until after protracted fighting among the ruins of Singapore city'
Prime Minister Winston Churchill to General Percival

Wednesday December 10 marks the first of a succession of increasingly grim days in the campaign in Malaya. A few days into the new conflict, protected from Japanese reconnaissance aircraft by monsoon cloud cover, the ships of Force Z under command of the 5ft 4in tall, 53-year-old Rear Admiral Tom Phillips, C-in-C Eastern Fleet had put out from Singapore. They sailed north with orders to intercept the invasion fleet. However the cloud cover lifted and the *Repulse* and *Prince of Wales* were located by Japanese aircraft and a submarine.

Now aircraft of the Japanese 22 Air Flotilla based in Indo China launched concerted and deadly attacks against the two capital ships. Captain George Tennant of the *Repulse* masterfully avoided 19 torpedoes, recalling afterwards, 'I found dodging the torpedoes quite interesting and entertaining, until in the end they started to come in from all directions and they were too much for me.'

Aboard the *Prince of Wales* the then Sub-Lieutenant Geoffrey Brooke remembered how 'It was agonising to watch the gallant battle cruiser, squirming and twisting her way through what we knew was a web of crossing torpedo tracks.

'Eventually, hit five times, she took a severe list to port and her speed came right down. Although she was still making headway, her bow began to go under. As the waves came aft along the fo'cs'le, tilted towards us and then engulfed the great 15 inch turrets, she listed

34

further; then rolled over, bridge, funnels and all splashing onto the surface of the sea.'[20]

The bombers then concentrated on *Repulse*, attacking simultaneously at different altitudes and directions. Shortly after midday she capsized and sank.

The *Repulse* lost 27 officers and 486 men, the *Prince of Wales* 20 officers and 307 men. Admiral Phillips and Captain John Leach were drowned, but Captain Tennant survived.

Few people in Singapore were aware of the departure of the *Prince of Wales* and *Repulse* so their loss came as a double shock. Wee Eng Tang a clerk at the naval base recalled, ' "Britannia rules the waves" or so we were innocently taught. We used to sing all these songs in school – but when the Japanese came along, all the bubbles burst . . .

'All our confidence in the British defences was shattered overnight. When we saw the headlines about the *Prince of Wales* I was shattered – morally, physically, mentally all sorts. Without all that confidence how could we fight?'

On the same day General Percival issued a Special Order of the Day:

In this hour of trial the General Officer Commanding calls upon all ranks Malaya Command for a determined and sustained effort to safeguard Malaya and the adjoining British territories. The eyes of the Empire are upon us. Our whole position in the Far East is at stake. The struggle may be long and grim but let us all resolve to stand fast come what may and to prove ourselves worthy of the great trust which has been placed in us.

The Japanese landing at Kota Bharu was a two-phase operation. On December 8 Takumi Detachment from 18 Division had landed and secured the area. Twenty days later it was followed by the men of Koba Detachment from the same division. The two detachments worked their way down the eastern coast via Kuala Trengganu, and Kuala Dungun to the port of Kuantan which they reached on December 31. Here the detachments split – Koba continuing the drive along the coast while Takumi cut across the jungle-covered highland of

Pahang State to add its weight to the thrust on the western seaboard. It was all a powerful demonstration of the aggression and flexibility that characterised Japanese operations in Malaya.

Though the landings in Malaya had focussed the attention of the British command, the Japanese main effort was actually at Singora and Patani in Thailand. Here Lt General Takuro Matsui commanding 5 Division had orders to get ashore on the 8th and push hard along the roads that led south to the towns of Alor Star and Kroh in Malaya and seize the key ground at Jitra. He was able to land tanks and other vehicles.

Jitra is at the junction of the Kangar road and the main trunk road. Control of the feature would deny the airfield at Alor Star along with other subsidiary airstrips. The Jitra was potentially an excellent defensive position with swamp on the left flank and higher ground on the right.

The formation tasked with holding Jitra was 11 Indian Division commanded by Major-General D. M. Murray-Lyon; however it had been training for a quick advance into Thailand in the Matador operation. It now had to go onto the defensive and take over the waterlogged positions that had been dug at Jitra. Worse still its stores were still in the rear where they had been held against a fast move into Thailand. With the Japanese approaching the division only had time to erect barbed wire obstacles, lay anti-tank mines and run out a minimum of telephone cables before the Japanese were on the position.

The core of the division were two regular British Army battalions, the Leicesters and the East Surreys. The rest of the forces consisted of four newly raised and half-trained Indian Army battalions and three Gurkha battalions, one of which consisted of 18-year-olds who had only recently arrived in Malaya.

Murray-Lyon opted for a two-up defence with 15 Bde astride the road and 6 Bde on the left flank with 28 Bde in reserve. It was a good plan in theory; however the men were spread very thinly on the ground. 15 Bde had a frontage of 6,000 yards including jungle, rice paddies and rubber plantations and the 6 Bde a huge frontage of 18,000 yards to the coast.

The first Japanese probing attack came in at 08.00 hours on

December 11 against 1/14 Punjab on the right flank of 15 Bde, other attacks followed against the boundary between the two forward battalions. Under pressure Brigadier K. A. Garret decided to withdraw the brigade to an intermediate position.

However before long 11 Division was in full retreat with the Japanese advancing so rapidly that their reconnaissance motorcyclists were often driving through the retreating columns. On one occasion Murray-Lyon was quick enough on the draw with his .38 service revolver that he shot one off his motorcycle as he sped past.

Murray-Lyon was taken prisoner when Singapore fell, and spent the rest of the war in captivity. Although a brave and competent officer he was not offered another command after 1945 much to the surprise of many of his brother officers in the Indian Army.

The first of a series of air raids hit George Town on the Malayan island of Penang on December 8. There were virtually no Air Raid Precautions (ARP) and consequently no air raid warning. In the fires that followed at least 1,000 people were killed. The civil administration collapsed and power, water and sewerage broke down and bodies of those killed in the air raids littered the streets. On orders from Singapore the evacuation of Europeans in small boats from Penang on the night of December 16, left the local Malays, Chinese and Indians to the mercy of the Japanese and was a source of shame for the British that alienated the local population. Three days later the Japanese secured the island and captured weapons, 24 motorised boats and other craft, supplies and even a working radio station that was quickly put to work broadcasting anti-British propaganda.

On December 17 British and Commonwealth forces fell back to the River Perak. It seemed a good place to halt the Japanese advance, the coastal plain was only 30 miles wide with the right flank covered by the jungle-covered Central Highlands. On the same day Percival sent urgent signals to London requesting reinforcements of troops and aircraft.

Thousands of miles to the east on December 22 on the Philippine Islands 43,000 men of the Japanese Fourteenth Army under General Masaharu Homma began landing near Manila on Luzon. Landings had already been made in the north on December 10 and in the east two days later. The Americans had retained bases on the islands and had treaty obligations to the government. Now a mixed force of one US division and nine Filipino commanded by General Douglas MacArthur faced veteran Japanese forces.

On December 23 Percival sacked Murray-Lyon replacing him with Brigadier A. C. M. Paris who had been commanding 12 Indian Infantry Bde and on the same day Air Chief Marshall Sir Brooke-Popham resigned and was replaced by Lt General Sir Henry Pownall. The elderly Brooke-Popham was described as 'past it' with a tendency to fall asleep at meetings who, even though he had 15 months in command in the Far East before the war with Japan, had not pressed the case for more modern aircraft for the RAF.

Pownall was almost immediately replaced by General Sir Archibald Wavell who, at the request of US President Franklin Roosevelt, had been given command of the new American-British-Dutch-Australian Command or ABDA. With Japanese forces rampaging through South East Asia and a stream of bad news reaching his HQ, Wavell remarked ruefully 'I have heard of men having to hold the baby, but this is twins'. ABDA was a short-lived command – established on January 15, 1942 it was disbanded on February 25. However as Basil Collier comments, 'The chief interest of the ABDA Command . . . is that it set the pattern for later systems of integrated command which worked reasonably well in more compact areas.'

When the Japanese crossed the River Perak on Boxing Day Yamashita sensed that his troops and commanders were in modern parlance 'inside the enemy decision cycle' – anticipating British defensive moves and defeating or outmanoeuvring them and consequently keeping British and Commonwealth forces off balance. On the same day Manila, the capital of the Philippines, was declared an open city.

On January 2 British and Commonwealth troops were outflanked at Kampar and were forced to withdraw to the Slim River. An encounter in the Japanese mechanised dash down the Malay Peninsula towards the Slim River was recalled by Lt Colonel Hōsaku Shimada commanding a tank unit.

We burst into the town streets. Enemy trucks were parked here and there, with bored soldiers sitting yawning in the driving seats.

Others, cheroots in their mouths, were fooling around with puppies not knowing what else to do . . .

'FIRE!' The tanks tore into the town centre, aiming for a building from which the British flag was flying, hardly sparing a glance for enemy troops on either side. Military vehicles were drawn up in front of the building. From a window, an officer poked his head out, an incredulous expression on his face. He stared at the tanks as they screeched to a stop. Heads peered out of windows, a dog began to bark.

Then the firing began. Shells smashed into the windows, shattering them into smithereens – windows blew apart. The whole town shuddered as the gunfire went on, as if it had been struck by an earthquake.

The MGs were waiting for the soldiers as they came out . . . The MGs chattered and they fell. From inside the building too, an enemy officer hurled himself into the street. This one could really run. Then he too fell forward – bullets poured into him. Three other officers who came after him were shot as they came out on to the steps . . . The guns kept up their fire. I looked out and selected new targets, but could not see any more occupied buildings. 'Right. Let's go!', I shouted. 'Cease fire!'

A puppy dashed out of one of the houses . . . It barked, turning towards the tanks which were heading out of town . . .[21]

Five days later the Japanese crossed the Slim and Percival was forced to order his forces to withdraw.

On the Philippines US and Filipino forces had withdrawn to the Bataan Peninsula where they planned to hold the mountainous feature and island fortress of Corregidor that dominated the approaches to Manila Bay.

When Wavell flew into Singapore on January 8 Percival was still optimistic and said that he hoped to hold Johore at least until mid February.

By the end of the first week in January, the entire northern region of Malaya was in Japanese hands. At the same time, Thailand officially signed a Treaty of Friendship with Imperial Japan, which completed the formation of their loose military alliance. Thailand was then allowed by the Japanese to resume sovereignty over several sultanates in northern Malaya, thus consolidating their occupation. Singapore Island was now less than 200 miles away for the invading Japanese Army.[22]

On January 11 the Japanese 5 Division entered Kuala Lumpur, the main supply base for III Indian Corps. Here the Japanese discovered train loads of military stores and rations in the marshalling yards. For Yamashita this windfall, that the troops quickly nicknamed 'Churchill Supplies', resolved his re-supply worries and allowed him to keep up the pace of his operations. The idea of basing operations on captured supply depots would be a feature of planning for operation HA-GO, the attempted invasion of India two years later.

Two weeks into January the Japanese had reached the southern Malayan State of Johore and it was then that they had their first encounter with the Australians of the 8 Division AIF.

The site of the first action between the Japanese and 2/30 Battalion, commanded by Lt Colonel Frederick Galleghan, who was universally known as 'Black Jack' because of his mixed race, was the Gemencheh Bridge. The bridge spanned the Sungei Gemencheh and connected the community of Gemas with the larger neighbouring town of Tampin.

The Japanese advance guard had crossed the bridge when B Company 2/30 sprang their ambush. As Japanese soldiers entered the ambush area designated as the 'killing ground', the bridge was blown behind them. A vivid account of the action was sent home in a letter by a young Australian gunner.

Dawn of the great day broke clear. A few straggling vehicles of our rearguard crossed the bridge – then nothing. The terse comment of the infantry commander telephoned back to the battalion that anything further coming would be Japanese gave us a thrill of anticipation.

We had not long to wait. At about four o'clock in the afternoon the look-out announced, 'Large party of cyclists crossing the bridge.' We froze and my heart stepped into 'high' as on the roadway 15 feet below passed the first of the enemy. Oblivious of the fate in store for them, they cycled easily under our gaze, laughing and chattering while Aussie fingers tightened around triggers and Mills bomb pins.

After some hundreds had crossed the river and entered the cutting, the captain gave the order. With a roar like the crack of doom, the bridge and the Japanese on it soared skywards on a dense column of smoke and fragments.

This was the signal for hellfire to break out. From each side of the road for a length of half a mile the Aussies poured into the congested, panic-stricken ranks of the Japanese cyclists a devastating fire with machine-guns, sub-machine-guns and rifles; the while our men leisurely removed pins from Mills grenades and rolled them over the lip of the defile to further rend the enemy ranks with their ear-splitting bursts.

After a brief but terrible few minutes, the order was given to retire. The job was done, the road a shambles on which no living thing remained.[23]

The fighting that followed, and a further battle closer to Gemas, lasted two days. It ended with the Australian withdrawal through Gemas to Fort Rose Estate. The Japanese had suffered up to 600 casualties but their sappers repaired the bridge within six hours.

As the Japanese attempted to outflank the Australians to the west of Gemas, on January 15 one of the bloodiest battles of the campaign began on the west coast near the Muar River. Bennett had allocated the new and half-trained 45 Indian Bde under Brigadier H. C. Duncan to defend the south bank of the river but it was outflanked by Japanese units landing from the sea.

The Australian 2/29 Battalion was now sent to Bakri to reinforce the brigade while 2/19 arrived at Parit Sulong about 12 miles further back down the road. The 2/19 commanded by Lt Colonel Charles Anderson MC,[24] was ordered forward to assist 2/29 and to re-establish contact with the isolated 14 Bde. Above the chaos, confusion, cowardice and ultimate humiliation of the Malayan campaign Lt Colonel Anderson towers as a real hero and a man who truly merited the Victoria Cross which he was later awarded.

His battalion managed to reach the rear of the Indian and Australian positions but were cut off when the enemy, employing their now proven tactics, moved in behind them and formed a new road block.

Eight Japanese Type 95 Ha-Go light tanks were ambushed and destroyed by Australian 2-Pounder anti-tank gunners on a jungle road at Bakri on January 18. Photographs that appeared of the burning tanks, with one pinned by a felled tree and the crew lying dead beside it, gave a false impression of a successful defence of the Malay Peninsula.

On the morning of January 19 when Japanese aircraft hit 45 Bde HQ putting it out of action Anderson took command of the battered brigade which was now designated Muar Force. He delayed their withdrawal until the recovery of the decimated Indian unit. By the morning of January 20, both 2/29 and 2/19 were involved in heavy fighting and had to break through Japanese forces who had worked round behind them. Anderson led the successful attack to extricate his units and conducted a fighting withdrawal to Parit Surong, which they discovered had been captured by the Japanese. Anderson attempted reopen an escape route for the column but by nightfall next day many of his men were wounded and ammunition was running low. The Muar Force was surrounded under artillery fire and air attack so Anderson ordered the men to destroy all vehicles and guns and split into small groups and escape to the British lines at Yong Peng. Over five days they fought their way back more than 25 miles but in the end only 500 of the 1,500-strong force reached safety.

More than 200 Australian and Indian soldiers were too badly wounded to be moved, and the only option was to leave them to surrender. When they reached the abandoned position the Japanese Imperial Guards kicked and beat the surviving wounded. Others were tied with telephone wire, dumped in the middle of the road, machine-gunned and then dead or alive doused in petrol and set alight. Local Malays said that others were tied together and forced to the edge of a bridge over the Simpang Kiri. A Japanese soldier shot one man who tumbled dragging the others with him into the river and their deaths.

Incredibly a young officer Lt Ben Hackney of 2/19 feigned death and managed to escape. Crippled, with both legs broken, he evaded capture in the jungle for six weeks before he was recaptured. More remarkably he then survived internment in Japanese PoW camps, and even work on the Burma Railway. In 1945 along with two other survivors he provided evidence to Allied war crimes investigators about the Muar River massacre which would ensure that Lt General Takuma Nishimura the commander of the Imperial Guards was brought to justice after the war.[25]

On January 19 Wavell warned Churchill that Singapore could not be held. With an eye perhaps to the ongoing savage defence of Stalingrad in the Soviet Union the Prime Minister insisted that 'no question of surrender be entertained until after protracted fighting among the ruins of Singapore city'.

By January 20 the final British and Commonwealth defensive line in Johore ran from Mersing on the east coast through Kluang in the centre to Bat Pahat on the west but it was now under attack along its full length. Unfortunately Percival had resisted moves to build fixed defences in Johore, as well on the northern shore of Singapore, dismissing them, it was reported, in the face of repeated requests to start construction from his Chief Royal Engineer (CRE), Brigadier Ivan Simson, with the comment, 'Defences are bad for morale.'

It would prove a bitter irony that the requests for more troops and aircraft that had urgently been requested for the defence of Malaya on December 17 now began to bear fruit. The low cloud of the monsoon and the redeployment of aircraft from the Japanese 3 Air Group to support operations in the Dutch East Indies meant that shipping was able to reach Singapore unmolested. On January 22 an Indian Army brigade landed followed two days later by the British 18 Division and Australian troops – less than a month later they would be dead or among the huge number of prisoners of war taken by the Japanese.

On January 27 Percival received permission from Wavell to order a general withdrawal across the Johore Straits to Singapore. A day later without consulting his Army counterparts Rear Admiral Spooner, the naval commander in Singapore, ordered the demolition of docks and fuel bunkers that contained a million gallons of oil. Soon a huge column of black smoke rose above the naval base reinforcing a feeling of doom and despair.

Shortly after 07.00 hours on January 31 the men of the Argyll and Sutherland Highlanders marched across the causeway between Johore in the Malay Peninsula and Singapore and with this ended the last organised Allied resistance in Malaya. Royal Engineers then blew a 70-foot-wide crater in the causeway. The gap was not a serious obstacle since in the following days a few stragglers managed to wade across.

The naval base of Singapore had opened on February 14, 1938. Work on the strategically important base had begun in the late 1920s but financial restrictions imposed by Winston Churchill, the then Chancellor of the Exchequer, had caused delays and cutbacks. Following the Japanese invasion of Manchuria in 1931 the rate of work increased but in the end the base had cost £30 million to construct.

Churchill boasted that it was the 'Gibraltar of the East' and, with 21 square miles of docks, by the standards of the 1930s it was remarkable. It had what was then the largest dry dock in the world, the third-largest floating dock, and enough fuel to support six months of operations by the entire Royal Navy. The coastal approaches were covered by batteries of 15-inch guns at Forts Siloso, Canning and Labrador, while there was a Royal Air Force airfield at Tengah.

On paper Percival still had a formidable force of nearly four divisions. He had divided the island into three sectors, Western Area (the Australian Imperial Force Malaya), Northern Area (III Indian Corps) and Southern Area (Singapore Fortress troops and other formations). However morale was low, many of the men had received only the most basic training and there was a grave shortage of weapons. Some of the 3,000 Australians who joined the 8 Division had not yet received any weapons training, while the British 18 Division had disembarked in Singapore exhausted and out of condition after a 13,000-mile voyage.

In hindsight the pace of events, like so much of the war in the Far East, resembles the remorseless plot of a Greek tragedy where the protagonist is doomed whatever course he adopts.

Despite reports of Japanese troops being seen on the western side of the Johore Straits Percival was convinced that the assault would come from the north-east. It was here that he sited 18 Division supported by the merged survivors of 9 and 11 Indian Divisions, with six regiments of 25-Pounder field guns and a regiment of 2-Pounder anti-tank guns.

In the north-west where the Strait was 800 yards wide he positioned three under-strength Australian battalions covering an 8-mile front with a coastline intersected with mangrove swamps and creeks.

On February 2 a staff officer from Southern Army arrived at Yamashita's HQ bringing plans for the invasion of Singapore. Following lunch he left without a word. Irritated, Yamashita tore up the useless plan and noted in his diary: 'Whenever there are two alternatives, Southern Army always insist on the wrong one.'

A day later from a tower in the Imperial Palace of the Sultan of Johore, now the invasion HQ, Yamashita looked right across to Singapore Island and observed Australian troops digging in.

The Japanese had assembled 200 collapsible boats with outboard motors, and 100 larger craft and concentrated on practising assault landings. The leading 4,000 men would all be veterans of amphibious operations in China.

On February 5 even though artillery ammunition stocks were running low, Japanese batteries opened fire against positions on the northeast of the island adding to Percival's conviction that this would be the beachhead. Two days later Japanese troops landed on Pulua Ubin Island off the east coat of Singapore, further reinforcing the deception plan.

On February 8 after an intense artillery barrage at 22.30 hours on a moonless night, men of 5 and 18 Divisions hit the north-west coast of the island, having crossed the Straits in a variety of craft.

Tsuji describes how Lance Corporal Kiyoichi Yamamoto of the 15 Independent Engineer Regiment was the helmsman on a boat with two open barges lashed to each side carrying assault troops. The two outer boats were destroyed by shell fire and 'Lance-Corporal Yamamoto's chest was torn open, exposing his right lung through his ribs. He continued, however, to direct the boat forward and singlehanded manoeuvred it to the disembarkation point, and without a hitch landed the troops aboard. Then, saying "Long live his Majesty the Emperor", and praying for the certain victory of the Imperial Army, he closed his eyes with composure and died.'[26] Though it has the same tone as the heroic propaganda tales of Soviet war heroes it does convey the aggressive determination of the assault.

Ashore the Australian troops fired Very lights, the signal for search-light illumination and supporting artillery fire, but there was no response. Despite heavy small arms fire the Japanese made it to the shore. The British and Commonwealth troops were pushed back to a line from Jurong in the south to the Kranji River in the north. This would be unhinged the following night when the Imperial Guards attempted to land at Kranji and men of the Australian 27 Bde raked the packed assault craft with machine gun fire. Those Japanese who reached the shore were trapped among the mangrove swamps of the Kranji River. Burning fuel oil from the adjoining naval base drifted westwards incinerating some of them. The situation appeared so disastrous that Major General Takuma Nishimura, who had been told incorrectly that a whole regiment had perished in the flames, wanted to call off his attack. Yamashita refused the request and when the Guards landed they found that the defences had melted away since 27 Bde had been ordered to withdraw.

The Japanese now had a strong lodgement on the island and the garrison had been forced back to a line from Nee Son in the north to Jurong in the south.

The first Japanese soldiers whom Kip Lin Lee, a 16-year-old Chinese schoolboy, saw were a marked contrast to the grubby, bewildered, wounded and exhausted Australian soldiers who had streamed past their home a few hours earlier.

'They (the Japanese) came, two of them, fully armed, fixed bayonets, fully camouflaged with red armbands, which we later learned was for military police.

'They walked into the house and looked it over. To our great relief, they were friendly smiling. They tried to make conversation and patted the little kids on the head. We said, "Look, its not so bad. They're quite friendly to us and to the children." '[27]

On February 10 Wavell flew in to Singapore from his HQ in Batavia Java to find Allied troops withdrawing and morale at rock bottom. Despite this he ordered that there should be no surrender, and the garrison should fight to the end.

Meanwhile, the Japanese had landed their Type 95 tanks, which rumbled through the hills, scattering Indian troops as they drove on the Bukit Timah depots, delayed only by the last survivors of the 2 Battalion Argyll and Sutherland Highlanders. The RAF flew out its last Hurricane fighters from the island.

In accordance with his orders from Wavell, Percival had prepared a plan for a withdrawal to a tight perimeter around Singapore City. The plan was issued to commanders of units holding the Jurong Line but in the confusion some thought it was an order and began to pull back. In the days that followed the Japanese continued their remorseless pressure, capturing the British base at Bukit Timah and critically the reservoirs in the centre of the island that supplied Singapore City.

Back in London General Sir Alan Brooke the Chief of the Imperial General Staff (CIGS) ruefully confided to his diary on the evening of February 12, 'News of Singapore far worse, and that of Burma rapidly deteriorating. We are bound to lose the former before long and I am getting nervous about the latter! We are paying very heavily now for failing to face the insurance premiums essential for security of an Empire! This has usually been the main cause for the loss of Empires in the past.'[28]

By February 13, a day that would be known as 'Black Friday', under air attack life in the city had degenerated with armed looters roaming the streets and fires from the bombing burning out of control. Civilians and soldiers were desperate to escape and some shot their way onto the boats.

Wavell signalled Percival to fight on but added it would 'be wrong to enforce needless slaughter'. If it is no longer possible to resist, 'I give you discretion to cease resistance . . . Whatever happens I thank you for gallant efforts of last few days.' The CRE, Brigadier Simson told Percival that there was now only enough water for two days.

'While there's water,' Percival said, 'we fight on.'

Early on Sunday morning Percival took Communion at Fort Canning. After the church service, he received a new signal from Wavell.

'So long as you are in a position to inflict losses and damage to enemy and your troops are physically capable of doing so, you must fight on. Time gained and damage to enemy by your troops are of vital importance at this juncture. When you are fully satisfied that this is no longer possible, I give you discretion to cease resistance. Inform me of your intentions. Whatever happens I thank you and all your troops for gallant efforts of last few days.'

Percival summoned his senior staff, and told them he had permission to surrender. There was almost no water, food reserves were only sufficient for a few days, and the only fuel left was in the tanks of vehicles.

General Gordon Bennett of the AIF was still bullish, urging continued resistance, but he had plans of his own in the event of a surrender.

The film of the British at the surrender negotiations on February 15 at the Ford Works at the foot of Bukit Timah Hill would later become a powerful piece of propaganda. In accordance with Japanese demands Percival arrived with a small staff with one officer carrying the Union Flag[29] and another a white flag. Yamashita appeared tough with a shaven head in a well-fitting green uniform while Percival who had started the day in freshly starched khaki drill shirt and shorts was now crumpled and tired.

Yamashita stated that if Percival did not surrender 'The attack will go forward if we cannot reach an agreement' – the Japanese would launch an all-out assault.

Finally losing his temper and banging on the table he shouted at the obviously intimidated Percival 'Is the British Army going to surrender or not? Answer YES OR NO!'

Percival apparently prevaricating requested that an armed force be retained under his command to keep order in Singapore. However at 19.00 hours local time he was finally bullied into accepting the inevitable and surrendered.

In fact Yamashita was a worried man playing a tough game of bluff. He had suffered more than 5,000 casualties including 1,700 dead and his forces on the island were outnumbered three to one. He feared that unless he could force a surrender he might be obliged to withdraw to the Malayan mainland to regroup and build up ammunition and stores for another attack.

British, Australian and Indian losses in Malaya and Singapore totalled 9,000 killed and wounded and 130,000 captured. Japanese casualties were 9,824 of whom 3,000 were killed. It is estimated that some 3,000 people escaped from Singapore in a desperate seaborne evacuation. Thousands of others were not so lucky; they were killed by bombs or bullets, drowned, shipwrecked or, like the nurses and staff of 2/13 General Hospital, murdered by the Japanese.

In Singapore the Japanese captured 55,000 rifles with 18 million rounds, and 2,300 machine guns with 500,000 rounds and 300 field guns. Half of the guns were modern 25-Pounders. In addition they took 49 of the 52 powerful fortress guns in working order.

It was Britain's greatest military humiliation since General Cornwallis surrendered to the Americans at Yorktown in 1781. In Japan there was jubilation and the city of Singapore was renamed Shonan – 'Southern Light'.

Australian gunner George Sprod, who after the war would make his name as a *Punch* cartoonist, recalled the moment of surrender.

'When the Japs came marching in it was something of an anticlimax. Could these be the mighty conquerors? Not for them the crash of jackboots, the blare of martial music – behind their fried-egg flag they padded along in their rubber boots, looking, with their bland faces, like a mob of schoolboys on an outing. These were our masters now; our pride could nose-dive no further.'[30]

Commenting on the demeanour of the British prisoners Tsuji wrote, 'Groups of them were squatting on the road smoking, talking and shouting in rather loud voices. Strangely enough, however, there was no sign whatever of hostility in their faces. Rather was there an expression of resignation such as is shown by the losers in fierce sporting contests . . . The British soldiers looked like men who had finished their work by contract at a suitable salary, and were now taking a rest free from the anxiety of the battlefield. They even bowed courteously to us Japanese, whom they hated.'[31]

In London Churchill broke the news to the nation and the world in a radio broadcast. He described the loss of Singapore as a 'heavy and far-reaching defeat'. He warned that many misfortunes and anxieties lay ahead but declared 'One crime only can rob the united nations of victory, a weakening in our purpose and therefore unity – that is the mortal crime'. Calling for a renewal of the spirit of June 1940 that followed the Fall of France and Dunkirk he said, 'Here is the moment to display that calm and poise combined with grim determination which not so long ago brought us out of the very jaws of death . . .

'We must remember that we are no longer alone. We are in the midst of a great company. Three-quarters of the human race are now moving with us. The whole future of mankind may depend upon our action and upon our conduct. We have not failed. We shall not fail now. Let us move forward steadfastly together into the storm and through the storm.'[32]

Following the surrender Bennett gave orders that the Australian troops under his command be issued with new uniforms and two days' rations, and then he handed over command of the division to Brigadier C. A. Callaghan. With his ADC and a staff officer, some planters who were officers in the Malay Volunteer Defence Force, Bennett commandeered a sampan at gunpoint and at 01.00 slipped away from the chaos of Singapore. The group crossed the Straits of Malacca, reached the east coast of Sumatra and transferred to the *Tern*, a harbour launch. They were about to set sail when they received a call for help from a Dutch doctor who had a broken-down launch and a group of wounded women and children stranded on Singkep Island. Three volunteers from the *Tern* took the launch and her passengers on a long and hazardous journey to India. Meanwhile the Australian officers reached Padang, on the west coast of Sumatra, where they were able to fly to Java. Bennett went ahead of them on a Qantas flight to Australia, arriving in Melbourne on March 2, 1942.

The response to Bennett's escape was mixed: Lt General V. A. H. Sturdee the previous commander of 8 Division believed he had deserted his command; Bennett asserted that he had learned useful tactical lessons in Malaya that needed to be communicated to the Australian Army. He had a valuable ally in Prime Minister John Curtin who issued a statement that read:

'I desire to inform the nation that we are proud to pay tribute to the efficiency, gallantry and devotion of our forces throughout the struggle. We have expressed to Major General Bennett our confidence in him. His leadership and conduct were in complete conformity with his duty to the men under his command and to his country. He remained with his men until the end, completed all formalities in connection with the surrender, and then took the opportunity and risk of escaping.'

Bennett's star appeared to be in the ascendant when on April 7, 1942, he was promoted to Lt General and given command of III Corps in Perth, responsible for guarding Western Australia. However what was initially a key command gradually became a backwater. Bennett transferred to the reserves on May 9, 1944 when General Blamey said that his chances of another active command were slim.

In 1944, now an embittered man, Bennett published his own account of the campaign in Malaya *Why Singapore Fell*. In it he explained that he had returned to Australia 'to tell our people the story of our conflict with the Japanese, warn them of the danger to Australia and advise them of the best means of defeating Japanese tactics'.

When the war ended, Percival released from captivity accused Bennett of relinquishing his command without permission. An Australian court of enquiry found that Bennett was not justified in handing over his command, or in leaving Singapore.

However the men of 8 Division who had suffered grim years in captivity were enraged at what they saw as a wider criticism of their performance in Malaya – a defeat they blamed on the British. To placate them Prime Minister J. B. Chifley appointed a Royal Commission on November 17, 1945 to report on the circumstances of Bennett's escape. It concluded that Bennett had not been a prisoner of war at the time and was under orders to surrender.

Percival survived three years in captivity, initially in Changi, where to restore morale and discipline he reconstituted the British command structure and arranged for lectures covering among various subjects the Fall of France in 1940. He was subsequently moved to Formosa and then to Manchuria where he was held with other senior PoWs including US General Jonathan Wainwright in a camp near Hsian, about 100 miles to the north-east of Mukden.

Following his release Percival wrote a detailed and self-critical account of the campaign in Malaya, though in reality the defeat was caused by a number of factors including pre-war neglect and an underestimation by senior soldiers and politicians in Britain of the threat posed by the Japanese.

Writing in *The War in the Far East 1941–1945* Basil Collier dismisses General Wavell's explanation that Malaya and Singapore fell because the area had been asleep for the past two centuries. The reasons for the defeat began with the reluctance of the Colonial Government to order tin mine and rubber plantation managers to release labourers to build defences. Later in Burma the tea plantation managers would put their work force at the disposal of the British and these tough acclimatised men would be invaluable building the vital roads and logistic links for the Fourteenth Army.

The Japanese in Malaya were not expert jungle fighters, the jungle was as inhospitable to them as it was to all of the combatants. From 1942 onwards a common saying among Japanese generals who feared that they were out of favour in Tokyo was 'I've upset Tojo, I'll probably end up in Burma'.

In fact in Malaya the Japanese made use of estate roads and jungle tracks and captured boats and fishing craft to infiltrate positions and cross rivers to outflank defences. Men on bicycles could make excellent time on the trunk roads and did not require fuel tankers and a large logistic tail. Like mounted infantry from an earlier century they simply dismounted for an attack and if they survived, instead of horses, they recovered their bicycles and pedalled on.

Yamashita's aggressive subordinates took quick decisions and 'were perhaps too unsophisticated to change their minds, as their opponents sometimes did, in the light of troublesome after-thoughts'.[33]

However Collier's main thesis is that Yamashita's forces were better organised and equipped for their role. Allied forces felt tied to the huge stocks of fuel, ammunition and stores that had been brought forward and were reluctant to abandon them – or the airfields that had in fact been vacated by the RAF. The very lack of this logistic support actually gave the Japanese greater flexibility – in an infantry heavy army that used the bicycle for mobility, all the soldiers required was food and ammunition. The former could simply be requisitioned from local sources.

In modern commercial parlance Japanese operations and logistics in

Malaya were based on a 'just in time' approach. They would try the same approach in Burma, and would find that though it was initially a winning formula it would contain the seeds of their defeat.

Finally as Meirion and Susie Harries explain in *Soldiers of the Sun*, 'The campaign for Malaya and Singapore that began the fighting could be taken as an epitome of Japan's war as a whole. The battles were fought with ingenuity, intelligence and irresistible determination, but they also betrayed unmistakable signs of the mentality which lost Japan the war – racial arrogance and a ruinous underestimation of the enemy.'[34]

CHAPTER 3

OUT OF BURMA
December 13, 1941 to May 25, 1942

Defeat is bitter.
Bitter to the common soldier, but trebly bitter to his general.
Defeat into Victory, Field Marshal Viscount Slim

Few could have imagined that December 13, 1941 when British forces evacuated the airfield and barracks at Victoria Point in the extreme south of Burma on the Kra Isthmus, it marked the beginning of the longest British campaign of World War II. Nor would they have believed that on May 3, 1945 the Fourteenth Army under General 'Bill' Slim would liberate Rangoon – the Burmese capital that had been hastily evacuated in March 1942.

However to describe the forces that fought in Burma as 'British' is a misnomer. The Fourteenth Army was principally an Indian army, though as John Masters describes it it contained many other nationalities.

'There were English, Irish, Welsh and Scots, and in the RAF, New Zealanders, Australians, Newfoundlanders, Canadians and South Africans. There were Chinese; there were tall, slender Negroes from East Africa, and darker, more heavily built Negroes from West Africa, with tribal slits slashed deep into their cheeks – an infantry division of each.[35] There were Chinese, Kachins, Karens, and Burmans, mostly light brown, small-boned men in worn jungle green, doubly heroic because the Japanese held possession of their homes, often of their families too.'[36]

Al-Haji Abdul Aziz Brimah, of 81 West African Division (Gold Coast) a sophisticated educated Muslim from northern Ghana recalled with tolerant amusement in an interview for The Memorial Gates

Trust. 'When we were coming into India on our ship, rumours went round among the Indians: "The Africans are coming! They are cannibals; they chop [eat] people; they have tails!" So when we went to bathe in the streams, people asked us not to take our pants off – our blue PT pants – in case they would be frightened by our tails! Then the British authorities themselves began to spread the story: "We are bringing in the Africans. When they catch you, they will chop you alive." This was the best way they had of putting fear into the Japanese.'[37] Masters noted:

> Lastly, and in by far the greatest numbers there were the men of the Indian Army, the largest volunteer army the world has ever known. There were men of every caste and race – Sikhs, Dogras, Pathans, Madrassis, Mahrattas, Rajputs, Assamese, Kumoonis, Punjabis, Garhwalis, Naga head-hunters – and from Nepal, the Gurkhas in all their tribal and sub-tribes, of Limbu and Rai, Thakur and Chhetri, Magar and Gurung. These men wore turbans and steel helmets and slouch hats, and berets and tank helmets, and khaki shakos inherited from the eighteenth century. There were companies that averaged five feet one inch in height and companies that averaged six feet three inches. There were men as purple black as the West Africans, and men as pale and gold-wheat of skin as a lightly sun tanned blonde. They worshipped God according to the rites of the Mahayana and Hinayana, of Sunni and Shiah, of Rome and Canterbury and Geneva, of the Vedas and the sages and the Mahabharatas, of the ten Gurus, of the secret shrines of the jungle. There were vegetarians and meat-eaters and fish-eaters, and men who ate only rice and men who ate only wheat; and men who had four wives, and men who shared one wife with four brothers, and men who openly practised sodomy. There were men who had never seen snow and men who seldom saw anything else. And Brahmins and Untouchables, both with rifle and tommy gun.[38]

To the young Lieutenant John Hudson who had taken command of his company of the Royal Bombay Sappers & Miners this Indian diversity came in the composition of the three platoons. 'The RBS&M recruited

Mahratthas, Punjabi Mussulmans (PMs) and Sikhs in equal propor-
tions. The Mahratthas (always No.1 Platoon) are strict Hindus from
the Bombay area, short and dark skinned with a happy nature, who
smoke and drink. The proud PMs (No. 2 Platoon) are Mohammedan,
tall, fair-skinned, teetotal and do not eat pork. They smoke through
their hands so that tobacco does not touch their lips. The Sikhs (No. 3
Platoon) never cut their hair, nor smoke, but drink alcohol . . . The
handling of three different religions, castes, tongues and customs in
one small company was an amazing feat that we officers had to
master.'[39]

It is indicative of the diverse ethnic character of the Army in Burma
that the first and last VCs were won by Havildar Parkash Singh of 8
Punjab Regiment on January 6, 1943 and Rifleman Lachhiman Gur-
ung of 4 Battalion 8 Gurkha Rifles on the night of May 12–13, 1945.

For all except the Burmese and Indians, Burma was a strange and
exotic place. In a world before television, cheap flights, the Internet
and satellite communications the only images that British soldiers
would have had of South East Asia would have been the short reports
that appeared on cinema newsreels and photographs from magazines
like *Picture Post*. No wonder then that for Ken Cooper, on patrol in a
humid tropical night in late 1944, there was a surreal moment when he
watched a Japanese ration party replenishing their water containers in
the Irrawaddy.

'Everything seemed strangely unreal in an unreal world.

' "God!" I thought, "what the hell are we all doing here? Those
scruffy, smelly creatures down there and us up here . . . in this remote
land." '

All the men of Fourteenth Army were fortunate to have in Slim a
commanding officer whose experience of soldiering was not based on a
British and European model but who had commanded Gurkhas and
served in the British Indian Army. He was in turn fortunate to have
tough, loyal men many of whom were naturally acclimatised and so
able to work and fight in this extremely demanding theatre.

They fought against Japanese soldiers, but also Burmese and even
fellow Indians – members of the Azad Hind Fauj – the Indian National
Army (INA). This force formed in July 1942 initially commanded by

Captain Mohan Singh was made up of 7,000 prisoners of war captured in Malaya and Singapore. They were promised by the Japanese that they would play an important part in the liberation of their homeland from British colonial rule. To the men of the Fourteenth Army they were simply 'Jiffs' or Japanese-Indian Fighting Forces or 'Japanese-Inspired Fifth-Columnists'.[40]

The main enemy however was the Japanese soldier, a tough opponent who fought through Burma and to the borders of India carrying between 65 and 70 pounds of personal kit and equipment; in contrast a GI in the US Army would stagger off a landing craft loaded with up to 132 pounds of kit. The Japanese soldier had a rifle[41] and ammunition, water bottle and water purification tablets, mess tin and rations, mosquito net, camouflage nets, gas mask, tent sheet, digging tools, first field dressing and sometimes a compass.

Laden with this kit, 'He walked rather "marched", picking up firewood en route and swigging from his waterbottle whenever he felt like it. His buttons were often undone, his cap at an irregular angle, and he was unshaven. But he was extremely fit; his unorthodox "marching" covered remarkable distances, and Allied troops found themselves shelled from unexpected directions as his regimental guns were manhandled deep into the jungle.'[42]

However overlaying combat experience and equipment was a formidable structure that made them probably the toughest army the world would see in the twentieth century.

In *Tank Tracks to Rangoon* Bryan Perrett asks of the Japanese soldier, 'What, then, kept him running forward in the hopeless attack, and why did he stay in his bunker knowing that he would be burned alive?

'The answers lie in a complex amalgam of iron discipline, national tradition, religion and philosophy, all of which were utterly alien to Western thought.'

Discipline in the Japanese Army was incredibly brutal – a man guilty of a minor military failing would be punished immediately. Punishment was physical – slapping, punching, kicking or a beating with the flat of an officer's or NCO's sword were commonplace. An order of the day for the Japanese 33 Division picked up on the Imphal battlefield in 1944 reads:

The coming battle will decide the success or failure of the war in
Asia. Regarding death as something lighter than a feather, you soldiers must seize Imphal. You must expect that the division will be
annihilated. Rewards and punishments must be given on the spot.
A soldier who puts up a good show must be decorated, a man guilty
of misconduct must be punished. In order to keep bright the honour
of his Unit a Commander may have to use his sword as a weapon of
execution, shameful though it may be to shed the blood of one's own
soldiers on the battlefield and though the shirker may be worth no
more than a horse's backside.[43]

Punishment took on an entirely different character when it was administered by the notorious *Kempei*, the Japanese military police.

However it is axiomatic that soldiers cannot be driven by fear alone
and will attempt to escape or surrender, the Japanese did neither of
these in any numbers until the very last months of the war. From
infancy Japanese children had been inculcated with a sense that
individuality was not a virtue, but rather that 'as members of the family, they must obey their parents implicitly and, forgetting their own
selfish desires, help each and every one of the family at all times. This
system of obedience and loyalty is extended to the community and
Japanese life as a whole; it permeates upward from the family unit,
neighborhood associations, schools, factories and other larger organ-
izations, till finally the whole Japanese nation is imbued with the spirit
of self-sacrifice, obedience, and loyalty to the Emperor himself.'[44]

On this foundation, the veneration of ancestors and military heroes,
a belief in the divine origin of the Japanese and of the Emperor had
been built. Throughout military training soldiers were also subject to
Seishin Kyoiky or 'Spiritual Training'. In many ways this was not
dissimilar to Communist political indoctrination. In the words of the
US Army Intelligence Manual TM-E 30–480, 'The object of all this
concentrated spiritual training is to imbue the Japanese soldier with a
spirit which can endure and even be spurred on to further endeavours
when the hardships of warfare are encountered.' With a run of stun-
ning victories over America and the European powers in 1941–42

Japanese soldiers had, in their eyes, every reason to believe that they were indeed the Asian supermen portrayed in the *Seishin Kyoiky*.

Writing of the British attitude to the Japanese following the debacle of Malaya and the retreat through Burma General Slim observed, 'Defeated soldiers in their own defence have to protest that their adversary was something out of the ordinary . . . that he had all the advantages of preparation, equipment and terrain, and that they themselves suffered from every corresponding handicap. The harder they have run away, the more they must exaggerate the unfair superiority of the enemy.'

However it was Japanese hubris that would eventually be turned against them by Slim and the men of the Fourteenth Army in the grim mountainous jungles of western Burma.

Burma is the largest country on the South East Asia mainland with an area of 262,000 square miles – a little smaller than the US State of Texas and about as large as France and Belgium combined.

It is a very varied land with high, jungle-covered mountains and hills, swampy coastal plains, cultivated alluvial deltas and a dry central plain.

The climate is tropical with cloudy, rainy, hot, humid summers and two monsoon periods: the south-west monsoon from June to September followed by a period of less cloudy, scant rainfall, mild temperatures, lower humidity during winter with the north-east monsoon lasting from December to April.

Rain and humidity contributed to tactical and logistic problems for the Japanese. Their ration tins rusted and food rotted when packaging broke open; the Allies with the benefit of US food technology had in the K-Ration a combat ration that was well packaged and so proof against the tropical heat and damp. Japanese small arms ammunition was plentiful but again there was no use of waxed or waterproofed packaging and consequently damp and dust led to numerous misfires.

The coastal regions receive about 197 inches of rain annually, the fertile delta region approximately 98 inches, while in central Burma the average annual rainfall in the dry zone is less than 39 inches. Northern regions of the country are the coolest, with average temperatures of

21°C while the wet coastal and delta regions have mean temperatures of 32°C.

This is a debilitating climate as Lt Sam Horner of 2 Royal Norfolks recalled when in 1944 his battalion was ordered to cut a trail over a 7,000-foot ridge south of Kohima.

'The heat, humidity, altitude and the slope of almost every foot of ground combined to knock hell out of the stoutest constitution. You gasp for air, which doesn't come, you drag your legs upwards till they seem reduced to the strength of matchsticks, and all the time sweat is pouring off you . . . Eventually, long after everything tells you that you should have died of heart failure, you reach what you imagine is the top of the hill – to find it is a false crest, and the path still lies upwards. And when you finally get to the top, there is a hellish climb down. You forget the Japs, you forget time, you forget hunger and thirst. All you can think of is the next halt.'[45]

'Getting soaked went with jungle life,' writes John Hudson. 'We were often so wet, night and day, that our whole bodies became white and wrinkled like an old washerwoman's hands.'[46]

On the open plains of central Burma in 1944 Captain Ken Cooper of the 2 Border Regiment recalled the heat before the monsoon broke.

'The Battalion plodded on in the intolerable heat which seemed to have reached its "stoking up" height, presaging the oncoming monsoon weather. The blinding, suffocating, glaring pressure of heat came down one's head and shoulders like a heavy weight. Legs and backs strained against the thin, tough material of our faded green uniforms. Dark, damp stains spread across the more permanent marks where constant perspiring left salt-dried white fringes.'[47]

One of the grim results of this climate was that bodies of the dead deteriorated very quickly in the heat. In fighting in the Arakan in 1945 at a feature named Snowdon East, Lt Dominic 'Nicky' Neill the Intelligence Officer with 3/2 Gurkhas recalled that 'All their bodies were shiny, translucent black, and bloated like a Michelin man.'

In fighting in central Burma Ken Cooper with The Border Regiment recalled the aftermath of an attack, 'B Company's dead could have been mistaken for giant negroes: their whole bodies were swollen and bloated, bellies bursting through the uniforms. The skin had a deep purple hue to it after the men had lain for so long in the scorching sun . . .

'Boots and equipment were removed, letters and personal effects dropped into empty sandbags. The blankets were then sewn up, using pull-throughs and boot laces.'[48]

Dominic Neill came upon the body of his friend Lt Steve Stephenson. 'He had been hit by an LMG burst and his entrails were hanging out. He was still wearing his signet ring, and I thought I would take it from him so it could be handed to his widow. With great care I started the awful task of taking the ring off Steve's decomposing finger. I got it partly off, when skin and ring fell into his exposed entrails. I was nearly sick on the spot. With the ring out of sight within Steve's poor body, I had neither the heart nor the courage to delve inside to find and recover the ring. I decided it would remain with Steve.'[49]

Burma has a 1,199-mile contiguous coastline along the Bay of Bengal and Andaman Sea to the south-west and the south, which forms one-third of its total border. In the north, the Hengduan Shan mountains form the border with China. Three mountain ranges, the Rakhine Yoma, the Bago Yoma, and the Shan Plateau, run north-to-south from the Himalayas.

The mountain chains divide Burma's river systems, the Irrawaddy, Chindwin, Sittang and Salween. There are fertile valleys and plains between the mountain chains. The Irrawaddy Valley, which is approximately 31,320 square miles in area, is largely used for rice cultivation. The Irrawaddy is Burma's longest river and is nearly 1,348 miles long, flowing into the Gulf of Martaban.

Mountains and rivers shape the communications – roads, railways and river transport run from south to north – lateral east-west movement is against the grain of jungle-covered mountain ranges – it was this barrier that would halt the Japanese advance in 1942. In some respects the terrain and climate played a similar role to the vast distances of the Soviet Union and its harsh climate that slowed down Operation Barbarossa, the German blitzkrieg against the USSR in 1941.

The natural hazards in Burma include destructive earthquakes and cyclones; flooding and landslides are common during the June to

September rainy season and there are periodic droughts. Food or waterborne diseases include bacterial and protozoal diarrhoea, hepatitis A, and typhoid fever, while mosquitoes and insects carry dengue fever and malaria.

The British first became involved with the kingdom of Burma in 1824 during the reign of King Bagyidaw. The capture in 1826 of Assam adjoining British territory in India, by the Burmese general Mahabandoola triggered the First Anglo-Burmese War. The outcome of which was defeat for the Burmese and a treaty that ceded control to the British of the coastal territories of Arakan. In 1851 when King Bagan imprisoned some British officials for murder, the Second Anglo-Burmese War broke out and again victorious the British annexed the remaining coastal provinces – that included Rangoon, Irrawaddy and Pegu. Four years later King Thibaw Min fined the Bombay-Burma Teak Company after Burmese tax collectors, acting for the King discovered that the company had been illegally felling teak and concealing it in order to evade taxes. However for the British in India this was the excuse in November 1885 for launching the two-week Third Anglo-Burmese War and the annexation of the rest of Burma as a province of British India. The King and the royal family were initially exiled to Madras and then to Ratnagiri. On January 1, 1886 Queen Victoria accepted the new province of India as a New Year's gift. Burma was administered through the Colonial Office with the infrastructure of a governor, residents and district officers. Railways, roads, port facilities and airfields were developed. The British retained control of the lucrative timber, oil and tungsten exports and in the twentieth century the dominance of lower levels of the civil service by Indians and business by Chinese, at the expense of the Burmese, fuelled a growing resentment of colonial rule. Japan was adept at fomenting this resentment, making secret contact with nationalist leaders long before the outbreak of war.

Burma became a separately administered territory on April 1, 1937 and was now independent of the Indian administration. It now had a degree of self-governance with a House of Representatives and a Senate; however the members of the Senate were appointed by the governor who from May 1941 had been Reginald Dorman-Smith.

Under British administration the most southern point of Burma at the northern end of the Kra Isthmus was named Victoria Point after Queen Victoria. Now known as Kawthaung it is described in modern travel guides as 'an unremarkable frontier town, dominated by Thai trade'. In 1941 it had a greater significance because of the airfield outside the town. However close to a now hostile Thai border it was regarded as indefensible and so British forces withdrew.

Responsibility for the defence of Burma had taken second place as the agony of the Malayan campaign was worked out. In the autumn of 1941 it had been with Far Eastern Command in Burma, on December 12 it reverted to India, however within eighteen days it came under the ABDA umbrella.

At the outbreak of war Lt General D. K. McLeod commanding land forces in Burma had under his command 1 Burma Division supplemented by 16 Indian Infantry Bde which was arriving in theatre. The Burma Division consisted of 1 and 2 Burma Bdes and 13 Indian Infantry Bde. The division was short of artillery, engineers and transport as well as signal units.

The Japanese forces tasked with the capture of Burma as far west and north as the capital and strategic port of Rangoon was Fifteenth Army under General Shojiro Iida. It comprised two divisions, 33 Division commanded by Lt General Shozo Sakurai, an experienced veteran of the war in China and former military attaché to France, and 55 Division under Lt General Yiroshi Takeuchi.

The invasion of Burma had two aims – the short term of cutting off the last overland supply route to China and the long term of securing the Japanese western flank. By 1942 Japan had captured the oil, tin, rubber and other essential raw materials it required in the British and Dutch colonies – however these needed to be defended by a military *cordon sanitaire*. In the Pacific these were island chains, while the rivers and mountains of Burma would block any attacks from India. However the capture of Rangoon would not only provide Japan with a very useful port, but effectively put the cork in the pipeline that was the Burma Road up which travelled ammunition and fuel for the Chinese. It is hard to underestimate the debilitating effect of the war in China that had dragged on since the Marco Polo Bridge incident in 1937.

Like invasions before and since what had appealed to Japan's leaders as a swift land grab was now consuming men and resources with no apparent end in sight. The Southerners offered the Japanese a solution to the insoluble – strangle China and secure the raw materials and resources for a secure future. In 1942 it looked as if they were right. It was only later, like a gambler playing for higher stakes, that some Japanese along with their Indian Nationalist allies envisaged an invasion of India from Burma.

A day after the British had evacuated Victoria Point it was occupied by men of Uno Force 143 Infantry Regiment, 55 Division. This prevented RAF aircraft staging to Malaya from India via the British-built airfields at Moulmein, Tavoy and Mergui and also provided the IJAAF with a valuable base for operations in Malaya.

The Japanese Army in Burma composed of 35,000 combat and support troops was a distinctly lean force with less than 600 trucks, 700 horses and 50 troop-carrying vehicles.

As Japanese forces concentrated on the drive down the Malay Peninsula to Singapore there was a lull until December 23 when Japanese bombers from 5 Air Division under General Hideyoshi Obata attacked Rangoon docks. The Allied air forces in Burma would from January 1, 1942 be commanded by Air Vice-Marshal D. F. Stevenson, an officer who had been plucked from his post as Director of Home Operations in the Air Ministry. Under command he would have only two fighter squadrons at this stage: one from the RAF No 67 Squadron equipped with 16 obsolescent Brewster Buffalo fighters and one from Chennault's American Volunteer Group (AVG) with P-40 Curtiss Warhawks and the RAF had No 60 Squadron with Blenheim light bombers.

The AVG had their first kill on December 20, 1941, when they shot down three Japanese bombers near Kunming and damaged a fourth that crashed before it reached its base in northern Indo China. On the same day two RAF Buffaloes flew over the recently vacated barracks at Victoria Point and in a low-level strafing run shot up the Japanese troops clustered around the buildings.

The 18 fighters of 3 Squadron AVG defended Rangoon from December 23 to 25 and claimed approximately 90 planes, most of them bombers. The other AVG squadrons were rotated through Rangoon between January and February 1942. Following the Japanese landings in Malaya three RAF fighter squadrons were diverted to Burma, and their Hurricane IIB fighters were ferried 4,000 miles to Rangoon. The first arrivals went into combat on January 23, 1942, with external fuel tanks still bolted to their wings. The successful defence by the RAF and AVG forced the Japanese, who in China had enjoyed a degree of air superiority bordering on supremacy, to switch to night attacks.

However the damage that the raids inflicted on civilian morale was incalculable. The attack on December 23 killed 1,250 with a further 600 dying from injuries. Though only 60 died and 40 were wounded in the third raid this was a reflection on the mass panic that had emptied the city. For the British the critical aspect of this civilian exodus was that the Indian dock labourers who fled north and west to the port of Taungup on the Bay of Bengal intent on escape home were no longer available in Rangoon docks to unload stores, vehicles and equipment. Many of the Burmese fled to the jungle where they were ill equipped to survive.

The Japanese invasion would highlight the fractured national character of the country. The northern non-Burmese tribal groups, who were Christian, remained loyal to the British; however a sizeable number of Burmese welcomed the Japanese and were prepared to fight alongside them.

However though Burmese served in Japanese-sponsored formations like the Burma Independence Army (BIA) and Burmese Defence Army, the men of the British Burma Army fought as part of the British Fourteenth Army.

In August 1943, Japan granted Burma nominal independence with Ba Maw as Premier. He had been Premier but had been imprisoned by the British during the war. The youthful Aung San was promoted to Major General and became Minister of Defence and Commander-in-Chief of the BIA, now renamed the Burma National Army (BNA).[50]

The BNA eventually consisted of seven battalions of infantry and a variety of supporting units with a strength that grew to 11,000. The force was composed largely of Burmans, but there was one battalion of

Karens. However the Japanese Army held the force in low esteem and insisted that BNA officers salute Japanese private soldiers since they were deemed to be their superiors.

Interestingly in *The Campaign in Burma* Colonel Owen is surprisingly generous when he writes 'British military authorities reckoned the Burma fifth columnists . . . at 4,000. As the Japanese invasion submerged the land and recruits flocked to join the winning side, this total swelled to 30,000. At its peak it represents two and a half per thousand of the population of Burma, which compares respectably with the percentage of collaborationists in most European countries overrun by the Nazis. Some of the young Burmese volunteers fought bravely against the British.'

The establishment of the BNA was in the future when on Christmas Day 1941 General Wavell replaced McLeod with Lt General Tom Hutton as commander of the Burma Army. Wavell as C-in-C India had the complex task of co-ordinating Allied operations across the theatre in his new post of C-in-C ABDA.

Early in January 1942 Major General J. G. Smyth VC, 'a tenacious little soldier' universally known as 'Jackie',[51] commanding 17 Indian Division disembarked at Rangoon. Hutton ordered him to deploy one of his own brigades which had arrived from India without its transport and two that were in the country to cover the 400-mile border with Thailand from Mergui to Papun.

On January 18 the 143 Infantry Regiment, 55 Division moved into Burma from Thailand to attack the port and air base at Tavoy north of Mergui. To do this they had crossed the steep jungle-covered Tenasserim Range. The defenders, 3 and 6 Battalions The Burma Rifles, were overwhelmed and forced to evacuate the town in disorder. The troops holding Mergui and its airfield were at risk of being cut off and were evacuated by sea. With air bases close to Rangoon the Japanese could mount many more sorties and be over the port before its early warning radar could alert the RAF and AVG pilots.

Smyth's appreciation of the situation was that the best way to defend Rangoon was to concentrate 17 Division near the wide estuary of the River Sittang. The 46 Indian Infantry Bde was already in place and with Hutton's approval the 16 Bde had been withdrawn from the frontier. However Hutton overruled Smyth who wanted to pull back 2 Burma Bde near Moulmein. Both Wavell and Hutton agreed that the longer Moulmein could be held – the more time would be available to reinforce Burma via Rangoon.

On January 20 the Japanese 55 Division invaded Burma from the Thai town of Raheng and ten days later began their attacks on the port and airfield of Moulmein on the confluence of the Rivers Aratan and Salween. The initial thrusts against 2 Burma Bde were overland from the south-east that took the Japanese to within 2 miles of the jetties on the Salween. Smyth reported to Hutton that given the choice of re-inforcing or evacuating Moulmein he favoured the latter. During the night Japanese forces crossed the mouth of the Aratan to land close to the town of Moulmein. 2 Burma Brigade were given permission to withdraw and 15 river steamers that had been requisitioned for this operation lifted the troops in daylight from the jetties. However a large amount of supplies and equipment were abandoned and some of the force was left behind in Moulmein and had to swim the river.

Hutton and Wavell were in agreement on the need to fight as long a delaying action as possible. The military stores and depots of Rangoon were being cleared and moved northwards to new depots around Meiktila, Mandalay and Myingyan where they were less vulnerable to air attack and would, it was hoped, be the basis for new offensive operations.

Smyth was ordered to hold a 100-mile line along the River Salween – in addition he needed to keep his coastal flank secure – inevitably his forces would be dispersed. Battalions were sited in depth across the Salween at Martaban, at Pa-an on the Salween and detachments at crossings points at Shwegun and Kamamaung. Depth battalions were positioned at Duyinzeik and Papun. The rear and reserve positions made up from men of 2 Burma Bde and 16 and 46 Indian Infantry Bdes covered the coastal railway line that crossed the River Sittang at its lowest bridging point at Sittang.

On February 10 Japanese troops from 33 and 55 Divisions, Fifteenth Army began to cross the Salween near to the mouth at Martaban and further north at Pa-an.

Five days later because the Japanese were now over the Salween in force, the outpost units of 17 Indian Division were pulled back west of the Bilin.

Leyland Stowe, the *Daily Telegraph* man in Rangoon, filed a belligerently optimistic report on February 3.

'The period of strategic withdrawals has now ended, and every yard held by our forces must be clung to grimly to avoid the possibility of disastrous consequences . . .

'Possible the enemy will not need troops from the Thai area before thrusting for Burma's central artery which Kipling immortalised as "the Road to Mandalay".[52]

'Anyway the day is now near when the dawn will come up with Japanese thunder from Thailand across Martaban Bay – and this month is likely to provide the answer to the Battle of Burma.'

Second Lt John Randle of 7/10 Baluch Regiment holding positions on the Salween saw things in a rather more realistic light.

'We were staked out there like a goat for the Jap tiger and sacrificed for no reason. The CO was killed and we lost 60 per cent of our officers. Only about fifty of the Battalion got away. With the exception of one officer, the Japs butchered all our wounded. News of this got back to us and this conditioned mine and the whole battalion's attitude towards the Japs. We were not merciful to them for the rest of the war. We didn't take any prisoners.'[53]

Between February 16 and 19 there was fighting along the Bilin River as the Japanese continued their advance. The river was not an effective obstacle being fordable at many points and the 33 Division had crossed near Paya working round the left flank of 46 and 48 Bde positions. The Japanese 55 Division employing proven tactics from the Malayan campaign used small craft to land behind the British positions. Despite this Smyth's troops fought well and held the position until February 20 before receiving orders for the withdrawal. However the Japanese got wind of these orders and pressed hard.

The delaying action on the Salween and subsequently the Bilin allowed 7 Armoured Bde to land at Rangoon. The brigade, on its way from North Africa where it had served with distinction, had been destined for Malaya. However when Hutton's staff reported that the dry paddy fields near Rangoon were good tank country the brigade was diverted to Burma. This decision saved 7 Armoured Bde from the fate of other reinforcements destined for the Singapore garrison. It was expected to reach Rangoon on February 21 and deploy three days later.

On February 20 Smyth pulled his three brigades back through the road junction and railway halt of Kyaikto and a day later began to fall back along the unsurfaced road to the Sittang. In *The Campaign in Burma* Owen recaptured the grim conditions of the withdrawal.

'Review the troops as they approach. Red eyes, grey faces, beards, their shirts torn with jungle thorns, striped black with to-night's wet sweat and white with yesterday's dried salt of sweat. Water-bottles rattle from their belts, as dry as their own lips. Many an ammunition pouch is empty, too, for these troops have come out of four days' battle. Dirt and blood stain the rags that bind their wounds. They have been marching with short halts for the past 24 hours, and there has been no time to wash, even if there was water. These soldiers are marching towards another battle.'[54]

Smyth realised that the Japanese might attempt to outrun 17 Division to capture the Sittang Bridge and then drive for Rangoon. However it was essential that the bridge should be properly guarded and effective traffic control in place to prevent chaos.

The Sittang Bridge spans the river where it is 800 yards wide and tidal. The bridge is a conventional box steel girder construction supported by ten stone piers and carries the railway from Martaban to Rangoon. On the east bank the railway passes through a cutting in the wooded feature known as Pagoda Hill. In order to make it passable for wheeled vehicles sappers had to lay timber over the tracks and sleepers. They also prepared it for demolition fixing charges to a span roughly in the centre.

In modern military parlance the Sittang Bridge was a Reserve Demolition – a target like a bridge, power station or lock gates to be prepared for destruction but kept operating for as long as possible. The oil installations around Yenangyaung that would be destroyed later in the campaign would be a Preliminary Demolition, one earmarked for demolition and which given sufficient time could be prepared for complete destruction.

February 21 was a day of intense heat and as 17 Division moved towards the bridge with vehicles skirting round potholes and bomb craters in towering clouds of red dust, they were attacked by Japanese aircraft. Tragically the RAF also hit the columns having been given inaccurate target designations. Lt D. H. West of 1/7 Gurkha Rifles noted in his diary, 'It is impossible to emphasize the effect these attacks had on the Indian troops. They had reached a stage where they could identify both our planes and the Japs and to be fired upon by planes bearing our markings completely shattered their convictions.'[55] Vehicles were ditched and the columns shuffled westwards towards the bridges.

The crossing continued into the night and in Frank Owen's words 'An army of sleepwalkers moves towards the bridge' but at 03.00 hours a nervous driver skidded off the decking and overturned. It took three hours to clear.

At dawn the rear section of the divisional HQ had just crossed when at 08.30 there was a burst of firing from the jungle on the eastern bank. Japanese troops had infiltrated towards the bridge and burst out of the jungle. Now 48 Bde had to turn about and face the attackers. Further east the enemy had split 16 and 46 Bdes strung out along the road. 16 Bde was fighting hard at Mokpalin to the south-east of Sittang.

By the end of the day less than a third of 17 Division had crossed. Brigadier N. Hugh-Jones of 48 Bde with his HQ had crossed and was in position on the right bank. At 04.30 hours a staff officer at his brigade HQ managed to contact the divisional HQ on a very poor public telephone line. At the other end an officer, using veiled speech because it was an insecure line, asked if 'Jonah' had reached the west bank. He wanted to know if Brigadier J. K. Jones commanding 16 Bde had crossed, however confusing Jones and Hugh-Jones the staff officer confirmed that 'Jonah' was across.

Confident that two-thirds of the division were across the Sittang, Smyth at the divisional HQ authorised Hugh-Jones to demolish the bridge at his discretion but as senior officer, accepted full responsibility.

A hour later he gave the order 'Blow the bridge'.

After the explosion a profound silence fell across the battlefield – the

Japanese had lost their prize and then 'a storm of excited chatter and yells rose from the Japanese lines. The effect on the isolated British-Indian brigades can be imagined: the fate of these troops was now sealed, and the disorder of the battle was complete.'[56]

On the east bank, the troops held off Japanese attacks until 14.00 hours at which point a general withdrawal to the riverbank was ordered. The troops at Mokpalin received the first and only radio message from the east bank. 'Friends waiting to welcome you at the East Gate' – from this they deduced the right bank was secure.

Fortunately the Malerkotla Sappers tasked with the destruction of the Sittang Bridge possibly lacking the necessary equipment were unable to prepare the piers for demolition or drop several spans to create what is known as a 'tactical gap'. This allowed men to cross the gap hanging onto a rope slung between the piers. However the sappers had diligently destroyed the local boats, two engined ferries and 300 sampans that had been collected on the west bank – craft that could have been used to ferry troops trapped on the left bank across the Sittang.

However the 17 Division survivors were able to cross using a variety of methods. Some built improvised rafts using empty petrol cans for flotation, others simply dumped their boots and kit and swam. Others took to the jungle further upstream and found crossing points. For many of the British soldiers who had stripped off clothing, equipment and boots to swim the river there was the agony of walking con-siderable distances in bare feet after they had reached the west bank. Incredibly the Japanese did not make a serious effort to attack the men as they escaped across the river.

On February 24 out of an authorised strength of 8,500 men 17 Division could muster 3,350 men and 149 officers of whom less than half had brought their rifles with them across the Sittang.

Striking a positive note Frank Owen asserts that despite this dis-aster, blowing the Sittang Bridge had delayed the Japanese advance on Rangoon for two weeks. The men who escaped were re-armed and equipped and 17 Division would live on to play a very significant part in the Burma campaign.

The circumstances surrounding the demolition of the Sittang

Bridge are still debated today. During the Cold War when reserve demolitions were seen as part of the NATO defensive plan for north-west Europe, the Sittang Bridge was held up as an example of how not to conduct such an operation. However another example cited was the capture intact by the US 1 Army of the Ludendorf railway bridge at Remagen, Germany on March 7, 1945. The Germans had been prepared for demolition, the charges were fired, failed to demolish the structure and US infantry raced across to seize the far bank and so gain a lodgement across the Rhine. The Sittang could have been an even greater disaster if the bridge had been captured intact.

At the time brother officers, aware of the confusion of the 'fog of war' and grateful that they were never faced by the decision that con-fronted Smyth and Hugh-Jones, were generally forgiving, though Hugh-Jones was haunted by his decision. Many years later he walked into the sea to drown. 'He was a Sittang casualty if ever there was one,' wrote Smyth.

On February 25 the ABDA Command was dissolved and Wavell reverted to the position of C-in-C India; a day later Japanese forces had infiltrated west of the Sittang. They now threatened the Rangoon to Mandalay railroad.

Chennault's Flying Tigers, who had done sterling work in the defence of Rangoon, were redeployed to the RAF bomber base at Magwe on March 1.

The indefatigable Leland Stowe filed for the *Daily Telegraph*, now with a dateline 'March 3, 1942 Burma'.

'Halfway up the Pegu-Toungoo road we met a barefooted dust-covered multitude. They were huddled by eights or tens in two wheeled bullock-carts, already laden with bundles of belongings, while hundreds of men and women trudged alongside. They gazed at us with bewildered pleading eyes . . .

'We could only tell them they must keep moving north – they must not stay in the war zone. One man asked, "Is there a good road all the way to Mandalay?" We saw a thankful look in his eyes when we said "Yes" . . .

'After all the refugees could not stay here. They must go on, day after day, perhaps for 600 miles – at the pace of oxen.' On the day he filed this story the Japanese began to cross the Sittang in strength.

On March 5 General the Hon. Sir Harold Alexander arrived from the United Kingdom to take over command from Hutton who became his Chief of Staff. With 7 Armoured Bde now in theatre it was grouped with 1 Burma Division and the battered 17 Indian Division as 1 Burma Corps or Burcorps.[57] It was at the same time that, following a request from Hutton for a corps HQ to take command of the corps, Slim set off for Burma. Wavell, who was increasingly out of touch with the rapidly changing tactical situation, ordered Alexander to hold Rangoon at all costs.

Alexander ordered 1 Burma Division to counter-attack from the north and 17 Division which had been reinforced by an extra brigade to attack Pegu the key railway junction north-east of Rangoon and about 8 miles from the Sittang. The counter-attacks launched on March 6 failed to relieve Pegu and Alexander confirmed the orders for the evacuation of Rangoon and a day later the evacuation began. As if to speed them on their way at 14.00 hours on March 7 a series of explosions rocked the city, as government offices, the post office, power station and dock installations were dynamited. On the night of March 7–8 the last trains pulled out for the journey north and launches carried the last colonial officials and demolition teams to ships off-shore to make the journey to Calcutta.

With the civilian population fleeing the city the civil authorities added to the confusion when, possibly for their own protection, they released the city's criminals from their cells along with the insane from their asylums.

Now with the city almost empty and unprotected John Randle received an unusual mission. His commanding officer ordered him to take a 3-ton truck and a small detail of men to bring back items that might be useful for the men – in effect authorised looting. First priority were cigarettes, tea, sugar and condensed milk – to make 'Chae' the rich sweet milky tea that was a staple for Indian soldiers.

'Burma Oil Company personnel, assisted by our sappers, had been given the job of destroying the large oil refinery at Syriam, just outside the city across the Rangoon River, and an enormous pall of black smoke covered half the sky. This ominous overcast sky and the miles of completely empty streets produced a chilling aura of defeat. I met no civilians at all; there were one or two other officers on a similar errand to my own with whom I exchanged information . . . Down in the docks a party of Royal Marines was heaving cases of whisky into the water: "Not going to let those buggers (the Japanese) get this lot!" '[58]

From 7 Armoured Bde the 7 Hussar's Chaplain Captain the Rev. N. S. Metcalf also ventured into the city along with the regimental transport officer to supplement the Hussars' vehicles with those reported abandoned by the RAF at Rangoon Zoo.

'Fortified by the report that all animals of a dangerous nature had been destroyed, we made our entry only to discover that some were very much alive, and *outside* their cages! There was a tense moment when it was discovered that a "tree trunk" was really a crocodile, and a "rope" hanging from a tree was a full size boa constrictor! There was also an orang-utan loose in the town itself, handing out a nice line in assault and battery to anyone who crossed its path.'[59]

It was at this juncture that the Japanese rigid adherence to orders prevented a disaster of the same magnitude as Singapore. The Japanese 33 Division under Lt General S. Sakurai planned to attack the city from an unusual axis. They would hook round to the north of the city and hit the defenders from the north-west. It was a sound plan since it had the element of surprise on its side. On his approach march his troops crossed the Prome road in rubber plantations at Taukkyan 25 miles north of Rangoon and it was here that they positioned a company strength flank guard. It consisted of automatic weapons and two 37mm Type 97 anti-tank guns[60] sited in depth. The anti-tank guns opened fire damaging one of the Stuart light tanks and despite joint infantry and armoured attacks by 1 Gloucesters and 20 tanks, the road block held firm. Now a mass of military and civilian traffic was building up and amongst the military vehicles was the staff car of General Alexander.

'All the Japanese commander had to do then,' observed Slim in *Defeat into Victory*, 'was to keep his road-block in position and with the rest of his troops attack the forty-mile column strung out along the

74

road. Nothing could have saved the British, tied as they were by their mechanical transport to the ribbon of road.'[61]

Over the night of March 7–8 a plan for an all-arms attack on the road block was prepared. A Squadron 7 Hussars would lead, with 1/10 Gurkhas and 1/11 Sikhs on the flanks, after an artillery barrage and air strikes by the RAF.

The night was quiet and with the dawn Major J. Bonham-Carter became suspicious about the silence and walked forward to investigate. Though the barrier was in place it was no longer manned. Following his orders, the Japanese flank guard commander had blocked the road long enough for 33 Division to cross and it had now moved off to rejoin the division. The Japanese had assumed that if the road block remained in place their plan for an outflanking attack might be compromised.

Though General S. Sakurai enjoyed the honour of capturing a deserted Rangoon on March 8, he had missed the chance of winning a major victory that would have shaped the course of the war in Burma.

'The Japanese division thus entered Rangoon from the west, according to plan; the British, finding the cork removed, flowed on, bag and baggage, to the north, also according to plan.'[62]

In 1942 the Japanese were however not unwelcomed by some political and nationalist groups in South East Asia offering the beguiling concept 'Asia for Asians'. The idea of liberation from British, Dutch and French colonial powers was very appealing to the leaders of the educated classes who aspired to national independence. However in a short time liberation became occupation and Japanese racism and brutality would quickly lead to them being regarded as being as bad or even worse, than Western colonialists.

After the fall of Rangoon, the Allies decided to make a stand in the north with the Chinese Fifty-sixth and Sixty-sixth Armies grouped as the Chinese Expeditionary Force in Burma, holding a front running through central Burma. Stores and ammunition were not a problem since early in the campaign Hutton had ensured that they were evacuated from Rangoon and moreover there were also large stocks destined to be sent up the Burma Road to China. Rice was plentiful and the oilfields in central Burma were still intact.

However with Rangoon in their hands the Japanese could reinforce quickly, sending ships carrying 18 and 56 Divisions, the victors of Singapore. Further reinforcements included 5 Air Division with more than 400 aircraft.

Two days after Alexander's narrow escape US Army General Joseph Stilwell was appointed to command the Chinese Fifth and Sixth Armies (the equivalent of European Divisions) then concentrated around Mandalay and Shan States.

Born in 1883 the chain-smoking Stilwell was a veteran of World War I, spoke Mandarin and knew China where he had been posted as military attaché. Immediately after Pearl Harbor he was sent by General George Marshall, Chairman of the Joint Chiefs of Staff to command US forces in China, Burma and India (CBI) and direct the training of Chinese troops to improve their combat effectiveness. Stilwell would thus become the first non-Chinese officer since the British General 'Chinese' Gordon to command Chinese troops. However he fell out with the Chinese nationalist leader Chiang Kai-shek whom he despised and he made no secret of his contempt for the labyrinthine politics of the nationalists. He disliked the urbane Mountbatten noting in his diary a visit to the ape cage in Colombo Zoo had put him in the right mood to meet 'Dickie'. However with Slim he enjoyed a good working relationship, since Slim had discovered if they talked alone, man to man Stilwell was completely reliable. Slim, a man who hated humbug, could see that Stilwell shared the same perspective.

On March 12 the British garrison on the Indian Andaman Islands was evacuated and less than a fortnight later they were occupied by the Japanese. A small piece of British India was now under Japanese control.

A week later Slim arrived in Burma to take operational command of Burcorps.

On March 21 Japanese aircraft caught the RAF and AVG on the ground at Magwe airfield near Prome and destroyed most of their surviving aircraft. Six days later the survivors were withdrawn from Burma.

What would follow was a northward withdrawal by Burcorps and the Chinese Fifth and Sixth Armies. The British and Indian forces along the line of the Irrawaddy and the Chinese the Sittang. On March 24 General Alexander and Chiang Kai-shek met to discuss plans for co-operation between the Chinese and British forces. The Chinese who had fought a vital ten-day holding action were now under considerable pressure near Toungoo and so on March 29 at the request of General Stilwell, British 17 Division attacked at Paungde and Prome in the Irrawaddy to relieve the pressure on Toungoo. However on March 30 the Chinese abandoned Toungoo and failed to demolish a bridge across the Sittang which left the way open to the Chinese border. The abandonment of the town also meant that on April 1 the Burcorps, fighting hard at Prome, were obliged to retreat to avoid being surrounded.

Three days later Japanese aircraft hit the completely unprotected city of Mandalay and in the ensuing fires more than 2,000 people were killed and a large part of the city was gutted. At the time this air attack, launched across 150 miles, was seen as a long-range operation. In a few years RAF and USAAF B-24 Liberators would almost double this range hitting targets deep inside Burma.

On April 5 there was another demonstration of the ability of the Japanese to project their power when in Operation 'C' a strong naval force under Admiral Chuichi Nagumo entered the Bay of Bengal tasked with destroying the British Indian Ocean Squadron based at Colombo, Ceylon. However Admiral Sir James Somerville had received early warning of the attack and had evacuated most of his fleet of rather elderly warships. The Japanese however inflicted damage on shore installations at Colombo and Trincamalee sinking a small aircraft carrier, two heavy cruisers, two destroyers, one corvette and six merchant vessels and destroying 39 aircraft. British forces withdrew to the Maldive Islands and the older slower warships were sent to Kenya.

On April 6 Chiang Kai-shek visited the Chinese Divisions and ordered them to hold positions around Pyinmana in the Sittang Valley. However the strategic balance was changing when a day later the

Japanese 18 Division began arriving in Rangoon by sea from Singapore. Despite the efforts by the British to wreck and sabotage anything of military value to the Japanese, captured trucks gave them new mobility, and on April 11 the new Japanese offensive began with attacks on the British positions between Taungdwingyi and Minhla on the Irrawaddy.

Despite support from the 38 Chinese Division, the British positions on the Irrawaddy were threatened by the Japanese capture of Migyaungye on April 12. Two days later the Japanese achieved a breakthrough and forces took new positions at Magwe. The plan to hold central Burma was unravelling as the Chinese Sixth Army in the Shan States was ordered back to Mandalay.

By mid April, Burmese working for the Japanese in a formation then called the Burma Independence Army (BIA), attempted to infiltrate across the Irrawaddy but were intercepted by a detachment of Royal Marines who shot up their boats. The five officers and 102 Royal Marines from the 1st RM Coast Regiment in Ceylon had volunteered for 'service of a hazardous nature'. Commanded by Major D. Johnston RM they were given the combative title of 'Force Viper'. Assisted by a Royal Naval Volunteer Reserve officer they took to the river in three platoons aboard a motley collection of launches and motorboats initially patrolling in the Rangoon area.

By now the oilfields at Yenangyaung were under threat.

Preparatory demolition work began on the installations around Yenangyaung in order to deny them to the Japanese. Under the direction of Mr W. L. Foster an official of the Burma Oil Company, oil was drained from the tanks into the bunds or ditches that surrounded them and equipment smashed. When all the oil had drained it was ignited.

The Japanese had managed to work round the British flank and blocked the road out of Yenangyaung in four places. For two days, under towering columns of black smoke pierced by a blazing sun, tanks and infantry of 1 Burma Division fought to break out. The light from the oil wells was so bright that 7 Armoured Bde crews could read their maps at night inside the turrets of their Stuarts. It was eventually extricated with help from the Chinese 38 Division.[63] The division had pushed down from Mandalay, but now both British and Chinese forces were under pressure. For a short time at the close of the fighting C Sqaudron 2 Royal Tank Regiment was under command of the 38 Division carrying out patrols and acting as divisional rearguard. When the two formations parted the Chinese gave the squadron second in command 85 rupees – one for each man in the squadron. The money had been collected among the poorly paid Chinese troops as thanks to the tank crews.

On April 18 the Chinese 55 Division retreating from Mauchi was effectively destroyed leaving the road to Lashio undefended. Vehicle-mounted Japanese troops of 56 Division pushed hard up through the Shan States.

The remains of the Chinese Sixth Army began to retreat from Taungyi towards Yunnan Province on April 23. The forces in the Sittang and Irrawaddy Valleys were forced to retreat because the Japanese advance from Taungyi towards Lashio threatened the left flank of the Allied Armies. To the west, General Alexander ordered the forces around Meiktila to withdraw north of the Irrawaddy.

When the Japanese entered Lashio on the Burma Road on April 29 China was cut off by land and consequently all supplies from the Allies would have to be flown in. Alexander decided to withdraw to new positions in the Chindwin and Irrawaddy Valleys. On April 30 after vehicles and tanks had crossed the bridge over the Irrawaddy at Ava demolition charges were fired by the Royal Engineers and two spans of this massive bridge dropped into the muddy waters of the river.

On May 1 Mandalay and Monywa fell to the Japanese. While Mandalay was the terminus of the Burma Road, Monywa on the Chindwin was the door to the escape route to India. Three days later on Burma's Arakan coast the port of Akyab was evacuated by the British. Chinese forces were defeated at Wanting on the Burma Road and at Bhambo on the Irrawaddy.

It was on May 5 that Stilwell learned the true extent of the Japanese advance further north of the Irrawaddy and decided that his forces should retire towards India and not China. The Japanese had in fact entered China via the Burma Road.

On the same day thousands of miles away across sea and jungle in

the Philippines the Japanese landed on the fortified island of Corregidor and two days later General Jonathan Wainwright ordered the
15,000-strong garrison to surrender. The fight for the Philippines had
lasted much longer than that for Malaya and Singapore but in the end
the outcome was the same.[64]

Wainwright had been placed in command of US forces in the
Philippines when MacArthur was ordered off the islands by President
Roosevelt and sent to Australia to become Supreme Allied Com-
mander for the South West Pacific.

On May 7 the Japanese captured Myitkyina in Burma and four days
later the retreating British forces fought a sharp action at Kalewa to
hold the ferry crossings open across the Chindwin before continuing
on to the Imphal area. It was the last action of 7 Armoured Bde with C
Squadron 7 Hussars supporting the attack to clear the enemy from
high ground.

At Kalewa Major Llewellen Palmer persuaded a ferry boat skipper
to tow a Stuart across on a raft. It was a slow crossing and the crew
threatened to strike if they were ordered to take any more tanks across.
The two regiments of 7 Armoured Brigade were therefore reluctantly
obliged to wreck their tough little Stuarts, some of which had travelled
2,400 miles with only the most basic maintenance. The one tank to
cross and reach India would return to help liberate Burma. Stripped
of its turret it became the command vehicle of 7 Light Cavalry. The
regiment's commanding officer Lt Colonel J. Barlow giving it the
name 'The Curse of Scotland' in reference to the former Royal
House of Scotland, the Stuarts.

The hard-driving General D. T. Cowan, who was universally
known as 'Punch' because of his distinctive nose, commanding the
rearguard 'arrived to take command; the presence of the Corps Commander in this tight corner, amid mortar and machine-gun fire, had a
most stimulating effect on both officers and men'.[65] It was a style of
leadership that would later characterise the Fourteenth Army at all
levels of command.

Two days later Japanese troops pursuing the Chinese Sixth Army,
crossed the Salween on the way to Kentung.

On May 15 the first British troops reached Assam in eastern India.

Casualties from the retreat had been about 30,000 out of a total force of 45,000. However some were men of the Burma Rifles who had returned to their homes. During the final stages of the withdrawal the British had been forced to abandon all their vehicles except 50 trucks and 30 Jeeps; however they had succeeded in saving 25 guns.

Slim watched the rearguard march into India.

'All of them, British, Indian and Gurkha, were gaunt and ragged as scarecrows. Yet as they trudged behind their surviving officers in groups, pitifully small, they still carried their arms and kept their ranks, they were still recognizable as fighting units. They might look like scarecrows, but they looked like soldiers too.'[66]

John Randle recalled that during the retreat 'We were often short of food and water or at least drinkable water . . . in my experience this never became critical nor indeed were we ever short of ammunition or petrol, the other sinews of war.

'One of the main problems of a prolonged series of forced marches is that fatigue becomes cumulative. After a while all one's thoughts, apart from carrying out one's military duties, become obsessed by the imperative desire to go to sleep, and stay asleep.'

The Chinese losses cannot be computed but must have been enormous. Stilwell crossed the border into Assam with his staff after a gruelling march on foot that would have tested a man half his age. Though about 95,000 Chinese soldiers had been engaged in the fighting, now only 38 Division remained a viable unit.

The human cost of the withdrawal through Burma was enormous particularly for the Indian community. The Indians had been brought in by the British administration as labourers or worked as merchants and money lenders in the cities. As they now trudged north Burmese Dacoits, armed criminal gangs, preyed on these vulnerable and unpopular groups. Dehydration, hunger and disease killed Europeans and Asians alike. Of the 400,000 refugees probably 10,000 died on the road. For the exhausted survivors who reached the border with India there was the ghastly prospect of a final journey on foot on tracks and paths through the steep jungle-covered mountains. Only the toughest and most determined survived the final slog through the Hukawng Valley in northern Burma.

The Japanese advance through Burma finally stopped, but their losses of less than 8,000 men reflected their superior training, tactics, equipment and crucially control of the air. In some respects their halt was imposed on them by the weather and terrain – the monsoon was about to begin and the jungle-covered mountains of eastern India were a barrier. However they could be well satisfied with the rapid conquest of Burma, and more significantly severing the last land link to China.

On May 20 Burma Army and Burcorps was formally stood down and a week later practically all the troops had crossed the border. When Slim visited them recovering in rough tented accommodation in Imphal 'he received an accolade reserved only for the likes of a Napoleon or a Wellington: his troops cheered him. "To be cheered by troops whom you have led to victory is grand and exhilarating," he commented. "To be cheered by the gaunt remnants of those whom you have led only in defeat, withdrawal and disaster, is infinitely moving – and humbling." In the depths of defeat, Slim was the victor.'[67]

CHAPTER 4

THE FIRST ARAKAN OFFENSIVE
September 17, 1942 to May 14, 1943

'A small part of the Army was set a task beyond their training and capacity'
Field Marshal Sir Archibald Wavell

According Lt Colonel Frank Owen the 'first Arakan campaign was conducted upon so narrow a terrain that its topography may be dealt with in a few words. Arakan is a land of steep little hills covered with jungle, of paddy fields and swamp. In such country advancing troops can walk over an enemy who is lying doggo and never be aware of him until they get a grenade or a burst of machine-gun fire in their back.'

He could also have added that the Arakan, the north-western coastal area of Burma that runs from the Naf estuary close to Chittagong on the Indian (now Bangladesh) border south to Cape Negrais, is probably the most inhospitable place in the world to wage war. The hills and coastal strip are intersected with twisting creeks or *chaungs* that according to the season or tide could be dry or water filled. For troops moving overland along the coast the *chaungs* present a succession of obstacles. On other parts of the coast mangrove swamp restricts movement. To this should be added the seasonal monsoons that can dump an annual rainfall of between 120 to 200 inches onto the swampy area.

This was brought home rather brusquely to Lt Michael Marshall joining 4/5 Royal Gurkha Rifles. 'We marched on a mule track over the Goppe Pass to Goppe Bazaar – it poured with rain all the time. I met the quartermaster of the 4th/5th before starting the march. I was wearing the trench coat I had brought with me from London and he said abruptly "We don't wear raincoats in the Arakan, we get wet." I took the point and never wore one again.'[68]

Finally if all this was not enough of a burden on the benighted soldier the Arakan is also highly malarial. In fact during the campaigns in the Arakan sickness would be a greater killer to both sides than combat.

'Everybody that went into the Arakan to start with would be pretty certain they'd have malaria three times in the first twelve to fifteen months,' recalled Sgt Reuben Kitson of the Royal Corps of Signals. 'Malaria was sometimes followed by jaundice.'[69]

Despite all these obstacles as the British opened up Burma in the 1890s a railway had been built from the small port of Maungdaw at the northern end of the Mayu Peninsula inland to the town of Buthidaung. To traverse the 2,000-foot Mayu Range that ran the length of the peninsula the enterprising railway engineers had constructed two tunnels. Though the narrow-gauge railway track had gone, bought and closed down by a shipping company who disliked the competition, the tunnels remained and would be of tactical significance in the fighting. To the north there was a trail that crossed the range through the Ngakyedauk Pass – soon known to British soldiers as the 'Okey-doke Pass'.

On September 17, 1942 Wavell ordered General Noel Irwin's Eastern Army to prepare plans for the capture of the Mayu Peninsula with the aim of securing Akyab in a joint amphibious and land attack. There was a desire in London that following the loss of Malaya and Burma the British should not remain on the defensive but should take the war to the Japanese.

Three days after Irwin had received his orders he instructed Major General Wilfred Lloyd, commanding 14 Indian Division, to move forward into the Arakan and seize a line from Maungdaw to Buthidaung.[70] This would be as a preliminary to the assault on the island port of Akyab that would take place when men and craft had been assembled. Lloyd had enjoyed a very successful career as a staff officer and brigade commander in North Africa and Eritrea.

The original plan would see an amphibious assault by 6 Bde from the British 2 Division against Akyab. However in 1942 the requirement for landing craft for the Operation Torch landings in North Africa and US amphibious operations in the Pacific took precedence and so the craft were not available. This would continue to be a problem in the war in Burma, and it was not until Germany had been defeated that aircraft, ships, guns and armoured vehicles would be fully available.

In 1942 a variety of lightly armed craft were available under command of Slim's XV Corps tasked with guarding the Hoogly River in India – Irwin chose to ignore them. In fact he had deliberately sidelined Slim, who had assumed that since XV Corps area of operations included the Arakan they would be tasked with the attack.

The reason for Irwin's deep antipathy to Slim appears over the distance of nearly 70 years and in the context of a major war, to be verging on the juvenile. Irwin had been commissioned into the Essex Regiment. It was while serving under Slim that 1 Essex Regiment had broken and run in 1940 at Gallabat in the Sudan. Slim had subsequently sacked the commanding office – a personal friend of Irwin's.

In his first meeting with Slim, Brigadier 'Taffy' Davies, Slim's Chief of Staff, recalled that 'Irwin adopted a hectoring and sarcastic attitude towards the Burma Corps generally'. When Slim complained that Irwin was rude the latter retorted 'I can't be rude: I'm senior'.

So if the terrain and enemy were not challenge enough for the men about to embark on the offensive in the Arakan the description of Irwin's character by Robert Lyman in *Slim, Master of War* suggests that it was a doomed enterprise even before it was launched.

'Irwin was also, by nature, a meddler. He trusted no one but himself, and involved himself constantly in detail which should have been no concern of an Army Commander. He gave little or no latitude to his subordinates to use their own initiative and ensured that in every point of detail his orders were carried out without discussion or deviation. This made him dangerously inflexible, finding it difficult to change his mind and approach when the situation demanded it.'

By October 23 the bulk of the forces had reached the coastal town of

Cox's Bazaar, but forward units had advanced as far as Buthidaung where they found Japanese units holding strong defences along the line of the road between Maungdaw and Buthidaung. They were then instructed to wait for the arrival of 123 and 47 Indian Brigades.

The original plan was to launch the attacks in November at the beginning of the period of good weather that lasted until May. However in early November 1942 the area received exceptionally heavy rain – on one day that month a staggering 13 inches of rainfall was recorded. The only road south was a 4-foot-wide track. However copying the tactics used by the Japanese in Malaya 14 Division used local craft to ferry troops and stores along the coast as men moved overland from the railhead at Dohazari. However much of the stores had to be carried by the troops themselves and so progress was almost imperceptible.

On November 17 Wavell decided to cancel the proposed major amphibious operation against Akyab, and instead two days later, issued orders for a more limited advance by 14 Indian Division down the Mayu Peninsula. It might then be followed by a shorter seaborne operation against the island port and airfield of Akyab.

The terrible weather that would normally be expected to clear during November had impeded road construction to Cox's Bazaar and so slowed the advance. The whole operation had been predicated on speed that would ensure that the small Japanese garrison from the 213 Infantry Regiment would be ejected or destroyed.

By December 16, 47 Bde and 123 Bde were in position at Cox's Bazaar to begin the advance to attack the Japanese lines between Maungdaw and Buthidaung. A flank guard of irregulars led by Lt-Colonel J. H. Souther would operate inland to report Japanese movements and provide intelligence. The modest Japanese forces pulled back in the face of the 14 Division advance to a more defensible line between Gwedauk and Kondon.

On December 22 Lloyd ordered 47 Bde to advance down the Mayu Peninsula while 123 Bde would push down the line of the River Mayu towards Rathedaung. A small detachment was to move farther inland in the direction of Kyauktaw. The terrain obliged him to split his forces and employ comparatively small numbers on a narrow front.

There was optimism on Christmas Day when patrols from 123 Bde reached Rathedaung and reported that the Japanese had moved out. In fact Japanese reinforcements were moving towards the area.

The Japanese waited and watched and even allowed a patrol from 47 Indian Bde to reach Foul Point, but when first a company and then a battalion attempted to follow up a week later they ran into well-sited defences concealed deep in the scrub.

Despite these setbacks 14 Indian Division pressed forward, more battalions of 47 Indian Bde followed on down the Mayu Peninsula and attempted to storm Donbaik and the Japanese defence line. Between December 27 and 28 troops from 123 Indian Bde attacked Rathedaung but were thrown back by the recently reinforced Japanese.

The fighting in the New Year took on something of the character of that in World War I. On January 7, 1943 14 Indian Division launched the first of four unsuccessful attacks over four days against the Japanese positions at Donbaik. In February there were renewed unsuccessful attacks. On February 18 the 2/1 Punjabis made a charge across open ground that penetrated the Japanese position with hand to hand fighting in the bunkers. 'But the impetus of the attack could not be sustained. Fewer than half the assaulting troops reached their own lines.'[71]

One attack was supported by a half squadron of Valentine[72] tanks under command of Captain da Costa 146 Regiment RAC. Unfortunately the tanks that had been shipped in to the mouth of the Naf River were not suited to the task that was required of them. Closed down they had very poor visibility with the driver relying on instructions from the commander. In the attack in support of a Dogra battalion the tanks initially did good work but some bogged in dried-up *chaungs*, one was knocked out and others caught by Japanese artillery fire.

March saw Wavell release the experienced 6 British Bde to mount an assault on Donbaik and a new force was created to guard the eastern Arakan flank.

On the 17th of the month troops from the Japanese 55 Division led, it was reported, in person by General Takeshi Koga attacked the 123 Indian Bde north of Rathedaung and forced them back.

A day later supported by troops from 71 Bde, men of 6 British Bde attacked Donbaik.

'It followed the same luckless pattern. The initial onrush pierced the Japanese defences, only to be broken up among the many underground strong-points which remained in action. The British regiments, which included the Royal Welch Fusiliers, Royal Scots, Royal Berkshire, Durham Light Infantry and an additional battalion of the Lincolns, fought with superb dash and determination. "I remember," writes a military observer, "how on the morning of March 18th men of the Royal Welch Fusiliers actually got on top of the two 'humps' which were strong points of the position. If any troops on earth could have stayed there and captured it they would have done so, for their attacking spirit that day was immense. But they were machine-gunned and mortared off the coverless ground." '[73]

Recruited from North Wales the Royal Welch Fusiliers had a linguistic advantage in their operations against the Japanese. While a considerable number of Japanese had a command of English, none spoke Welsh. The Fourteenth Army would later use bilingual Welsh/English speakers as radio operators knowing that they could speak in clear.

By the end of the month British and Indian units in the Arakan had lost over 3,300 killed and wounded during the attack on Donbaik. Some were convinced that the whole enterprise had been ill-advised from the start and now there were reports of a powerful Japanese threat growing across the Kaladan River.

These were correct; the tough Japanese 55 Division, though only at two-thirds strength because its 144 Regiment had been transferred to New Guinea, had been ordered to reinforce the 215 Regiment in the Arakan. The division under Lt General Takeshi Koga had marched 600 miles across the Arakan Yomas mountain range arriving in late March.

Wavell rejected the advice of Lloyd that the operations should stop, dismissed him and replaced him with General C. E. N. Lomax who was more optimistic about the offensive.

Wavell and Lomax now exhorted the units east of the Mayu Range to 'stick it out' and the survivors of 6 British Bde to hold fast around

Donbaik. Both men felt the approaching monsoon period would enable the brigades to build up their strength. They did not take account of the rising toll from malaria and plunging morale.

On March 24 the Japanese grouped around Rathedaung crossed the mouth of the River Mayu and, faced with the prospect of being cut off and trapped, the British were forced to pull back from Donbaik.

On April 1, Brigadier Wimberley the 47 Bde commander realised that the Japanese were infiltrating between his positions and moving towards the coast. He abandoned his heavy equipment and made for the coast. However a Japanese column was ahead of him and set up a road block at Indin. Men from 6 Bde destroyed it and the orders were finally issued for a complete withdrawal from the peninsula back to the Buthidaung–Maungdaw line. However two nights later a strong Japanese force from 112 Regiment, 55 Division surrounded the 6 Brigade HQ, overran it and captured Brigadier Ronnie Cavendish and some of his staff.[74] Wimberley and 47 Bde evaded the enemy and after a ten-day march on starvation rations reached British lines. The surviving British and Indian troops marched northwards as the Japanese planned to occupy the Tunnels of the Buthidaung position and pursue the British out of the Arakan.

On April 14 Lt General Slim was appointed to command all troops in the area. At the beginning of May, the survivors of 14 Indian Division were back behind the Maungdaw–Buthidaung line and the Japanese 55 Division was pressing them hard. Slim had a hope of salvaging something and sent down two fresh brigades but once he realised the condition of the men of 14 Division he decided that the only wise course was a further gradual withdrawal.

On May 3, a battalion of Lancashire Fusiliers was attacked in their positions on the left flank. The Japanese drove through and across the Tunnels road and there was no practical alternative to a hasty withdrawal to the new line curving up from Nhili to Bawli and Goppe Bazaars, then down across the Mayu. A day later the Japanese had infiltrated between Buthidaung and Maungdaw, disrupting British communications.

Slim had hoped to establish a defensive 'Box' here to draw the Japanese into a costly action; however the British and Indian troops were exhausted and orders were issued to abandon Buthidaung which fell to the Japanese on May 7. The British 26 Division pulled back from Maungdaw on the 11th and it was occupied by the Japanese three days later.

By the time the 1943 Arakan campaign was over the British and Indian casualties were 3,000 killed and seriously wounded – more than twice that of the Japanese. The morale of 14 Indian Division was depressingly low and the men were exhausted and many suffering from recurrent bouts of malaria. Generals Irwin and Lloyd were relieved and Slim was appointed to command Fourteenth Army with effect from May 15, 1943.

It was now a time to learn lessons, retrain and rebuild morale. Those troops who had met and fought the Japanese no longer saw them as jungle supermen. The Japanese had two advantages, fanatical bravery and tactical mobility based on the ability of their infantry to march long distances at great speeds with minimal logistic support.

The British and Indian forces had not lacked courage, as Gurkha officer Lt Michael Marshall remembered.

'It was the first time I had heard the Gurkhas actually shouting "Ayo Gurkhali!" (The Gurkhas are coming!), a fearsome noise at close quarters, which undoubtedly scared the Japs. It was also the first time I had seen them using their kukris at close quarters. They mostly went for the throat. The Japs ran.'[75]

The Fourteenth Army would soon begin to benefit from logistic support that would completely nullify the Japanese tactics of road block and encirclement. By the close of the Arakan campaign the advantage of air superiority had shifted in favour of the Fourteenth Army.

Faced by a growing air threat from strategic bombers hitting bridges, shipping and railway links as well as close air support that targeted bunkers and front-line positions Colonel Seizo Tanahashi of 112 Regiment fighting in the Arakan issued orders to the Japanese troops under his command.

'There must be no fear of aircraft. As long as you are not discovered you must seek to remain so. If once our position is revealed, the enemy planes must be shot down. It is not permissible to suppose that our soldiers are no match for aircraft.'[76]

It would prove a vain hope.

CHAPTER 5

CHINDITS

February 13 to April 29, 1943

There are men who shine at planning, or at training, or at leading:
here was a man who excelled at all three

Bernard Fergusson on Wingate, *Beyond the Chindwin*

Following their victories in Malaya and the bloody stand-off in the
Arakan the men of the Imperial Japanese Army still enjoyed a reputation of being expert jungle soldiers, albeit among those men who had
not met them in battle.

A man whom some would call visionary and others verging on
insane would give the lie to the superman reputation and help to
rebuild the confidence of British and Indian forces in Burma.

In the summer of 1942 Wavell summoned Orde Wingate, a charismatic, but troubled Royal Artillery Lt Colonel and instructed him to
raise local forces and plan a guerrilla campaign against the Japanese
forces in Burma. The speed of the Japanese advance overtook these
plans, but assisted by Major J. M. Calvert[77] commandant of the Bush
Warfare School, the 40-year-old Wingate had been able to conduct a
reconnaissance of the terrain and had more imaginative and ambitious
plans.

Wavell knew that Wingate had plenty of valuable experience in
guerrilla operations. In 1936 in British-administered Palestine, a
passionate Zionist Wingate had led Jewish 'Special Night Squads'.
These groups had waged a counter-terror campaign against Arab
groups who had attacked Jewish communities. In 1940 British and
Imperial forces attacked Ethiopia, which had been overrun by the
Italians in 1936. As part of a Special Operations Executive (SOE)
team Wingate was sent as a liaison officer to the exiled Ethiopian

Emperor Haile Selassie. Wingate raised an irregular force of Ethiopians which he named Gideon Force and in parallel with Wavell's conventional operations waged a successful guerrilla campaign against the Italians. With the defeat of the Italians he accompanied Haile Selassie on his victorious return to the capital Addis Ababa.

Wingate had exceeded his SOE brief in Ethiopia and his critical report on operations made enemies within the British military establishment. Writing in 1945 Bernard Fergusson said of his former commanding officer,

'. . . he had only one standard, and that was perfection. He seemed almost to rejoice in making enemies, and in erecting additional barriers through which to break. By some, chiefly journalists, he has been idealised; by others, chiefly professional rivals, he has been decried.'[78]

After Ethiopia Wingate was almost dismissed, but instead was given a lowly staff job. Exhausted and ill, he cut his throat in an attempted suicide and then spent several months in hospital.

In India in discussions with Wavell, Wingate proposed that a force supplied by parachute drops of food and ammunition could penetrate Japanese lines and attack targets like railways and bridges, targets that he called 'the vulnerable artery . . . winding through the jungle'. The aircraft were in short supply in Burma, but pressed by Wingate, Wavell authorised a self-contained overland operation code named Longcloth. It was originally intended to be a diversion while an amphibious attack was launched in the Arakan – the Arakan attack was cancelled and Wingate feared that this would happen to his plans.

Later in the war, Slim would say of Wingate's commitment and passion, 'He could impart his belief to others. Above all, he could adapt to his own purposes the ideas, practices and techniques of others once he was satisfied of their soundness.

'To see Wingate urging action on some hesitant commander was to realise how a medieval baron felt when Peter the Hermit got after him to go crusading. Lots of barons found Peter the Hermit an uncomfortable fellow, but they went crusading all the same.'[79]

Sergeant Harold Atkins of the Queen's Royal Regiment who would fight in the Second Chindit expedition said of his commanding officer, 'Each time I saw Wingate, he looked a rather scruffy individual for a very senior officer. He used to wear an old sort of topee – the old-fashioned topee – and it seemed to sit well down on his ears. He had his customary beard and his khaki drill was normally crumpled. He wasn't a big, imposing figure at all, so the first appearances didn't impress one really.'[80]

Promoted to Brigadier, Wingate organised the British and Indian forces in 77 Indian Infantry Bde into eight self-contained columns each made up of four patrols of four sections. Though they were to undertake an unprecedented operation, the men of 77 Indian Infantry Bde were ordinary soldiers from 13 Battalion The King's (Liverpool) Regiment, 3/2 Gurkha Rifles, 142 Commando Company, 2 Burma Rifles, eight RAF sections, Brigade Signal Section from The Royal Corp of Signals and a mule transport company. Only the men of No 142 Commando Company and men of the Bush Warfare School in Burma could be called dedicated special forces.

Wingate pushed all the soldiers under his command very hard.

Wavell would write of him in June 1944, 'He was not, I think, easy to know. His forcibly challenging personality invoked antagonism – he often exasperated my staff by the vehement importunity with which his demands for priority of equipment and personnel were pressed; nor did his subordinates find him an easy man to serve. His troops had full trust in his ability, but he had not the power to win their affection, though his occasional addresses, which were vivid and compelling, could stir their imagination. The truth is, I think, that he had in him such a consuming fire of earnestness for the work in hand that he could spare no effort to soothe or conciliate those with whom he worked.'[81]

Wingate called his forces Chindits, a name suggested by Captain Aung Thin DSO of the Burma Army. Chindit is a corrupted form of the Burmese *Chinthé* or *Chinthay*, the mythical winged stone lions which guard the gates of Burmese temples. The *chinthe* became the brigade's insignia.

Bernard Fergusson would say of Wingate and the Chindits, '. . . no other officer I have heard of could have dreamed the dream, planned the plan, obtained, trained, inspired and led the force. There are men who shine at planning, or at training, or at leading: here was a man who excelled at all three, and whose vision at the council-table matched his genius in the field.'[82]

Longcloth began on February 6, 1943 and to accomplish the tasks given to him by Wavell, Wingate divided 77 Bde into two groups, the Northern and Southern. The groups were in turn broken down into columns of about 400 men built around an infantry company. In addition there was a reconnaissance platoon of the Burma Rifles, two 3-inch mortars and two Vickers medium machine guns, mule transport platoon of 100 mules and 15 horses, RAF liaison officer and radio operators to direct air supplies, a doctor and radio detachment to provide communications between columns.[83]

The Southern with 1 and 2 Columns and 142 Commando Company under Lt Colonel L. A. Alexander was to cut the railway south of the town of Wuntho. Its role was also to divert Japanese attention from the operations of the Northern Group. It was then to march 250 miles across Japanese-held territory to rendezvous with the Northern Group that would have cut the railway near Nanken. Wingate had five columns under command, of which two commanders Majors Mike Calvert No 3 and Bernard Fergusson No 5 were to play important roles in the Second Chindit Expedition.

If conditions were favourable for Longcloth, the combined force would then cross the Irrawaddy River and sever the Mandalay–Lashio railway. They were also to exploit 'any opportunities created by its presence within enemy territory'.

The two Groups set off into Burma on February 8, 1943. On February 14 they crossed the Chindwin, the Southern at Auktaung and Northern at Tonhe with Wingate in command of the larger Northern Group. Behind them were hundreds of pack mules carrying stores and ammunition. As a deception plan to cover the operation 23 Indian Division simulated an attack on Kalewa.

By March 1 the two groups were making slower progress than had been hoped, partially because they were concerned to find clearings for supply drops when in fact, it was discovered later that it was possible to recover supplies even if they were dropped in the jungle.

After Alexander had crossed the Chindwin his group skirmished with Japanese patrols and made a long detour in order to avoid further contact with the enemy. On March 3, No 1 (Gurkha) Column of the Southern Group commanded by Major Dunlop cut the Mandalay to Myitkyina railroad just north of Kyaikthin though a clash on the night of March 2–3 had led to No 2 Column being scattered and forced to return to India.

Tilbahadur Thapa a Gurkha in No 1 Column recalled the attack.

'One night we camped and started to cook our meal. As we were cooking, the Japanese attacked us on all sides and a free-for-all developed man to man, kukris, bayonets, swords, hand-to-hand. Both sides fired blindly, even killing each other, Gurkhas killing Gurkhas and Japanese killing Japanese by mistake in the confusion. It was like a nightmare. So noisy was it that we could not hear each other clearly. The jungle was set alight. Pandemonium all round. We were all shouting . . .

'The next day we took stock of the situation and by evening we were organised enough to move off into the night. We walked till dawn when we stopped in some low-lying ground. We opened our wireless and were told to return to India. We went back the same way and, on reaching the Irrawaddy, started making boats and rafts from cane and bamboo.'[84]

Betrayed by villagers Tilbahadur Thapa was captured but after being held in Rangoon jail was able to escape from a work party after an RAF attack.

The Southern Group crossed the Irrawaddy unopposed on March 9–10 at Tagaung and arrived at the designated rendezvous but were unable to find Wingate or contact him by radio.

Wingate's group, which had enhanced its transport with an elephant and its handler or *oozie*, crossed the headwaters of the Mu River and attacked the railway north of Wuntho according to plan.

On March 6, Fergusson's No 5 (King's) Column attacked the three-span steel girder railway bridge across the river at Bonchaung. His demolitions expert explained that the sequence of the demolition at 21.00 hours would be a 'big bang . . . preceded by a little bang. The little bang duly went off,' he recalled, 'and there was a short delay; then . . . The flash illuminated the whole hillside. It showed the men standing tense and waiting, the muleteers with a good grip of their mules; the brown of the path and the green of the trees preternaturally vivid. Then came the bang. The mules plunged and kicked, the hills for miles around rolled the noise of it about their hollows and flung it to their neighbours.'[85]

Fergusson's column also brought down a landslide onto the railway blocking at Bongyaung Gorge while Calvert's No 3 (Gurkha) Column cut the track at Nankan.

Attracted by the idea of making a permanent base for raiding in the area, Wingate lingered north of Wuntho. He sent one column back to India since it had expended most of its ammunition in a diversionary action near Pinlebu on March 4 and two columns across the Irrawaddy. No 1 Column of the Southern Group crossing on March 10 at Tagaung and the Northern Group between March 10 and 13 at Tigyaing. Though the delay had allowed the Northern Group to inflict considerable damage on the railway, the Japanese were now aware there was a real threat to their lines of communications.

By March 18 Wingate's columns were across the 1,000-yard-wide Irrawaddy but it was now the dry season and vegetation offered less natural cover, moreover the tracks and roads allowed the Japanese to use vehicles to concentrate their forces. The aerial re-supply, which had worked effectively in the jungle, became less reliable as radio communications became difficult and the columns were forced to keep moving by Japanese pressure.[86] From the south the Japanese 18 Division commanded by Lt General Renya Mutaguchi[87] pressed north in an attempt to cut off the Chindits' escape route to India, while from the east the 56 Division under General Yuzo Matsuyama drove westward across the Kachin Hills towards Wingate's Northern Group.

Wingate still hoped to penetrate further east to demolish the 1,000-foot-high Gokteik viaduct that carried the Mandalay–Lashio road and rail link that had been laid down by Wavell as the ultimate objective. Nos 3 and 5 columns were ordered to press on to the viaduct but reported that the area was now alive with Japanese. Wingate therefore ordered No 5 to act as an advanced guard while No 3 under Calvert, who was familiar with the area, would attack the viaduct.

Many of the mules had been slaughtered for food and to save water but in turn this meant that heavy equipment had to be abandoned. After six days, short of water and supplies Wingate realised that he would have to abandon his plan to attack the Mandalay–Lashio road. On March 24 he received orders from General Geoffrey Scoones, commanding IV Corps which was responsible for northern Burma, that instead of attacking Gokteik he should withdraw to India.

Wingate ordered the column commanders either to take their men north to China or make their way back to India. As an alternative they could split into dispersal groups as they had been trained and infiltrate back to friendly territory.

No 7 (Kings) Column commanded by Major K. D. Gilkes chose the longer and safer route into China, while No 8 under Major W. P. Scott a Royal Engineer, constructed an airstrip and were flown across the Irrawaddy. Some of the dispersal groups that reached the west bank of the Chindwin were unaware that the IV Corps had pulled back and assuming that they were in friendly territory relaxed and were killed or captured by Japanese patrols.

Summing up Operation Longcloth or the First Chindit Expedition Bernard Fergusson strikes a low key.

'What did we accomplish? Not much that was tangible. What there was became distorted in the glare of publicity soon after our return . . .

'But we amassed experience on which a future has already begun to build.'

In the light of the experience gained by the Chindits Wingate wrote of the Japanese in his report: 'His mind is slow but methodical. He is a reasoned, if humourless, student of war in all its phases. He has carefully thought out the answer to all ordinary problems. He hates a leap in the dark to such an extent that he will do anything rather than make it.'[88]

Operation Longcloth had proved the viability of long-range penetration operations, had taken the war to the Japanese and exposed their overly rigid tactics. In his report Wingate wrote 'a weapon has been found which may well prove a counter to the obstinate but unimaginative courage of the Japanese soldier and which will give scope to the military qualities which the British soldier still shares with his ancestors. These qualities, hitherto unsuspected by the world, are firstly intelligence in action, that is originality in individual fighting, and secondly, on the moral side, self-reliance and the power to give of his best when the audience is smallest.'

On May 21, 1943 from his office in New Delhi L. Marsland Gander[89] of the *Daily Telegraph* filed a news story that, if cheerfully upbeat, also reflected Fergusson's jaundiced view of the publicity that the Chindits had attracted. With the headline 'BRITISH JUNGLE FORCE KEPT JAPANESE ON RUN' Gander wrote 'To-night I am able to reveal details of a daring three-months' campaign carried out behind enemy lines deep in the heart of Central Burma by a mixed force of British, Indian, Gurkha and Burmese troops . . .

'Among them were Commando men who had raided Norway and France. Now, beating the Japanese at their own game of infiltration in the dark solitudes of the Burmese forests . . .

'The Japanese command was bewildered, and put out broadcasts saying these men were the remnants of Gen. Alexander's defeated Burma Army.'

Mr Gander may have allowed himself to be carried away with his journalistic enthusiasm at the expense of accuracy, but his story encapsulates the optimism that Operation Longcloth had generated in both the Army in India and civilian population in Great Britain. The soldiers of the Japanese Army were not unbeatable and nor were they masters of the jungle.

Wingate identified the weakness that had beset the British in Malaya and Burma. 'The vulnerable artery is the Line of Communication winding through the jungle.' Uniquely he was now in a position to rectify this. 'Have no L. of C. on the jungle floor. Bring in the goods like Father Christmas, down the chimney.'[90]

In this way Longcloth had proved the viability of aerial re-supply and had made long and vulnerable lines of communications redundant and so laid the ground for a subsequent bigger Chindit operation in Burma in 1944.

However these lessons had come at a high price.

Many of the sick and wounded had to be left behind with friendly Burmese in the hope that they would care for them. Some would be betrayed and murdered by the Japanese, others die in grim solitude.

One remarkable tale of survival was that of 19-year-old Second Lt Ian MacHorton of 8 Gurkhas, probably the youngest British soldier in the expedition. 'He had been left for dead, for worse than dead because the smashed leg he had sustained in battle had doomed him to death by starvation or Jap torture.'[91] Rather than see him doomed to this fate a teenage Gurkha soldier Kulbahadur Thapa had chosen to stay with the young officer. It required a direct order from MacHorton before he would leave him to join the other Chindits. Now alone MacHorton had dragged himself back to the Chindwin and after swimming the river he collapsed exhausted at the feet of a British patrol.

Of 3,000 men and 800 mules that crossed the Chindwin only 2,182 men and two mules had reached India by the first week in June, some of them travelled as far as Paoshan in southern China. 'The Chinese people feted them and the Americans flew them home to India.'[92] The men had marched between 750 and 1,500 miles carrying 70 lb packs or roughly half their body weight in one of the most debilitating climates in the world.

The operation was controversial, critics said that Wingate was a self-publicist who had destroyed a brigade. Of the men who reached India 600 were unfit for any further service. All that Wingate could show for it was some damage to railways in Burma that within a month were operating again. It would be many months before 77 Indian Infantry Bde could be reconstituted as an effective force with fresh troops.

What, moreover, the public and the Army in India did not know was how ruthlessly discipline had been imposed in the jungle.

Wingate and the column commanders had been given special disciplinary powers by the C-in-C India for the duration of the operation. Lt Colonel Jeffery Lockett who commanded the Commando group in Calvert's No 3 Column wrote:

Ordinary army discipline did not apply in Long Range Penetration . . . One column commander I knew found a sentry asleep, so endangering the safety of the whole of his column, which was asleep at the time. He gave the offender three choices: to be shot; to be flogged; to walk back to our own lines the other side of the Chindwin by himself (a distance at the time of some eighty miles). I suppose

100

the Chindits were the only force in this war in which flogging was allowed. I myself, when I was a column commander in 1944, had two men flogged (again for being asleep at their posts). It was a distasteful task, but there was no alternative.[93]

Ironically Mutaguchi Wingate's opponent also looked at the lessons of Longcloth. He had lost face when earlier he had asserted that the jungle-covered mountains of northern Burma were an obstacle and now the British had proved him wrong. On promotion to General and command of Fifteenth Army in March 1943 he decided to play the British at their own game and take the offensive pushing across the inhospitable Indian border to Imphal in March 1944.

It would prove a fatal decision and at midnight on November 15, 1943 the new Allied command that would prove his nemesis came into existence.

The South East Asia Command (SEAC) took over the operations in Burma, Thailand, Malaya and Sumatra and the defence of North East India and Ceylon.

The Supreme Commander was Acting Vice Admiral Lord Louis Mountbatten (he held the substantive rank of Captain and was the youngest Vice Admiral in the Royal Navy). The Deputy Supreme Commander was Lt General J. S. Stilwell with Lt General Sir Henry Pownall the Supreme Commander's Chief of Staff. Lt General R. A. Wheeler of the US Army was the Principal Administrative Officer, with a British deputy.

Mountbatten had hoped that he could address long-term strategy and the three Commanders in Chief could handle the day-to-day operations on sea, land and in the air.

'In practice,' writes Basil Collier, 'he found that he had often to smooth over difficulties arising from an imperfect and anomalous organization.

'Mountbatten was only forty-two years old at the time of his appointment. Tall, handsome, a close relative of the royal family, he had distinguished himself as commander of a destroyer flotilla early in the war . . .

'A man of immense personal charm with a genius for public

relations, Mountbatten was considered something of a lightweight by some of the more senior generals and admirals, who resented his swift rise to prominence. His new command was far from being the smoothly running Allied team which Eisenhower would soon command in Great Britain.'[94]

Mountbatten had his critics and indeed enemies, but in late March 1944 he would take a bold decision that would shape the course of the campaign in Burma.

CHAPTER 6

CHINDITS AND MARAUDERS

February 5 to August 3, 1944

'Any place, Any time, Anywhere'
Motto of No 1 Air Commando USAAF

Following the string of disasters in Malaya and Burma, the success of
the first Chindit expedition had delighted the British public and caught
the attention of Winston Churchill and in 1944 Wingate was promoted
to Major General. He accompanied Churchill to the Quebec Conference in August 1943 where the United States offered to support the
second Chindit offensive with American air power.

General Henry H. 'Hap' Arnold, USAAF Commander was keen to
explore novel ways of employing air power, so he selected two young
veteran fighter pilots, Lt Colonel Philip G. Cochran[95] and Lt Colonel
John Alison, to devise and assemble an aerial task force to meet the
needs of the next Chindit operation. He was also horrified by the
stories of wounded men being left behind with Burmese in the first
expedition because there was no way of evacuating them.

Now aged 41 Wingate took command of a force drawn largely from
70 Division, but named for deception purposes 3 Indian Division,
Long Range Penetration Group. It was actually the equivalent to two
divisions which for the operation would be divided into 300-strong
self-contained columns. Most of the troops were British, the remainder were Gurkhas or West African while US Army engineers would
assist in the construction of jungle airstrips. Wingate was dismissive of
Indian soldiers whose dietary requirements he felt added an additional
and unnecessary logistic load.

This time many of the men on his second Chindit expedition, code
named Operation Thursday, would not have a six-week march into

central Burma, since with the huge assets of the USAAF now available they would be flown into jungle airstrips. This was to be an aerial invasion that in its range and complexity would dwarf the German airborne assault on Crete on May 20, 1941. Not only would men be flown in but also signals equipment, anti-aircraft guns, 25-Pounder batteries as well as engineer units with bulldozers and graders to prepare the airstrips.

Cochran and Alison identified the main roles of the aerial task force as: fly in troops and equipment, evacuate casualties, re-supply by air, give close air support and impose air superiority.

Once in India the unit was re-designated the 5318th Provisional Unit (Air). The unit's aircraft were given markings of five white diagonal stripes banding the fuselage behind the cockpit to give it an identification and also 'to let the Japanese know who was dominating the skies of Burma'.

When, during training in India two gliders collided during takeoff killing three Americans and four British soldiers, the USAAF crews were concerned that the British might be reluctant to fly with them. However immediately after the accident they received a note from a Chindit commander.

'Please be assured that we will go with your boys any place, any time, anywhere.'

It was a phrase that would become the motto of the unique force now designated No 1 Air Commando.

Some Chindits however would be required to make the journey on foot and so 16 Bde under the blue-eyed 6-foot-tall Brigadier Bernard Fergusson set off from Ledo on the Indian border and began the arduous journey south. The oldest man in 16 Brigade was 45 and the youngest 19.

Captain James Dell of 2 Queen's Royal Regiment described the overland approach. 'It took us a whole day to get the column up the first mountainside – it was as steep as the roof of a house . . . In places the slope was so steep that the mules had to be unloaded and their loads passed up hand-to-hand. It rained all the time . . . Despite the rain and the saturated ground, we were short of water – but we could hear the streams thousands of feet below.'[96]

During a single week in early March, 77 and 11 Chindit Bdes flew into Landing Zones (LZ) in the Kaukkwe Valley deep inside Japanese-controlled northern Burma. To achieve this it was estimated required 660 Dakota sorties and 78 Waco gliders that would transport 9,052 troops, 1,360 pack-animals and 250 tons of equipment. In the event, of the 67 gliders that flew, 32 landed safely on the LZ, nine came down in enemy territory and 11 on friendly soil. Some 15 were turned back because of congestion on the LZ. The casualty rate was 121 men but for the loss of no aircraft.

The LZs for Operation Thursday were code named 'Piccadilly', 'Broadway' and 'Chowringhee'. In an air reconnaissance mission flown just prior to the operation it was discovered that 'Piccadilly' that was to be used on the first night had been apparently obstructed by felled trees. This caused concern in India since the year before in Operation Longcloth a Dakota had landed on this site and consequently there was concern that the Japanese might have anticipated an aerial operation of this kind.

Slim assessed the information and with his sound good sense said 'things are seldom as bad as they seem' and the landing was switched to Broadway. The felled timber, it later emerged, was simply the work of Burmese foresters.

At 06.02 on March 5 four Dakotas each towing two gliders took off for the LZ.

At Broadway unseen deep ruts in the grass caused two gliders to land badly and temporarily block the Landing Zone. At Chowringhee all was ready and the fly in the following day proceeded smoothly.

Japanese reaction ranged from arrogant confidence to concern. The commander of IJAAF air units in Burma, Major-General Noboru Tazoe, urged Mutaguchi to divert troops from U-GO, his offensive against Imphal and Kohima in India, to secure the Japanese rear areas against the Chindits. When Mutaguchi, the driving force behind U-GO, heard of the landings on March 9 he boasted 'When I get to Imphal, I'll have their supply base. They'll be rats in a trap.'[97]

In place behind enemy lines the Chindits set to work to build fortified positions or 'Strongholds' named 'Aberdeen' and 'White City'. Probing attacks were beaten off and Chindit patrols from

White City pushed west to cut the Rangoon to Myitkyina railway line in several places.

Fergusson's column, after its arduous approach march attacked the logistic base and airfield at Indaw. A fourth Chindit brigade, No 14 was flown in as 16 Bde attempted to capture Indaw. Defended by well-sited bunkers manned by the recently arrived 24 Mixed Independent Brigade it proved an impossible objective for the lightly armed men and they were withdrawn to India.

On March 24 news reached the Chindits that Wingate had been killed when the USAAF Mitchell bomber in which he was travelling along with Stuart Emeny of the *News Chronicle* and Stanley Wills of the *Daily Herald* had crashed into mountains. Brigadier W. D. A. 'Joe' Lentaigne who had commanded 11 Bde now took over command, but the force had lost its charismatic leader and moreover a man with a direct line to the British Prime Minister.

For five days White City, the position that blocked the railway at Henu, came under a concerted attack by the Japanese 18 Division under General Tanaka. The fighting was described as 'medieval' but, with cheerful understatement, Calvert later said it was 'just like an officers' mess guest night'. It was hand-to-hand combat with rifle butts, bayonets, and kukris and with the Japanese officers wielding their traditional swords.

It was during this brutal fighting that Lt George Cairns with 1 South Staffordshire Regiment won his posthumous VC. A sword-wielding Japanese officer had hacked off the young officer's left arm but Cairns killed the officer, picked up his sword and led an attack slashing to left and right killing and wounding before he fell to the ground. He later died of his wounds. Since two officers who witnessed the bravery were later killed it was only pressure from Calvert after the war that led to the waiving of the principle of three witnesses for a VC. In May 1949 Cairn's widow received the last VC to be awarded in World War II.

Lentaigne decided to abandon Aberdeen, Broadway and White City and set up a new position further up the railway line near Hopin 60 miles south of Mogaung code named Blackpool. It would be held by 111 Bde, with 14 and 77 Bdes with mobile columns supporting the Chinese and American troops under Stilwell. The Japanese had now established a separate command to take on the joint Chinese, American and British threat from the north.

At the same time that the Chindits were in training for Operation Thursday, the United States Army, which was providing weapons, training and leadership for the Chinese, formed a force with the rather cumbersome title of 5307th Composite Unit (Provisional) with the code name Galahad. It was under the command of Brigadier General Frank Merrill.

He seemed well qualified for this new and testing command.[98]

In a piece of journalistic hyperbole the force of 3,000 men, grouped in three battalions, was dubbed 'Merrill's Marauders' by the *Time/Life* war correspondent James Shepley. The men in the force did not use this name. In training they worked with the Chindits and planned to use similar deep-penetration tactics in Burma. Though Merrill enjoyed good relations with the British, his superior Stilwell remained an Anglophobe, suspecting like a number of influential Americans that British long-term plans for India and Burma was re-colonisation after the war had been won.

The soldiers who made up the Marauders were volunteers from the US Army Pacific and Caribbean Commands. Many were fine men including Sioux Indians and Japanese Americans who were the backbone of the intelligence and reconnaissance platoons, while locally recruited and trained Burmese Kachin tribesmen worked as guides and scouts. However within the 5307th were some men who were entirely unsuitable. The unit's medical officer said it contained 'the misfits of half a dozen divisions . . . We expected picked troops, instead we found many chronically ill men. Many brave men came, but also numerous psychiatric problems as well as men with chronic disturbances who believed they might get treatment if they could get away from their outfits.' Because attacks of malaria in the Pacific 'were given little more nursing care or rest than the average common cold at home' many Pacific veterans 'volunteered in the hope that they would get hospital care'.[99]

'A strong motivation for some volunteers', noted the American historian Ronald H. Spector, 'was the thought that assignment to a dangerous overseas mission ought to bring them home leave. It didn't.'[100]

Stilwell now Deputy Supreme Commander SEAC pressed for the Galahad force to be committed to action. On January 11 Mountbatten finally agreed 'because', in his words 'it seemed to mean more to Joe than the bickering was worth'.

When Wingate heard about Galahad he was less diplomatic, he told the unit's temporary commander, Colonel Francis G. Brink, 'Brink, you tell General Stilwell he can take his Americans and stick 'em up his ass.' A statement with which, Spector noted, Wingate impressed 'the colonel and his staff with his surprising command of colloquial American expressions'.[101]

The 5307th had an 18-day march into their area of operations and it was at Lanen Ga that they had their first contact with the Japanese. In an ambush Private Robert Landes, who was at point, was killed in a burst of machine-gun fire. He became the first American infantryman to be killed in action on the continent of Asia since the Boxer Rising in Peking in June–August 1900.

Once in action they suffered from many of the problems that beset the Chindits. Fatigue, disease and poor diet took a toll. The 5307th fought bravely when in February 1944 they were committed against the Japanese 18 Division at Kamaing and later Mogaung and Myit-kyina in the Hukawng Valley in northern Burma. They were initially ordered to block the Japanese withdrawal routes, and though the full strength of 18 Division was hurled against them, they held their positions along the banks of the River Nampyek Nha. When Chinese tanks under US command entered the battle the Japanese commander Lt General Shinichi Tanaka ordered a withdrawal leaving over 800 dead on the battlefield.

In the spring the Japanese turned to counter-attack at the village of Nhpum Ga. Under heavy mortar and artillery fire the Marauders dug deep and fought a siege battle. Merrill placed one battalion on a hilltop near the village of Nhpum Ga and another at Hsamshingyang 3 miles away to protect the airstrip. The airstrip was the Marauders' only means of supply and communications. The attacking Japanese cut the trail from Hsamshingyang to the airstrip and access to the defenders' water hole. Dehydrated K-Rations[102] and water were delivered by airdrops. By early April the Japanese conceded defeat and melted back into the jungle. The surviving gaunt Marauders who had endured a poor diet, debilitating climate and fatigue had suffered a weight loss of over 20 pounds a man. By the end of the battle the force was down to half its original strength but Stilwell wanted it to capture Myitkyina.

The town that had been captured by the Japanese on May 8, 1942, had an airfield, was a terminus for trains from Mandalay, river communications on the Irrawaddy and an important staging post on the Ledo Road.[103]

On April 9 following a meeting between Mountbatten, Lentaigne, Slim and Stilwell the Chindits came under the latter's command. The Chindits were suffering badly, but covered the right flank of the US forces from Japanese attacks around Indaw and Mogaung for over three months.

For the Marauders to attack Myitkyina they had to cross the 6,000-foot Kuman Mountains and make a three-week jungle approach march carrying 60-pound packs. On May 17 supported by Chinese forces the US forces captured Myitkyina airfield 4 miles from the town, surprising the few defenders and quickly overwhelming them.

Delighted by the news Stilwell noted triumphantly in his diary 'THIS WILL BURN THE LIMEYS'. Churchill cabled Mountbatten demanding to know how 'the Americans, by a brilliant feat of arms, have landed us in Myitkyina'.

The exhausted men of the Galahad now awaited the USAAF aircraft, which would fly in food and ammunition. A rumour circulated that on Stilwell's orders these aircraft would evacuate the Marauders to rest camps in India.

The aircraft did arrive, but they were carrying an anti-aircraft battery and aviation engineers. On May 24 units of the Japanese 144 Regiment Eighteenth Army were quickly reinforced and launched strong counter-attacks south of Myitkyina. This stabilised the situation and on June 2 the Japanese moved about 2,500 reinforcements into the town and dug in. So instead of scoring a lightning victory, the Americans were besieged in a situation made more miserable by the onset of the monsoon. Fighting was so localised and intense in the railway sidings that at times it was fought between individual defended goods trucks on a single train.

By now the Marauders in Stilwell's terse description were 'shot' and were being evacuated at a rate of 75 to 100 men a day. Malaria and dysentery was widespread and one platoon suffered so severely from dysentery that they cut away the seats of their trousers so as not to be hampered in combat.

Stilwell confided to his diary 'US troops are shaky. Hard to believe. Either all our officers are rotten, or else Boatner [his chief of staff] is getting hysterical.'

As the fight for Myitkyina dragged on Stilwell even ordered men in hospital suffering from fatigue and disease to return to the front. Reluctant US Army engineers who were working on the Ledo Road were ordered off their construction work and issued rifles and ammunition to join the fight as infantry.

Stilwell was equally harsh with the Chindits and the Chinese under his command. He demanded that the Chindits stay in the jungle to keep the pressure on Myitkyina and made almost impossible demands on Morrisforce, a composite group of about 1,000 Chindits who were fighting on the east bank of the Irrawaddy, urging them to intervene in the battle for Myitkyina. He was constantly pressing the Chinese for more men and greater commitment to the campaign.

However he seemed particularly uncaring with the Marauders. Up to the battle for Myitkyina 'no member of Galahad had received a combat decoration, no member received a promotion, a candy bar, a bag of peanuts, an issue of cigarettes, a can of beer, a bottle of whiskey or a pat on the back by anyone'.[104] Yet they had fought in five major actions and 30 minor ones.

By June 13 the battalions of Brigadier 'Mike' Calvert's 77 Bde were down to company strength but timing his attack on Mogaung to coincide with one by the Chinese on June 24 they were able to take the town. By now uniforms were so faded and tattered that they were almost unrecognisable so Chinese and British forces attached strips of parachute material to their uniforms for quick identification in the heat of action.

On June 23 Rifleman Tul Bahadur Pun of 3/6 Gurkha Rifles was part of the force ordered to attack the railway bridge at Mogaung and the Japanese position known as the Red House. In a demonstration of awesome personal courage as his comrades were cut down by automatic fire, the Rifleman picked up a Bren gun[105] and alone covered 30 yards of open ground across ankle-deep mud and over fallen trees before he reached the Red House bunkers. Here he killed three, put five to flight and captured two light machine guns and ammunition. He then gave accurate supporting fire for his platoon that allowed them to reach their objective.[106]

Stilwell's HQ announced that Mogaung had fallen to the Chinese and then demanded that 77 Bde join the battle for Myitkyina. Calvert closed down his brigade's radio sets and marched to Stilwell's army's headquarters in Kamaing. A court martial was threatened, but after he and Stilwell finally met in person and Stilwell appreciated for the first time the conditions under which the Chindits had operated, 77 Bde was evacuated to India to recover.

The Chindits marched out of Burma and in *The Campaign in Burma* Frank Owen is perhaps less than generous when he writes of the survivors.

'When the men came out of the jungle after five months they were pretty tired, and they showed it. Bearded troops seem always to look more gaunt, and most of these had shed many pounds of weight.'[107]

The siege of Myitkyina ended on August 3, 1944. The Japanese were now completely isolated but the garrison commander who committed suicide on August 1, arranged for the surviving 900 Japanese soldiers to escape. The besieging Americans and Chinese suffered about 6,150 battle casualties and by then few of the original Marauders were still fighting.

An area of northern Burma was now again under Allied control and Myitkyina an important logistics centre and an airfield was denied to the Japanese.

With the end of the campaign the 5307th Composite Unit (Provisional) was disbanded amidst some acrimony and integrated into the US Infantry as the 475th Regiment. Only later did they receive the recognition they deserved, a Presidential Unit Citation, six

WE GAVE OUR TODAY

Distinguished Service Crosses, four Legions of Merit and 44 Silver Stars.[108]

In October 1944 at the insistence of Chiang Kai-shek, Stilwell was recalled to Washington. He died two years later a bitter man, convinced that neither he nor the soldiers of the Chinese Fifth and Sixth Armies had received sufficient credit for their operations in Burma.

Thursday, like Longcloth, was an operation that still generates strongly held opinions. There are those who assert that it disrupted the Japanese attacks on Kohima and Imphal by diverting troops and cutting road and rail communications. This however makes no allowance for the operations of the RAF and USAAF attacks against road, rail and river links behind the Japanese front-line.

Captain Richard Rhodes-James of 1/6 Gurkha Rifles who fought in Operation Thursday holds a different view.

'Although the Second Chindit Expedition did have an effect, it was not cost-effective to achieve this with six brigades. The 77th Brigade achieved great things, the other brigades did not. Two or three brigades would have been enough to commit to the LRP (Long Range Penetration) task, and Slim could have used the other three more brigades to much better effect in the main battle . . . At times you see and hear in the media that Wingate turned the tide of the war in Burma. I think it was turned at Kohima and Imphal by the Fourteenth Army.'[109]

CHAPTER 7

ARAKAN – THE FIRST VICTORY
February 6 to March 3, 1944

'The enemy has been challenged and beaten in jungle warfare.
His boastfulness has received a salutary exposure'
Prime Minister Winston Churchill to Vice Admiral Lord Louis
Mountbatten

After the poor performance of tanks in the first Arakan offensive there were many who doubted the effectiveness of armour in the jungle. However tanks had their champions and the tank that would be a real war winner in Burma was the American M3 Lee/Grant.[110] The M3 was obsolescent in the battlefields of Europe and had been replaced by the M4 Sherman[111] that would later be deployed and prove very effective in both the Pacific Islands and the dash across Burma in 1945.

Advancing down jungle tracks the crew of the M3 Lee/Grant could use the 75mm gun to fire directly at the embrasures of bunkers covering the tracks, while the 37mm gun could be employed against threats from the flank or rear. In defence they were mobile pill boxes that could carry vastly more machine-gun ammunition than the infantry and be lethally effective against the clumsy and repetitive Japanese attacks. In attack they could move in to near point-blank range and blast the incredibly robust Japanese bunkers.

In what would be known to all as the battle of the 'Admin Box' and officially as the Battle of Sinzweya, tank advocates would be more than vindicated. At the 'Admin Box' and other positions, both the soldiers and Slim's tactics of standing firm in all-round defence and relying on aerial re-supply, would be tested and proved in the grim terrain of the Arakan.

In 1944, XV Indian Corps commanded by Lt General Philip Christison, who had been an instructor with Slim at the Staff College at Camberley in 1936, launched a three-pronged attack into the Arakan. Their mission was to push south to clear the Mayu Peninsula as far south as to be able to command the mouth of the Naf River. The Mayu Peninsula consists of a flat coastal plain, indented by several *chaungs*, and separated from the fertile valley of the Kalapanzin River by the steep jungle-covered hills of the Mayu Range. The Corps was to capture the port of Maungdaw that could be opened up for sea-borne supplies. In addition the Maungdaw–Buthidaung road was to be secured along with the Tunnels. A longer term aim was the capture of Akyab and its airfields that could be used to support future operations against Rangoon.

This time the troops who were to be committed were better trained and equipped than the men who had fought the first grim campaign. Under Slim's overall guidance, experience and confidence had been built up by realistic training and then patrolling against the Japanese. British, Indian and African troops were learning that the Japanese were no jungle supermen. Japanese jungle drills had become sloppy and document security even sloppier – maps, orders, diaries and letters provided a wealth of intelligence – there were almost none to be gained from prisoners, because there were no prisoners to be interrogated.

One problem that initially faced intelligence officers was a lack of men who could read Japanese. Academics from the British Museum were flown out to India and soon a programme teaching rudimentary Japanese to intelligence officers was set in place. Often knowledge of military symbols and initials was sufficient to interpret the information on a captured map. The Japanese were confident that their language even when written in clear was impenetrable to non Japanese.

By 1944 the Allies in Burma had a sophisticated code-breaking and radio-interception programme based at HMS *Anderson* a shore station in Ceylon. The Japanese were their own worst enemy when using the radio, speaking slowly, repeating themselves and confining their transmissions to straightforward information or orders.

The plans for the renewed British attack on the Arakan began to take shape. The force that would take on this challenging mission was the XV Indian Corps commanded by General Philip Christison. It consisted of the veteran Indian 5 Infantry Division under Major General H. R. Briggs, a division that had already seen heavy fighting in East Africa and the Western Desert. It would attack along the coastal plain. To the Indian 5 Infantry Division fell the task of capturing Razabil and Maungdaw.

The other formation in the XV Corps was the comparatively inexperienced but well-trained Indian 7 Infantry Division under Major General Frank Messervy.[112] It would attack down the Kalapanzin Valley to occupy Buthidaung and isolate the inland town of Letwedet. Out on the right flank the British 81 (West Africa) Division under Major General Woolner would advance down the Kaladan River Valley. Unlike the two Indian divisions 81 would rely on aerial re-supply by the newly established Anglo-American Troop Carrier Command since the roads and tracks it was following would not support a large-wheeled logistic train. The British 36 Infantry Division and Indian 26 Infantry Division were available as reinforcements.

Christison's aim with the three-pronged attack was to ensure that his forces covered as wide a front as possible and did not run the risk of an attack down a narrow axis – leaving them vulnerable to the Japanese tactics of outflanking and encirclement.

The advance that had begun cautiously at first picked up momentum and on January 9, 5 Indian Division had captured Maungdaw, the small port 'that had degenerated into a cluster of huts sinking into a swamp'. Fighting continued south of the port where a Japanese position on a hill, known as the 'Tortoise' because of its distinctive shape, took the brunt of a joint land and air attack.

It was hit by dive bombers followed by an artillery bombardment by medium, field and mountain artillery. Then the Lee/Grant tanks of 25 Dragoons advanced with their infantry support. The tanks crushed one Japanese anti-tank position and blasted another with their main and secondary armament. The fighting lasted three days and by then the 'Tortoise' was a pulverised mound of sand and shredded jungle – but the Japanese hung on.

As well as the bunkers on the surface the hill had a complex of tunnels beneath it and accommodation for soldiers and officers, some 30 feet underground that were invulnerable to the heaviest bombardment.

The incredibly robust construction of the Japanese bunkers led some soldiers to believe that concrete or armour plate had been incorporated. In reality layered tree trunks and rammed earth made them almost invulnerable. In a bizarre experiment in August 1944, classified 'Most Secret' the British Directorate of Tactical Investigation presented the findings of tests against bunkers. The aim was to explode a projectile inside the bunkers or close enough to the embrasure to ensure that fragments went into the interior or the weapons slit was blocked. To test the effect animal occupants were introduced – two white rabbits, one already 'somewhat dull in behaviour and suffering from mange', two cockerels, and two half-grown billy goats one 'salivating freely'. The animals had some protection inside, so when a 2-inch mortar bomb was detonated they were found to be 'coated in dust; they appeared mildly surprised but in other respects were apparently normal. The goat was coughing slightly.' When an anti-tank PIAT bomb was exploded the blood pressure and pulse rate of one of the goats actually went down. Pushing the experiment harder three bombs were detonated simultaneously. 'Both the goat and the observer started, while the cockerel and the rabbit remained apparently unaffected.'

It was in the Arakan that the tank crews developed what would be called a standard operating procedure (SOP) for bunkers. They would first engage the area around the bunker with high explosive (HE) shells with super quick fuses. This would strip off or set fire to the vegetation that camouflaged the position and expose the embrasures. Solid-shot armour-piercing (AP) rounds would then be fired at the bunkers to loosen the earth and timber structure. Finally HE with delayed fuses would be fired through the embrasure or against the structure to burst inside. When working with infantry tanks would use AP in the final assault to ensure there were no friendly casualties.

Patrick Davis who fought in Burma from 1943 to 1945 with 3

Gurkhas says 'Bunkers in the end could become death traps. We evolved a battle-drill for dealing with them . . . Once a couple of bunkers from the interlocking chain had been knocked out, the rest fell quickly, for they could be approached from a blind side.'

The next major objective to confront XV Indian Corps was part of the Tunnels position on Mayu Range that linked Buthidaung and Letwedet in the Kalapanzin Valley with Razabil and Maungdaw. To reposition troops and resources for this attack, Corps engineers had improved the narrow track through the Ngakyedauk Pass, across the hills. It was near the eastern end of the pass that Indian 7 Division had established its main administration area at Sinzweya.

From captured documents the XV Indian Corps intelligence officers knew that the Japanese were planning a counter-offensive, to the Japanese this was part of an 'offensive defence'. However the intelligence staff could not give Christison a date or an idea of the strength of the enemy forces.

The Japanese envelopment tactics had been studied and General Messervy produced an unusual and original analysis.

'. . . our brigades and the Japanese regiments will become interposed with one another like layers of a Neapolitan sandwich. Our tactics will then be quite straightforward. We will fight back towards our own people and in doing so will destroy the Japs between us.'

His opponent Lt General Shozo Sakurai commanding the Twenty-eighth Army in the Arakan and southern Burma had positioned 55 Division under Lt General Tadashi Hanaya in the Arakan. However since a Japanese division had a separate headquarters to administer its infantry units most of them were grouped as *Sakurai Force* in the Mayu area. The Infantry Group headquarters was commanded by Major General Tokutaro Sakurai.

Tokutaro 'Tokuta' Sakurai was known for his eccentric social manners and ruthless and unscrupulous behaviour, confusingly had the same name as the Army commander but was no relation. As a Major he had headed the Intelligence Section of the China Expeditionary Army and used 'rough and ready means to gather intelligence'. He liked to lead his men personally in the attack.

General Shozo Sakurai was confident that the operation would be a success: 'As [the British] have previously suffered defeat, should a portion of them waver, the whole of them will at once get confused and victory is certain.'[113]

The counter-attack, code named HA-GO or Operation Z, that was in the offing was part of a larger theatre-wide operation. By launching it in the first week of February, they would oblige the Fourteenth Army to send reinforcements from the Central Front. This meant that this front would be weakened just before the main Japanese offensive in the first week of March.

Before the operation the men received an inspirational order of the day which typified the Japanese concept of 'Faith as Strength'. They were told that though they would die and their bodies lie rotting in the sand-dunes, they would turn to grass which would wave in the breezes blowing from Japan.

'Promises like these,' observe Meirion and Susie Harries, 'would not have put fire in the bellies of many Allied troops.'

Like so many plans HA-GO looked good on paper but made no allowance for what the enemy might do, and crucially the superb asset that the Fourteenth Army enjoyed in air mobility – reinforcing and re-supply by air now took hours, not weeks. Though timing was critical the Japanese were so confident of success there were orders to ensure that vehicles were to be captured intact to be used in follow-up operations. Gunners were assured that they would not need to bring their artillery with them since they would soon be firing captured ammunition from abandoned British guns. Hanaya divided his force into columns named after their respective commanders.

On February 3 Sakurai Column began infiltrating the front-lines of the Indian 114 Bde, which was widely dispersed, and moved north on the small town of Taung Bazaar. Contact was made by British and Indian forces on February 4 with a number of units including one group of Japanese soldiers heading for Goppe Pass. Here they 'bumped' a Royal Indian Army Service Corps mule column but the tough Pathan muleteers stood their ground and drove them off. In Christison's opinion the fight put up by these modest heroes was crucial to the battle that followed. Had the Japanese crossed the

Goppe they could have pushed west and threatened HQ 5 Indian Division and HQ XV Corps at Bawli Bazaar.

At Taung Bazaar, *Sakurai Force* swung west and south, and on the night of February 6 they attacked 7 Division HQ.

Messervy recalled the attack. 'I was awakened by an outburst of yells and groans, though oddly enough I heard very few shots. I jumped out of bed, and walked about in pyjamas for an hour or so trying to find out what was going on. The whole camp was aroused, but there was confusion all around us. It was very dark. Suddenly the Japanese, with a cheer which you hear when Arsenal scores a goal at home, charged the Signals quarters. The Signalmen, with a company of Indian Engineers, were acting as Divisional Headquarters Defence Force. The Japanese came on in a waist-high mist which partly concealed them. They pierced only the outer fringe of the position in force, however. No Japanese actually came my way, though some who approached were shot by the Liaison Officer's batman; the others ran back.'[114]

The fighting intensified as the Japanese brought up mortars. Signallers and clerks from 7 Indian Division commanded by Lt Colonel Pat Hobson fought hard and inflicted around 40 casualties on an estimated force of 200. However the pressure became too great and the decision was taken to break out to the larger Admin area. Documents were destroyed and equipment wrecked. At 11.20 hours signallers at the Corps Administration Area monitoring the 7 Division HQ frequency heard a voice say, 'Put a pick through that radio', followed by silence.

The men of the 7 Indian Division worked their way back to the Admin area in small groups. Messervy earned his reputation as a front-line general when 'dressed in a vest and trousers, and carrying a grenade in his hand [he] led his men by devious paths, wading shoulder deep through a flooded chaung, or creek. They reached the Box in four hours.'[115]

The Admin area which, as the Admin Box, would be the site of the first Japanese defeat of the Burma campaign was an area of dried-up paddy fields about 1,200 yards square. A low hillock about 300 feet high in the centre, covered in scrub, which would become known as

Ammunition Hill, further to the east was a second feature that was named Artillery Hill. The whole area was surrounded by low wooded hills.

As would be expected the Admin Box contained stocks of fuel, ammunition, rations, a hospital, a mule company and even an officers' shop. At the divisional hospital located on a hillock known as M.D.S. (Medical Dressing Station) Hill Major B. G. A. Lilwall would perform 252 operations during the siege.

Sakurai Column then followed up towards Sinzweya and the rear of 7 Indian Division. A Japanese battalion 1/213 Regiment also known as Kobo (Koba) Column after its commander Colonel Toba Koba, crossed the Mayu Range at a seemingly impossible place. They hauled their guns up a 1,000-foot cliff face, over the mountains and down the other side, to set ambushes on the coastal road along which Indian 5 Division was being supplied. 'In the end these raiders had to be liquidated to the last man. They interfered with communications less than they had hoped, for much of the supply of 5 Division, continued to flow in (through Maungdaw) by sea.'[116] Koba himself survived to fight in Burma until the end of the war when he surrendered his sword to 1/10 Gurkha Rifles at Paung, Burma on October 28, 1945.

The Japanese still holding the Tunnels area which had been designated Doi Column launched raids and diversions, while unexpectedly large numbers of Japanese Nakajima Ki-43 'Oscar' fighter aircraft flew from Akyab to contest the skies over the battlefield. It would prove to be the final gesture by the depleted IJAAF.

The situation was serious but now Fourteenth Army had the leaders, trained and confident men and the resources to defeat the standard Japanese tactics of infiltration and encirclement. The forward divisions of XV Corps were ordered to dig in and hold their positions rather than retreat, while the reserves were moved up to counter-attack.

Command of the Admin Box was assumed by Brigadier Geoffrey Evans, commander of Indian 9 Bde, part of the 5 Division. He reinforced the defenders, who were mainly headquarters and line of communication troops, with 2 West Yorkshire Regiment and men from 4/8 Gurkha Rifles. However his major assets were two troops of

M3 Lee/Grant tanks of 25 Dragoons who were protected by men of 3/4 Bombay Grenadiers. There were two batteries of 6 Medium and a troop of 8 Heavy AA Regiments RA.

When Messervy reached the Admin Box, followed by several of his HQ he met the commanding officer of the Dragoons, Lt Colonel H. R. C. Frink with the grim words 'Frinkie, I've lost my Division'. However hot tea and whisky revived him and the Dragoons' tank radios enabled him to re-establish control over the scattered division.

It was now that Fourteenth Army planning paid off. Major General A. H. J. Snelling, who headed the administration for the army, had ensured that ten days' rations for 40,000 men had been stockpiled close to airstrips in India. His superb planning, and the efficiency with which ration supplies were handled, earned him the affectionate titles of 'Grocer Alf' and 'The Fourteenth Army's Grocer'.

Dakotas of the Troop Carrier Command took off and began dropping rations and ammunition to the cut-off troops, including the defenders of the Admin Box. The first airdrop missions met opposition from Japanese fighter planes, but three squadrons of Spitfires from 224 Group, operating from new airfields around Chittagong, took on the Japanese. For the loss of three Spitfires the RAF claimed 65 Japanese aircraft – while this may be an optimistic overestimate, it was a pointer to the way the air battle was going. RAF Wellingtons and USAAF Liberators hit Japanese air bases and by mid February the skies belonged to the RAF and USAAF.

Heading the Troop Carrier Command was Brigadier-General William D. Old USAAF, a man who believed in leadership by example. When, on February 8 Dakotas of 31 and 26 Squadrons were attacked by Japanese Oscars that shot down one transport, forced another to crash land and disrupted the supply operation, Old took the controls of a Dakota and flew in on the next sortie.

Old's aircraft returned pitted with shell splinters, but he had set the style and 60 tons a day were being parachuted into the Box. In the end 900 sorties delivered 3,000 tons of stores that not only included important items such as fuel, ammunition, rations and spare parts but morale-boosting items like mail, cigarettes and beer.

The Japanese had not foreseen this development. While they

themselves began to run short of supplies, the British and Indian formations fought on. In a pointer to what would happen at Imphal and Kohima there was an attempt to supply Sakurai Column using pack mules and Arakanese porters, who were instructed to use Sakurai's original infiltration route, but the supply column was ambushed.

The time allocated for the successful completion of Operation C was fast running out and on the ground, the fighting for the Admin Box was savage.

In an attack just after last light on February 7, 60 Japanese led by six officers captured M.D.S. Hill. They murdered 35 medical staff and patients in the cramped divisional hospital but fortunately a number of the casualties had been moved to a safer location during the day.

Six of the doctors who had been captured were lined up and shot dead with a bullet in the ear. One man Lt S. N. Basu of the Indian Medical Service miraculously survived when the Japanese officer's pistol misfired twice and when it fired the round passed through his left ear. He tumbled to the ground. 'I knew I was dead. I fell down, but after a time I realised I could see and think.'[117] He feigned death and smeared blood over his face. A Japanese soldier turned him over with his boot and assuming he was dead did not, as was customary, bayonet him. Basu managed to crawl away and hide in a slit trench.

The men of 2 West Yorkshire Regiment counter-attacked at dawn and rescued the few survivors; it fell to the Yorkshiremen and particularly the Regimental Sergeant Major (RSM) Jim Maloney and the regimental HQ administrative staff to avenge the murders. A day later, soon after the sun had set, a group of Japanese were detected moving along a gully beneath the regimental HQ. The RSM positioned his ambush and briefed the men. One group were to throw grenades and a second to pull the pins; 'otherwise', he explained, 'we would not get the stuff into the chaung quickly enough'.

In fifteen minutes of screams and explosions 45 Japanese died in an area only 40 yards square. In the flash of exploding grenades a Japanese officer scrambled up the bank and lunged with his sword at the Orderly Room Sergeant – the Sergeant, a man more commonly associated with a typewriter and paperwork, parried the blow with his rifle and proceeded with his corporal to bayonet the assailant.

When the dawn came up the British could see blasted from the tattered Japanese packs the remains of British rations and white sugar – loot from the murderous attack on M.D.S. Hill.

Among the grisly remains of the gully, which would earn itself the name Blood Alley, intelligence officers found a marked map that showed how far behind schedule the Japanese were now running, but also that Blood Alley was a forming-up point for attacks on the Admin Box. Poor communications and the Japanese inflexible adherence to orders meant that in succeeding nights more Japanese assembled in the gully – to die in the darkness under a hail of exploring No 36 grenades. Eventually the stench from their bodies became so unbearable that the site was bulldozed.[118]

When the rapid tropical nightfall enveloped the Admin Box men extinguished their last cigarettes and braced themselves for the Japanese attacks. Even with the reliable aerial re-supply, morale was uneven and there were tensions within the command.

Evans drove the garrison hard and even instituted an award for the sector that had killed the most Japanese in the preceding 24 hours. After a violent argument with Frink relations with the 25 Dragoons were only smoothed over by sending Major Hugh Ley as a liaison officer. However the Brigadier knew that the tanks were the lynchpin of the defence and to ensure they were used effectively installed himself in Ley's trench.

Enter one of the minor heroes of the Admin Box – Trooper John Evans, Ley's soldier servant who before the war had been a 'gentleman's gentleman'.

Even in the front-line Evans did not allow his standards to slip. After the violence of a night attack he would enquire solicitously, 'Will you be requiring a new slit trench dug today, Sir?' The Brigadier was informed by Evans that if he wanted a mug of tea after dawn 'Stand To', he should remember that he was a guest in the major's trench.

'It is believed,' writes Jon Latimer, 'Brigadier gave the Trooper no further cause for complaint.'[119]

Japanese fire caused heavy casualties in the crowded defences and twice set ammunition dumps on fire. However all attempts to over-run the defenders were thwarted by the tanks, to which the Japanese had no counter once their few Mountain Guns were out of ammunition. The British anti-aircraft guns used in the ground role were a formidable part of the defence and the tanks evolved an ingenious technique for using dust to shield their movements in the cramped perimeter.

On the night of February 14 the Japanese tried an all-out attack with three battalions and succeeded in capturing C Company Hill on the perimeter. Under Major Chris O'Hara, A Company West York-shires with support from ten tanks recaptured it the next day. By combining high explosive followed by solid-shot armour-piercing rounds, tanks and infantry were able to get within feet of the Japanese positions.

By February 22 the Japanese supply system had broken down and they had been without food for several days. Men were foraging for wild rice and many were sick. Colonel Seizo Tanahashi, commanding 112 Infantry Regiment the main body of Sakurai's force stated that his 2,150-strong regiment was now down to 400 men. He had ordered a withdrawal and over the radio told Sakurai, 'I regret doing this, but am determined to do it; there is no alternative.'

Meanwhile, Christison had moved up 26 and 36 Indian Divisions, XV Corps's reserve divisions to relieve 5 Division, which in turn sent a brigade to break through the Ngakyedauk Pass to relieve 7 Division.

Although total Allied casualties were higher than the Japanese, when the Japanese withdrew they had been forced to abandon many of their wounded to die. For the first time in the war, the Japanese tactics had been countered and indeed turned against them.

In early February the lightly armed 1/1 Guerrilla Regiment of the Indian National Army left Rangoon for Prome, marching across the Chin Hills to Taungup and then along the coast to Akyab which it reached in early March. However by now 55 Division was beginning to wind down its unsuccessful operation. The battalion subsequently marched up the Kaladan River where assisted by local Arakanese they enjoyed some low-level successes against the isolated 81 West African Division. At a feature known as Pagoda Hill they attacked 1 Gambia

Regiment and after three days forced them off the position and obliged the division to withdraw to the eastern bank of the Mayu River covering Taung Bazaar. The INA unit then crossed the Burma–India border to occupy Mowdok near Chittagong – the nearest the Indian National Army came to 'liberating' India.

Now the Indian 26 and British 36 Divisions resumed the offensive in late March and early April. They captured the much fought-over Tunnels but at this point, operations had to be curtailed to free transport aircraft and troops for the Imphal battle. It was on March 11 in the fighting near the Tunnels that Naik Nand Singh of 1/11 Sikhs won the VC clearing three heavily defended trenches which were part of a position defended by 40 men with medium and light machine guns and a light mortar.[120]

A high narrow ridge known as '551' because of its height on the map was reckoned to be the key to the Tunnels: a company of 14 Baluchistan Battalion used ladders to conduct a fighting patrol at night against the position. As they returned the company commander realised that one man was missing and went back to the ridge. Here he bumped into a Japanese patrol who attempted to take him prisoner. In a frenzy of hand-to-hand combat in the darkness the Major shot one man, and then grabbed the little body and 'swung it round in the fury of battle like a flail against the next two assailants. He knocked them both over the cliff. He resumed his search for his own lost soldier, and found him. Of such', writes Owen, 'was the army in Arakan.'[121]

After three days of shelling and dive bombing the Tunnels would be captured following an attack on March 26 by 72 Brigade. On April 4 a Sherman tank from C Sqaudron 149 Regiment RAC manoeuvred into position and fired a round into the mouth of the Tunnels. A huge explosion followed as stored ammunition detonated – bodies and debris were blasted out and fires burned for hours afterwards.

By now tank crews had further refined their tactics.

'Half-way through an assault and by pre-arrangement the infantry would halt and the tanks would cease fire. This was almost always more than the inquisitive little NIP could stand, especially as the tanks "revved up" their engines and gave the appearance of moving off. He almost inevitably came up from underground to have a look and then, by radio-telephony to all tanks, "WALLOP".'[122]

With the onset of the monsoon it was found that the low-lying area around Buthidaung was malarial and unhealthy and the Allies actually withdrew from the area to spare themselves losses to disease.

The fighting continued in the Arakan area and on the night of December 15–16, 1944 in the Kaladan Valley, Havildar Umrao Singh was in command of a field gun detachment of 33 Mountain Battery in a forward position. In the darkness the position came under sustained fire from 75mm guns and mortars and then for two hours it was attacked by two companies of infantry. Singh was twice wounded, and while firing a Bren gun directed the fire of the surviving mountain gun. The 24-year-old held the gun pit until dawn when his apparently lifeless body was found surrounded by the bodies of ten Japanese soldiers. The small arms ammunition had run out and he had used one of the gun hand spikes in hand-to-hand combat – he lay face down in the mud still clutching it.

He recovered and survived to be awarded the VC. Known in his village as 'VC Sahib' when Umrao Singh died on November 21, 2005 a link with the Indian Army that had fought and defeated the Japanese in Burma was severed. He was the last surviving Indian VC.[123]

Long after the war in old age, struggling to eke out a living on his small farm it was suggested that he could sell his VC for a very good price. An indignant Singh said selling the medal would 'sully' the *izzat* (honour) of his fallen comrades.[124]

The Japanese held Akyab until January 1945, when a combined land and amphibious operation drove the Japanese from Arakan. The Japanese found themselves victim of their tactics when troops were landed to cut off their retreat down the coast.

In the Arakan campaign of 1944 the three British and Indian divisions suffered nearly 8,000 casualties while the one Japanese division lost just over 5,000. If the campaign and the battle of the Admin Box were to be judged by the bare statistics of this grim butcher's bill this would have been counted a defeat – it was a victory. The Japanese 55 Division had attacked confident that the tested tactics that had given *below:* This postcard of a Japanese soldier, with the face blank so the sender might either sketch in his face or stick a photograph, is an interesting piece of propaganda and a take on how the Japanese perceived themselves in 1942. The soldier holds children representing Malaya, the Pacific Islands, China and the Dutch East Indies – territories that the Japanese have 'liberated' in their drive south and west. (Author's collection)

above: One of eight Japanese Type 95 Ha Go tanks burns following an ambush by Australian 2-pounder anti-tank guns on January 18, 1942 north of Bakri in Malaya. Against trained and effectively armed opposition thinly armoured Japanese tanks were very vulnerable. (Australian War Memorial)

below: Sunday February 15, 1942, Singapore: carrying the Union Flag and a white flag Lt General Arthur Percival's party make their way to General Tomoyuki Yamashita's HQ to negotiate a cease fire. (Cody Images)

above: A Japanese painting shows the moment when General Yamashita demanded that British forces on Singapore surrender. General Percival was in no position to bargain and was forced to accept Japanese terms – it was the greatest British military humiliation for over 100 years. (Cody Images)

left: The triumph of the Japanese saluting the Emperor following the capture of Singapore. The success of the Japanese Army in 1942 and 1943 would earn it a formidable reputation as an invincible force. (Cody Images)

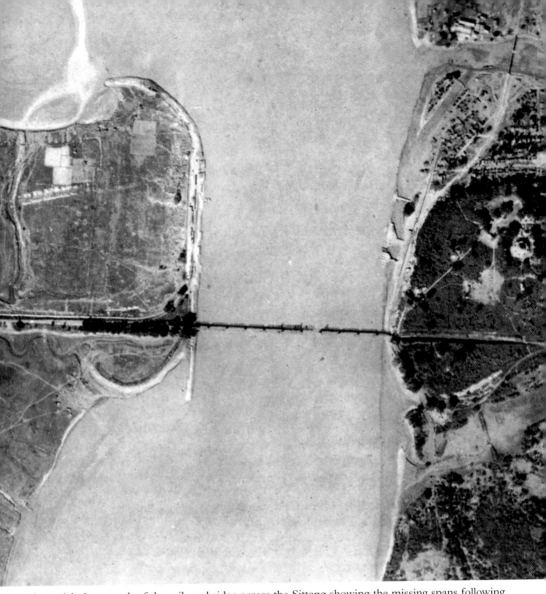

An aerial photograph of the railway bridge across the Sittang showing the missing spans following the premature demolition on February 23, 1942. Despite the fact that men of 17 Indian Division were still on the left bank many managed to find their way to safety using improvised flotation devices or by swimming. (South East Asia Command)

Orde Wingate in typical
eccentric style takes his
ease in a mule stall
constructed aboard a
Dakota. His unorthodox
training methods turned
ordinary soldiers into
men who could fight in
the jungle and beat the
Japanese. (Imperial War
Museum)

A Chindit, in many
ways a typical soldier
of the Burma campaign,
with his battered felt
bush hat, shovel and
SMLE rifle. For the
infantryman the shovel –
and ideally the big
GS shovel – was a vital
bit of kit: digging in
quickly could be a life-
saver. (Cody Images)

Men of the 5307th Composite Unit (Provisional) under the command of Brigadier General Frank Merrill. The US media would give them the more dramatic name of Merrill's Marauders and General Stilwell would make demands of them that were almost impossible to fulfil. (Cody Images)

A contrast in transport systems: loading a reluctant mule aboard a Dakota. While the Dakota and other transport aircraft gave superb strategic mobility in Burma, the humble mule allowed loads to be carried in some of the most inhospitable and inaccessible terrain in the world. (Cody Images)

above: General Renya Mutaguchi was in his late 50s when he launched the fatal 'March on India'. (Author)

right: Men of the Indian National Army in Burma in 1944. Indian troops captured in Malaya were persuaded by pro-Japanese nationalists to join a force that would liberate India from the British. (Cody Images)

below: Camouflaged Japanese soldiers use a river as a route through the jungle. The ability of the Japanese to dig in and conceal themselves in the jungle made them formidable enemies. (Cody Images)

A blasted tree frames the view of one of the most unusual battlegrounds of World War II: the tennis court at Kohima. Now neatly marked out it has been incorporated into the Commonwealth War Graves Commission cemetery. (Cody Images)

Parachutes fall from a Dakota as the crew deliver stores and ammunition. With air superiority over Burma the 14th Army was able to exploit the tremendous logistic flexibility of airpower that could be used to move troops and equipment and parachute supplies directly to the front line. (Cody Images)

Vice Admiral Lord Louis Mountbatten inspects a 25-pounder battery. Though Mountbatten was regarded as a light-weight by many British and American senior officers he would give valuable support to Slim at some critical times in the Burma campaign. (Cody Images)

This muddy road, with Indian troops and ambulance Jeeps, illustrates many of the logistic problems that faced the 14th Army. Heavy rain triggered landslides that blocked the road, carried it away or bogged down vehicles up to their axles in soft mud. (Cody Images)

General Slim, described as a man with the brains of a general but the heart of a soldier. An almost unique military leader who earned the affection of all the men under his command and the nickname 'Uncle Bill'. (Cody Images)

In a scene that could have come from an earlier century General 'Bill' Slim receives a captured Japanese sword from a Gurkha officer. The officer has the distinctive 'Black Cat' flash of 17 Division on his tunic. (Cody Images)

Tough, with a robust sense of humour Gurkha soldiers proved formidable fighters in the jungles of Burma. Here a Gurkha uses a traditional method to carry his kit slung from a carrying pole. (Cody Images)

Bomb craters punctuate the line of a railway track in Japanese occupied Burma. Strikes by the RAF and USAAF disrupted Japanese logistics and forced men to march long distances before they had even reached the front line. (SEAC)

A RAF Hawker Hurricane IIE is loaded with 60lb rockets. The slow-flying Hurricane that had been withdrawn from service in Europe was an ideal aircraft for ground attack missions and rockets could be delivered with greater accuracy than bombs. (Cody Images)

Sunlight and shadow in the Burmese jungle breaks up the outline of a 14th Army soldier.
Untypically for 1944 he has a steel helmet – the felt bush hats had become a widely worn and
popular headgear. They were nicknamed IWT hats from the column 'I Was There', since back
in India they indicated that the wearer had served in Burma. (Cody Images)

A British soldier examines Japanese dead in a drainage ditch in the Arakan jungle. This coastal area which had seen an Allied defeat would later see effective all-arms cooperation in a campaign that would capture key airfields. (Cody Images)

Indian Army Sappers removing a bomb from the road north of Rangoon in 1945. Lacking large quantities of anti-tank mines the Japanese improvised with shells and bombs in an attempt to delay the tanks of the 14th Army. (Imperial War Museum)

With the background of Buddhist temples a column of Ghurka soldiers moves through a Burmese town in the steady and remorseless southwards drive towards Rangoon. (Cody Images)

above: The grave of Lt George Knowland VC at Taukkyan Commonwealth War Graves Cemetery Rangoon, Burma. Knowland was 23 and serving with No 1 Commando when he was killed in action at Kangaw in the Arakan on January 31, 1945. (Col Mike Bradley OBE)

left The memorial at Kohima that bears the haunting words commemorating the men 'who gave their today' and that still challenge those who have lived to enjoy a tomorrow. (Commonwealth War Graves Commission) victory in Malaya and Burma would again be successful but it had been fought to a standstill and then forced to withdraw.

Churchill's growl of satisfaction echoes down the years in the words of a special message to Mountbatten.

'The enemy has been challenged and beaten in jungle warfare. His boastfulness has received a salutary exposure.'

CHAPTER 8

IMPHAL

March 8 to July 3, 1944

Petty discipline ceased to have any meaning. When you are walking
hand in hand with death all day reprimands no longer matter

John Hudson, Royal Bombay Sappers and Miners

The pear-shaped Imphal plain is a 300-foot-high plateau in the
Manipur Mountains on the eastern border of India. The plain is
about 600 miles square and is formed by an opening in the gorges of
the Manipur River that flows south to join the Chindwin at Kalewa.

John Hudson arrived at Imphal before any fighting had begun.

'Instead of "Green Hell" of the media,' he recalled, 'I found myself
in "a garden eastward in Eden". Imphal was tranquil and beautiful on
a rich alluvial plain where villages dozed in the brilliant air surrounded
by palm groves, paddy fields, banana, mango and bamboo.'[125]

Slim was far less complimentary: Assam and the Imphal plain
was 'some of the world's worst country, breeding the world's worst
diseases, and having for half the year at least the world's worst climate'.[126]

'Christmas day', recalled Hudson, 'was a watchful holiday for the
division. The Brigadier, commanding 37 Gurkha Bde, turned up with
a live duck under his arm . . . Because of his exalted rank he had been
issued with this bird for his Christmas dinner, and now it was his pet. I
was allowed to give it a sip of my gin. The blazing heat, inebriated
duck, the Japanese army just over the hill and the false Christmas spirit
was unreal to me, like a comedy film.'[127]

Back in 1942 with the onset of the monsoon, the retreat by Burma
Corps had stopped at the mountain plain of Imphal in India. In the
intervening two years engineers from IV Corps, with the assistance of

a huge labour force from Indian tea plantations, had improved the communications working with shovels and spades and baskets. The steep all-weather two-way road north through Kohima linked up with the logistic centre at Dimapur on the Bengal–Assam railway.

Dimapur itself was a 'beautiful township, adorned with pine trees' recalled John Hudson to British soldiers returning to India after the grim fighting in Imphal and Kohima the town had 'clean and colourful shops and a Victorian atmosphere that was nostalgic and homely'.

An all-weather road ran south and east from Imphal across the mountain spine via Palel down to Tamu on the India border. A southern all-weather road exited from the plain as far as Torbung and then continued south as a fair-weather road via Tiddim and Fort White – though some engineers described the fair-weather road as 'a series of boulders joined together by dust'.

At the beginning of 1944, Fourteenth Army, the Chinese Army in India and Chinese Expeditionary Force were poised to invade Burma from the west, north and east. To support Fourteenth Army, Imphal held by Lt General Geoffrey Scoones's Indian IV Corps had been built up to be a substantial logistic base, with supporting airfields. Confident, well-trained and equipped British and Indian troops were well forward, almost to the Chindwin River and poised to invade Burma.

In the past two years Slim had emphasised the value of intense and realistic training knowing that it would build confidence and morale.

Captain Alexander Wilson one of the directing staff at the British 2 Division infantry jungle warfare school recalled one of the unusual benefits of this training.

'Most British people, many brought up in towns, have never really been in the dark, because there are always street lamps, or some sort of light. Few of our soldiers had ever been alone at night. We have lost our sense of hearing and smell. These are basic animal-like instincts which are vital in the jungle. The Japs smelt different to us, and you could smell them in a defensive position, or if they had recently passed down a track. The Japs smelt rather like scented powder. Indians smelt different to us too – it depends on what you eat.'[128]

Training in the jungle warfare school concentrated on night operations, realistic live firing exercises and communications. Radio, which was now a vital tool in modern war, posed problems as Wilson recalled.

'Radio communications were a problem in jungles and hills. You found an enormous number of blank areas for communications, especially at night. You had to find the right spot for siting wireless sets by moving around.'[129]

In late March 1943 despite waging what had been recognised as an effective campaign against the first Chindit expedition General Iida had been posted back to Japan. On April 8, the 58-year-old General Masakasu Kawabe replaced him in command of the Japanese forces which were now organised as the Burma Area Army.

The Japanese planned to extend their hold on northern Burma and among the logistics operations to support this, was the construction of new rail-lines using Allied PoWs and conscripted local labourers. A single-line metre-gauge railway linking the Thai system to the Burmese railway south of Moulmein was begun with a completion date of November 1943.

It would be a strategic asset for the Japanese since it ran across the northern neck of the Malay Peninsula. This reduced the need for shipping from Thailand, Indo China and ultimately Japan to make a long and increasingly hazardous journey south around Singapore and then north to Rangoon.

However now the Imperial General Headquarters (IGHQ) Tokyo insisted that it should be ready by August so that reinforcements for the Fifteenth Army could be brought up. Now with shouts of 'Speedo!' the guards and engineers on the railway piled on the pressure on the already starved, sick and overworked 61,000 Allied PoWs of the labour force.[130] In the end about 15,000 would die during the construction through neglect and ill-treatment and the health of many of the survivors would be permanently undermined. About 32,000 men were retained on the railway as maintenance crews once the work was completed.

To complete the rail link the spans of the Sittang Railway Bridge across the wide mouth of the Sittang River, that had been demolished by the British in the retreat in 1942, were rebuilt.

One of the subordinate formations of the Burma Area Army

responsible for the central part of the front facing Imphal and Assam, was Fifteenth Army under a new commander Lt General Mutaguchi.

Ambitious and aggressive his natural instinct was to mount an offensive against Imphal. Ever since the naval battle of Tsushima between May 27–28, 1905 in which Imperial Japan defeated the forces of Tsarist Russia, senior Japanese naval and army officers had been fascinated by the idea of the single war-winning decisive battle. He intended to cut off and destroy the Allied units in their forward positions and then capture Imphal with its wealth of stores and rations. For Mutaguchi this would be his decisive battle – but one that he was destined to lose.

In launching this attack however the Japanese were unwittingly dancing to General Slim's tune. He wanted them to embark on an offensive that would over-extend their forces and critically weaken them.

'I wanted a battle *before* we went into Burma,' Slim explained, 'and I was as eager as Kawabe to make it decisive.'

In war games at the Burma Area Army HQ Mutaguchi pressed for this offensive into Assam instead of advancing to the Indian border and securing a defensive line as proposed by other officers. He submitted his own plan without the prior approval of General Kawabe.

All Mutaguchi's divisional commanders had objections to the plan. Kotoku Sato commanding 31 Division distrusted Mutaguchi, and Genzo Yanagida of 33 Division, who even though he had no combat experience when he took command of 33 Division in late 1943, openly derided him as a 'blockhead'. Masafumi Yamauchi commanding 15 Division was suffering from the onset of tuberculosis and was grimly fatalistic.

Yamauchi was almost the mirror image of the bully Mutaguchi. A gentle frail man he had studied at West Point and later served as military attaché in Washington. Here he had become attached to western food and hygiene and like other more widely travelled Japanese understood the strength of the industrial power of the United States. In Burma he had a western-style latrine and continued to insist under almost siege conditions that he should be served with milk, oatmeal and fresh-baked bread. He was removed from his command by Mutaguchi on the grounds of ill health. By the end of the campaign it was reported that Yamauchi had died leaving behind as his obituary the short poem 'The hills of Arakan I have crossed, my journey to the next world'.

By the end of the disastrous campaign Sato and Yanagida were demanding to be court-martialled to expose Mutaguchi's incompetence.

Their main reservations concerned supply and logistic support. Aggressively confident Mutaguchi had assumed that the operation would be successfully concluded in three weeks. Supplies would then be available from captured Allied dumps – as he had experienced in Malaya. However as his subordinates knew, if they were not captured, the spring monsoon rains would turn the rudimentary supply roads and tracks into mudslides.

Back in July 1942 following the Japanese triumph in Burma C-in-C Southern Army General Terauchi had proposed to the commander of the Fifteenth Army Lt General Shojiro Iida should push on into India with 18 and 33 Divisions in a three-pronged attack code named Operation 21.

The southern thrust of Operation 21 would be along the coast towards the port of Chittagong, in the centre there would be an attack on Manipur in Assam, while to the north the base at Ledo would be captured. The capture of Ledo would cut off the air supply route to China known as the 'The Hump' that linked Ledo to Kunming. The plan was regarded as too ambitious by commanders on the ground who considered the terrain a major obstacle even in the dry season. Divisional commanders in the Fifteenth Army shelved the plan.

The Japanese Army had a very low ratio of service to combat troops, almost one to one. In the US Army it was estimated that 18 men were required to keep one man in the front-line, and the average ratio for western armies was one to eight. What officers of the Imperial Japanese Army saw as an austere strength would in fact prove its undoing in the fighting in Burma in 1944 when a robust and effective logistic 'tail' would support British and Indian troops in Burma while their Japanese enemies starved.

The new invasion plan proposed by Mutaguchi suffered from all the drawbacks of Operation 21 as well as new ones that were revealed as the campaign progressed. The Japanese assumed that the British would be unable to use tanks on the steep jungle-covered hills around Imphal. For the sake of ease of movement and supply, the Japanese would leave behind most of their field artillery, their chief anti-tank weapon. As a result, they would have very little protection against tanks.

Mutaguchi had a deep contempt for British and Indian troops and had made no allowance for their improved training and morale. However possibly a greater error was to underestimate the importance of the air superiority enjoyed by the Allies and the flexibility that aerial re-supply would give the Fourteenth Army. It would be a unique advantage. In the past in Malaya when formations had been outflanked and cut off they collapsed when stores ran low – now as the soldiers in the 'Admin Box' had shown they formed all-round defence and continued to fight with rations and ammunition delivered from the air. A major factor for morale was that front-line casualties did not face a gruelling overland journey but could be evacuated quickly from jungle airstrips to secure hospitals.

It is a bitter irony that as the brutality of the Japanese towards prisoners and wounded quickly became known, Allied soldiers in Burma fought with greater determination. The hatred for the Japanese and determination not to surrender would be one of the factors that would ensure the British victories at Kohima and Imphal.

John Randle recalled: 'The war in Burma was fought with a savagery that did not happen in campaigns in the Western Desert, Italy or North-West Europe, though it certainly did in the fighting between the Germans and Russians . . . Thus, throughout the Burma campaign, I never once recall burying Jap dead. If there were sappers about, and there were when we captured Meiktila, the large number of Jap dead were simply bulldozed into pits. Otherwise we just shoved them in nullahs, or well away from our positions, for the jackals and vultures to dispose of.'[131]

As a form of supplies on the hoof Mutaguchi proposed that 15,000 cows and other animals could be driven across the Chindwin as a mobile source of fresh meat, so called 'Genghis Khan' rations.

However it would emerge that lack of forage meant that many of these unhappy animals either died or were eaten by rear area formations miles from the front-line. The RAF photo reconnaissance flights that produced pictures of these herds being assembled would be one of the indications that an offensive was in the offing. Another indicator were numerous rafts hidden in a camouflaged creek near Homalin.

Mutaguchi's proposed offensive had initially been firmly rejected by the staff at Burma Area Army. However the Southern Expeditionary Army Group, the overall headquarters for all Japanese forces in South East Asia, were in favour. Kawabe's staff attempted to alert the Southern Expeditionary Army Group to the logistical risks with Mutaguchi's plan, only to find that IGHQ Tokyo now supported it. In conversation on March 22, 1943 with War Minister Hideki Tojo, Kawabe had explained, 'The measures we take in relation to Burma are really the first steps in our policy towards India. I'd like to stress that our main objective lies there, in India.'[132]

In the end, the various Japanese headquarters allowed the plan to proceed, because a mere passive defence of Burma against the various developing Allied threats would require as many reinforcements as would an attack on Imphal. It would become part of the 'Absolute National Defence Zone' the islands and occupied territory around Japan that must be held at all costs to protect the Japanese home islands. If the attacks were successful, almost all the Allied operations in Burma would have to be abandoned.

So despite these reservations the plan was accepted in June 1943. A month later table-top tactical exercises were held at the HQ at Maymyo and final war games at Rangoon on December 23, 1943. On January 7, 1944 IGHQ Tokyo gave authorisation for occupation of an area around Imphal with Order No 1776. Operation U-GO or C was now scheduled for between March 7 and 8.

For some Japanese U-GO was logical as a spoiling attack to disrupt the impending Allied offensive. However Mutaguchi had larger ambitions and in these he was abetted by the pro-Japanese Indian nationalist Subhas Chandra Bose, the leader of the nationalist Azad Hind movement with its military arm the Indian National Army or INA.[133]

Bose was eager for the INA to participate in any invasion of India, and persuaded several Japanese senior officers and politicians that the victory that Mutaguchi anticipated would lead to the collapse of British imperial rule in India. He assured the Japanese that large formations of Indian troops would defect to the Japanese in order to play a part in the liberation of India. From a spoiling attack U-GO would now become the grandiloquent 'March on Delhi'.

The operation had three strategic objectives. The first was to cross the frontier and capture the Allies' advance base at Imphal, destroying the British position on the central front. The second was to cut the Bengal–Assam railway, which was the supply line to southern China and so neutralise Chinese operations under the direction of General Stilwell and force him back to Ledo. The third was to overrun the Assam airfields, disrupt the USAAF aerial supply operations 'Over the Hump' that supplied fuel for Major General Chennault's 14 Air Force and ammunition and stores to the Chinese.

In detail U-GO was a three-pronged attack. In the south 33 Infantry Division under Lt-General Motoso Yanagida would cross the Chindwin at Kalewa and advance west and north to destroy the Indian 17 Infantry Division at Tiddim, then attack Imphal from the south.

In the centre *Yamamoto Force*, formed from units detached from 33 and 15 Divisions under Major General Tsunoru Yamamoto, would destroy the Indian 20 Infantry Division at Tamu, then attack Imphal from the east.

Finally from the north 15 Infantry Division under Lt-General Masafumi Yamauchi would envelop Imphal.

In a separate subsidiary operation, 31 Division under Lt-General Kotoku Sato would cross the Chindwin at Homalin, advance through the Somra Hills and isolate Imphal from the north and the road link to the railhead at Dimapur by capturing Kohima. The division would then push on to Dimapur.

In typical style Mutaguchi issued a bombastic Order of the Day.

'The Army has now reached the stage of invincibility – and the day when the Rising Sun shall proclaim our definite victory in India is not far off. This operation will engage the attention of the whole world and is eagerly awaited by 100 million of our countrymen. By its very decisive nature, its success will have a profound effect on the course of the war and may even lead to its conclusion . . .

'Aided by the Gods and inspired by the Emperor and full of the will to win, we must realise the objectives of this operation.

'Conscious of their great responsibilities and of their duty to emulate our heroic ancestors, both officers and men must fight to the death for their country.'

It was reported that his confidence was so high that the Fifteenth Army 'Comfort Women' – women, many of whom were from Korea, who had been forced to provide sexual services to the Japanese Army – were to be ready to be flown into Imphal ten days after the attack.

The British were well aware that the Japanese planned an attack, but they underestimated the strength of the force to be used. Imphal was defended by IV Corps under General Geoffrey Scoones. The Corps consisted of three divisions known not only by their numbers but the distinctive divisional flash or badge worn on the upper shoulder and painted on vehicles: 17 (Black Cat), 20 (Mailed Fist) and 23 (Fighting Cock). In addition the corps had 254 Tank Brigade comprising 3 Carabiniers with Lee-Grant tanks and 7 Light Cavalry with Stuarts.

The plan was for 17 and 20 Indian Divisions, both in fairly advanced and therefore exposed positions, to fall back around Imphal where they would protect and live off the large base organisations that had been established in the valley. The Japanese would then be worn down in defensive fighting until the monsoon broke which would isolate them as their tenuous supply system already under sustained air attack broke down completely.

The men of 17 Division knew themselves by names other than 'Black Cat': as veterans of Burma they were proud of the nickname 'God Almighty's Own'. In 1942 a competition had been run for the design of a divisional flash. For a formation that had been buzzing around all over South East Asia some wags in the division suggested that it should be a 'Blue-Arsed Fly on a Green Background'. In the end it was the Divisional Commander's wife's suggestion of a black cat that decided the insignia.

On March 6 Sergeant Eric Murrell cipher specialist with the Devonshire Regiment in the Kabaw Valley watched soldiers swimming in the River Yu. It was a bucolic scene that would soon become a distant memory.

'The river is good fun – the "coloured" troops bathe in quantities. Several here are "Johnnie Gurkhas" as we call them. (War and roughing it seem just great fun for these grand little fellows.) And many more here are Sikhs, who wear their hair long; and when we see a group shrieking and laughing while bathing in their bright-coloured shorts, we usually call out "Hello, girls". Teams of horses and mules are ridden down by Indians in khaki turbans to join the humans in a bathe, while the big guns boom and whistle overhead, sending their salvos over the ridge opposite to the Japs on the Chindwin.'[134]

If Slim and Mutaguchi stand like protagonists in a drama with the Japanese doomed to be defeated by their hubris, the battle for Imphal is like a play in four acts.

Act one is the Japanese attack.

Slim and Scoones had decided that they would withdraw into the Imphal plain and force the Japanese to fight with their logistic supply chain stretched to beyond its limit. However they misjudged the timing and strength of the Japanese attack. On March 8 the first Japanese forces began to cross the Chindwin River.

Four days later patrols from 33 Division had appeared west of the Tiddim Road, but Scoones only gave his forward divisions orders to withdraw to Imphal on March 13.

The Indian 20 Division under Major-General Douglas Gracey withdrew without difficulty, mainly because two of Yamamoto's battalions from the Japanese 15 Division had been delayed at Indaw in northern Burma by Wingate's Chindits who were now in action behind Japanese lines. Gracey, who with a stick and black Labrador dog looked rather like an English country gentleman, had taken his men into his confidence explaining the broad outline of how the campaign was to be conducted. They therefore understood the reasoning behind the withdrawal. His division halted at the Shenam Saddle a feature that covered the approaches to the all-weather airfield at Palel and held this key 15 Division objective throughout the campaign.

However to the south it initially looked as if U-GO might be going according to plan. Reports came in that the road along which Indian 17 Division, under Major-General David Cowan was withdrawing, had been cut in several places by the Japanese 33 Division.

Cowan had received the order to withdraw but it was not passed down to formations in the field until 13.00 hours March 14 and they were given four hours to start moving. The division included 4,000 mules and 2,000 motor vehicles. Cowan marched with his men – he had given orders that vehicles were to be used for the wounded. Hooking round to the south along a fair-weather road and tracks the Japanese 215 Regiment captured a supply dump at Milestone 109, 20 miles behind Cowan's leading outposts.

The Japanese 214 Regiment advancing along tracks to the north seized Tongzang and a ridge named Tuitum Saddle across the only road, a few miles behind the Indian 17 Division's position.

Fighting around Milestone 109 was even more severe, but Cowan had taken steps to secure the most vulnerable point in the rear of his division, the bridge over the Manipur River. Once the division crossed safely on March 17 they blew it up behind them. Though they were forced to abandon large amounts of stores these were not the vital 'Churchill Supplies' that the Japanese had been banking on capturing. Crucial stores like food, ammunition and vehicles that would have sustained the Japanese had been back-loaded leaving behind only clothing and blankets.

Uncharacteristically at Tuitum Saddle, the Japanese had not dug in completely because the ground was rocky and they were hit by a counter-attack on March 18. The Japanese suffered heavy casualties and were forced away from the road.

In radio news broadcasts the Japanese were already reporting the destruction of the division gleefully announcing that 'only the commander and 26 men escaped to tell the tale'. In *The Campaign in Burma* Owen explained that it was a Japanese custom to make such boasts and then try to live up to them.

Scoones had been forced to commit the bulk of his only reserve, the Indian 23 Infantry Division under Major-General Ouvry Roberts, to support 17 Division. For John Hudson with 23 Division this was the beginning of his part in the Imphal battle. Taking aim at a sword-wielding Japanese officer who was urging his men forward he fired.

'I knew that it was my bullet that threw him down, and the words of the recruiting sergeant in a freezing school hall in Derby came back to me:

'"There are three things you never forget, Laddie! Your army number, your first woman, and your first 'Un!" Little did I know at that time that my first would be a Jap and not a 'Un".'

The two divisions, now supplied by parachute drops, withdrew along 167 miles to the Imphal plain, which they reached on April 4. The parachute drops included not only ammunition, water and rations but even mail and newspapers.

Meanwhile, Imphal appeared to have been left vulnerable to the attacks by Yamamoto's 15 Division in the north. The Japanese 31 Division had blocked the main road south of Kohima by the start of April, cutting off IV Corps.

Even before the Japanese Fifteenth Army launched its three-pronged attack on Imphal and Kohima, Slim had anticipated that IV Corps would need to be rapidly reinforced if Scoones had to commit his two reserve brigades. These reserves were now in action helping 17 Division clear the road back to Imphal.

Slim had already discussed the requirement for rapid reinforcement using aircraft on March 14 and four days later he contacted Mountbatten as SEAC Supreme Commander with an urgent request that aircraft of the USAAF Air Transport Command be transferred to assist No 194 (Transport) Squadron RAF. Within a day, on Mountbatten's orders, 20 big USAAF Curtiss C-46 Commando transport[135] aircraft joined the 25 RAF Dakotas and in only 11 days the now battle-hardened Indian 5 Infantry Division with all its artillery and transport was flown fresh from its triumph in the Arakan to the Central Front. Two of its brigades went to Imphal, and their leading troops were in action by April 3.

Such was the speed at which the operation was put into motion that many of the soldiers and even the USAAF pilots had little idea of what was going on.

'"Say, where do you want to go?" asked one pilot. *"Malum nahin*

Sahib" ("I don't know") was the reply of the Indian officer in charge of the soldiers. "Where are we off to and what is the name of the place we have just left?" enquired another when he was airborne. "Never mind, we'll take a chance."'[136]

Mountbatten, who was recovering from a nasty eye injury that had put him in hospital,[137] now had to square this operation with the American Joint Chiefs of Staff (JCS) in the United States. They agreed retrospectively to the re-assignment of the USAAF aircraft that were normally used for flying men and equipment 'Over the Hump' to China, but their telegram stated that they did not agree that he had the right to make such diversions without consulting them.

However the way that the battle for Imphal shaped up with the timely arrival of reinforcements makes Mountbatten's decision to act first and then consult the JCS a critical moment in the war in Burma.

Act two of the drama begins in April. By April 4 the whole of IV Corps was in position around Imphal. The defence was shaped like a horseshoe with 17 Indian Division covering the south and the road from Tiddim, 20 Indian Division covered the south-east and 23 Indian Division the north-east.

The Japanese launched their attacks on the Imphal plain from several directions: the 33 Division attacked 17 Indian Division, where a fighting patrol cut a secondary track from Silchar into the plain on April 15–16 in a suicidal attack on a suspension bridge – the destruction of which took three Japanese soldiers to their death. However Yanagida was already pessimistic and depressed by the failure to trap the Indian 17 Division. He had also been rattled by a garbled radio message which suggested that one of his regiments had been destroyed in fighting at Milestone 109 and consequently he advanced cautiously. This hesitancy may have cost him a significant victory. While the Indian 17 Infantry Division was resting after its retreat, Bishenpur was held only by Indian 32 Bde detached from 20 Division.

Yamamoto Force attacked the Shenam Saddle on the main road from Tamu into Imphal. The Shenam Saddle was ideal defensive terrain. Despite using heavy artillery and tanks, Yamamoto could not break through Indian 20 Division's well-sited defences. This was the setting for the only armoured action of the battle; it was distinctly one-sided with little Type 95s pitted against Lee-Grants of the Carabiniers. The Japanese tank crews had used cover very effectively but when they emerged from the jungle the big British tanks quickly knocked out five and a sixth was captured undamaged.

The defences on the saddle were built around hills that were soon given nicknames Nippon Hill, Sita, Crete East and West, Gibraltar, Malta and closest to the enemy Scraggy.

In depth was the lower Sapper Hill. 'If Scraggy fell (God forbid!),' recalls John Hudson, 'Malta had to hold out, but if Malta fell, Scraggy was untenable. They were interdependent and to look down on Scraggy from the heights of Malta was like viewing a low aerial photograph of the Somme in 1915.'

It was in this sector that the Japanese used formations from the INA.[138] The initial enthusiasm of most INA soldiers, who had been promised they would liberate their homeland, quickly waned and there were surrenders and desertion.

John Hudson had grim memories of the British defences. 'Malta was much worse than Gibraltar; it was lower, muddier and more frequently under attack. A single battalion occupied Malta and Scraggy so that they could rotate three companies between the two fortresses . . .

'If I hated Malta I detested Scraggy. It was so bad on Scraggy that the turn-round was cut to two nights on the hill itself and half an hour in the forward trenches.'[139]

When Ken Cooper joined 2 Border Regiment after the Imphal campaign his Platoon Sergeant described the fighting for 'Scraggy' as a 'duffy'.

'Another ferocious "duffy" had occurred on Scraggy Hill. Many of the forward posts had been overrun by the Japs, leaving a no-man's-land of not much more than ten or twenty yards. This had made digging impossible, and the men nearest the enemy were barely two feet underground, until mortar boxes filled with earth were brought up at night to provide extra cover . . . Apparently the men in the forward position had been relieved every half hour. The strain was that bad.'[140]

To the north 15 Division encircled the Imphal plain. Its 60 Regiment had captured a British supply dump at Kangpokpi on the main

Imphal–Dimapur road. The depot was also known as The Mission because of the little chapel built by Methodist missionaries before the war. However once again, the depot held no 'Churchill Supplies' and had already been emptied of food and ammunition.

A serious threat developed when the Japanese 3/51 Regiment seized Nunshigum Ridge, which overlooked the main airstrip at Imphal. The 1,000-foot feature had been held by 60 men of 3/9 Jats. They counter-attacked on April 7 and held it until a strongly reinforced Japanese force recaptured it on April 11.

Since the Japanese now had time to dig in and consolidate, it was clear that a full-scale, all-arms assault would be required. All the artillery and aircraft that could be mustered were on call to support the attack. So while Hurricane fighters strafed the hill and Vultee Vengeance dive bombers hit identified positions with their 1,000-pound bomb loads, the men of 1/17 Dogras supported by the M3 Lee-Grant tanks of B Squadron 3 Carabiniers began the long and hazardous climb.

By 11.15 hours tanks and infantry were on the ridge line, the fire lifted and with that the Japanese emerged to attack tanks and infantry at close range.

By now the Dogras had taken heavy casualties and all the tank commanders had been killed or wounded. The fighting hung in the balance – a moment when the deeds of one or two clear-headed and brave men can change the course of the action.

Two such men – Squadron Sergeant Major (SSM) Craddock of the Carabiniers and Dogra VCO-Subadar Ranbir Singh were by now the surviving senior ranks on the ridge. They agreed that if the tanks could get in closer to the bunkers the Dogras could go in with the bayonet.

To do this Craddock had to ensure that tanks that had been immobilised were moved, this included towing one under heavy small arms fire. The first attack stalled. This time a tank commanded by Sgt Hannan climbed a very steep slope to the centre of the Japanese position while the SSM worked round to the right. Between them the two tanks beat down the opposition and the Dogras went in. At the close of the fighting 250 bodies were found among the bunkers.

As a tribute to this action fought by NCOs alone B Squadron Royal

Scots Dragoon Guards parades on the anniversary of Nunshigun under command of its Sergeant Major and NCOs.

Act three in the Imphal drama began on May 1 the date on which Japanese major attacks came to a halt.

On May 2 Kawabe, out of touch with the reality of the situation, assured IGHQ Tokyo that U-GO still had an 80 to 85 per cent chance of success. Ill with amoebic dysentery, he visited the Fifteenth Army HQ at Indainggy on May 5 and finally realised that U-GO was doomed.

From a set of captured orders and other intelligence Slim and Scoones had identified the exhausted Japanese 15 Division as the weakest of the Japanese formations, and knew that a successful counter-attack against it would break the siege. However progress was slow in part because the monsoon had broken making movement very difficult. Also, IV Corps was suffering some shortages. Although rations and reinforcements were delivered to Imphal by air, artillery ammunition was by now rationed. However neither 31 Division fighting at Kohima, nor 15 Division, had received adequate supplies since the offensive began, and their troops were starving. At the end of May XXXIII Corps began to drive the Japanese from Kohima and advance south.

Lance Corporal Muragishi serving with 15 Division found his platoon under attack by four tanks.

'The men held their breath and went rigid with fear as the tank caterpillars grated towards them – ready to trample down the trench sides. At that moment, one of our men heaved himself up out of the trench and seemed to prance in front of us. It was Lance Corporal Uehara of 6 Company. Just before leaping out of the trench, he said in a low urgent voice, "I'm going to get that tank. Just watch me!" . . .

'He was clutching in his right hand a globe the size of a fist. He closed up to the tank and, from about ten yards, hurled the globe.

'Immediately, for some reason, the British tank was enveloped in white smoke, like steam . . . white smoke poured straightaway inside the tank which was covered in it . . .

'The tank crew, giving queer screams, jumped out and down from the tank . . .

'From the turret of the now empty tank a terrific amount of black smoke gushed. Uehara had climbed up the side of the tank, slipped the pin of a hand grenade and flung it inside.'[141]

The Japanese corporal may have used a glass Frangible Smoke Grenade containing a mixture of titanium and silicon tetrachloride. The tank crew must have assumed they were under chemical attack and would indeed have been justified in their fears. In the US Army Handbook on Japanese Military Forces TM-E 30–480 a glass grenade that contained approximately a pint of Hydrocyanic Acid almost identical in appearance is described and illustrated.[142]

Though there were local successes the troops of Japanese 15 Division were forced to abandon their defensive positions to forage for supplies in local villages.

Relations between Mutaguchi and Yanagida had now reached such a low ebb that the two generals no longer communicated directly. When he wished to talk to 33 Division the commander Fifteenth Army spoke to the divisional Chief of Staff Colonel Tanaka Tetsujiro. Yanagida was sacked on May 9 and replaced by General Noburo Tanaka on May 23.

Yamauchi, now mortally ill and still attempting to run operations from his sick bed, was finally dismissed by Mutaguchi on June 23.

Yamauchi's health was not helped by the aggressive operations of 23 Division who were now pushing up the road to Ukhrul forcing his HQ to make several hurried withdrawals by night.

A staff officer from IGHQ who visited the Central Front in Burma returned to Tokyo and presented a report that began bleakly 'The Imphal operations stand little chance of success'.

However the fighting went on relentlessly and on the night of May 20–21 in driving rain an attack was launched against a feature known as Red Hill in the 17 Division area near Bishenpur by men of the 2/214 Regimental Group, 33 Division. A force of 500 infantry, 100 gunners with three light-calibre guns supported by 40 sappers. It would be the closest the Japanese got to Imphal. They were stopped by a platoon of D Company 10 Baluch Regiment who held the hill under the heroic leadership of Subedar Ghulam Yasmin. The feature was known as Red Hill because shell fire had stripped away the vegetation and exposed the red laterite earth below.

When the dawn rose the Japanese who had been unable to capture the crest dug in on the southern slope. This small force under mortar and artillery fire sustained three attacks of increasing strength and ferocity by seasoned troops between May 22 and 23, May 26 and two days later without re-supply of food or ammunition or casualty evacuation. It was after the third attack the Japanese pulled back – their force of 640 had been reduced to 37.

'It was not fashionable in those days to heap praise on our enemy,' writes John Randle, 'and it has not really been fashionable since. Nevertheless, to my mind the exploit of that Japanese battalion in holding out for so long against repeated attacks was one of the finest feats of arms that I ever saw. There was much to dislike and despise about the way the Japs conducted the war, but no one who actually fought them on the battlefield could deny their courage and fighting prowess . . .

'The last word must surely be with General Slim . . . who after visiting the recaptured Red Hill, praised their courage. No soldier who fought in Burma on either side could ask for higher praise than that.'[143]

The final act in the drama of Imphal opens on June 6.

On the day that, far across the world, Allied forces landed in Normandy in the European war against Japan's ally Nazi Germany, Mutaguchi met Kawabe. The Japanese had realised that operations ought to be broken off as early as May but neither officer could face the shame of the responsibility of ordering a retreat.

'The sentence "The time has come to give up the operation as soon as possible" got as far as my throat,' he wrote later, 'but I could not force it out in words. But I wanted him to get it from my expression.'

This was *hara-gei*, an unspoken form of communication using gesture, expression and tone of voice. However as the Harrieses' observe, 'Combined with the conspiratorial secretiveness bred of faction fighting, this kind of obliquity was a real obstacle to lucid policy-making and decisive action.'[144]

Three days later Kawabe informed IGHQ Tokyo that there were problems with U-GO.

On June 22 the leading troops of IV Corps and XXXIII Corps met at Milestone 109 and the siege was raised.

'We met the Imphal garrison coming north,' recalled Major Alexander Wilson of the Durham Light Infantry. 'We were clearing road blocks quicker than the Japs thought we could. The Japs would blow the little culvert between two ridges, and sit on the other side – there were no bunkers, but foxholes, and they fought hard. The technique was to fix them in the front and climb above them, and outflank them. The Japs were getting short of men. Artillery support was very important. Sometimes the guns fired direct over open sights. The Jap artillery was very sparse – they were an army in disarray . . . but it didn't mean they didn't fight.'[145]

Although there was now no realistic hope of success, Mutaguchi and Kawabe ordered renewed attacks. Both men were under pressure from C-in-C Southern Army General Terauchi.

Mutaguchi issued an Order of the Day that would become famous for its unrealistic appeal to mysticism and the Japanese spirit.

'The struggle has developed into a fight between the material strength of the enemy and our spiritual strength. Continue in the task till all your ammunition is expended. If your hands are broken fight with your feet. If your hands and feet are broken use your teeth. If there is no breath left in your body, fight with your spirit. Lack of weapons is no excuse for defeat.'

By now Mutaguchi, clearly mentally unstable, was transmitting orders to Sato that included phrases, dutifully translated by British intercept teams as 'Get off your fat arse' and 'Pull your finger out'.

At his HQ at Indainggy five miles north-east of Kalemyo 'He had a little clearing made near his tactical headquarters and stood bamboo in it pointing in the four directions of the compass, which he then decorated. Early in the morning, he would approach the bamboo and call on the eight hundred myriad gods of Japan. His batman said that he would get up in the middle of the night and shout out, "There's some strange thing under the floor of my hut, get troops here at once and chase it away!" The batman promptly had the place scoured by troops, who of course found nothing untoward.'[146]

Reinforced by a regiment from 53 Division and a battalion from 54 Division, under a new forceful commander, the freshly promoted Lt-General Tanaka, 33 Division attacked Indian 17 Division's positions at Bishenpur, but failed to break through since by now 70 per cent of the division had been killed or were wounded or sick.

At the end of June Tanaka confided to his diary 'Both officers and men look dreadful. They've let their hair and beards grow until they look exactly like wild men of the mountains. Over a hundred days have passed since this two-month operation began. In that time the men have had almost nothing to eat – they're undernourished and pale.

'The weather's been clear for two or three days, but last night it began to pour, which adds to the men's hardships . . .

'Since 15th June I've not used a watch. Watches aren't much use on the battlefield. The rain pours endlessly, but enemy aircraft are still flying. They're at it 24 hours a day, almost as if the skies were clear.'[147]

Yamamoto Force also made repeated efforts, but by the end of June both formations had suffered so many casualties that they were unable to make any progress.

A Japanese diary was picked up in the area. It had been kept by Second Lt Taiso Nishikawa of No 5 Company 33 Division. Incredibly as late as June 28 the division was still thinking of offensive operations.

The whole Division, including the Divisional Commander, fought ten days without rice, and, because of things like this, the date of the general offensive, originally 10 June, was postponed ten or twenty days, and left indefinite . . .

The enemy stands firm, having plenty of weapons, ammunition and food. His attacks with tanks and mortars are something terrific – so are his air raids, and we can do nothing.

Today is the 28th of June. Gradually the general offensive is getting under way. My unit is in the front-line of all and has begun the final attack, but this is the toughest going, and if we do manage to take a position, the enemy bombards it with mortars, and bombs it from the air to a heart-shaking degree; so that those who have dug deep trenches are buried in them, and those who have dug shallow, have hands and feet blown away . . .

The wounded men were sent back but the sick were not. Kept in the front-line, they have to pound the unhulled rice. Up to the time of their death they have to pound the unhulled rice, and when they die, they die from sheer exhaustion.[148]

However it was symptomatic of the collapse of morale that Major Ito commanding a company in the *Yamamoto Force* on receipt of the order to press an attack under impossible conditions said 'The Emperor cannot possibly give orders as foolish as these'.

When they received orders to make a renewed attack 15 and 33 Divisions refused to obey since they were in no condition to comply.

On July 3 when Mutaguchi realised that his formations were no longer obeying his orders he finally ordered the offensive to be broken off. The Japanese divisions, reduced in many cases to a rabble, fell back to the Chindwin River, abandoning their artillery, transport, and soldiers too sick to walk. Yamamoto was ordered to withdraw into the Kabaw Valley on July 13. He refused to obey this direct order from the Fifteenth Army HQ and acting on his own initiative, retreated with what remained of his division to Sittang on the Chindwin and set up his HQ at Yazagyo on August 2.

The defeat at Kohima and Imphal was the largest defeat to that date in Japanese history. They had suffered 55,000 casualties, including 13,500 dead. Most of these losses were the result of starvation, disease and exhaustion. By contrast, the Allies suffered 17,500 casualties and many of these were men who had been evacuated to base hospitals and would return after they had recovered. Both Kawabe and Mutaguchi were relieved of command.

'Though few believed it at the time,' writes Frank Owen, 'here in the

"Bloody Plain" the spine of the Japanese Imperial Army in South-east Asia was broken.

' "They will never come back," said Slim addressing one of his victorious divisions. "In this year we have thrashed the Japanese soldier, man for man, and decisively. Next year we shall smash the Japanese Army." ' [149]

CHAPTER 9

KOHIMA

April 3 to June 22, 1944

'Stuff your bloody thoughts, General! What about reinforcements?'
British signaller, Indian Parachute Brigade, Sangshak to General Ouvry
Roberts

On his way to join his regiment at Imphal John Hudson had passed through the town of Kohima, the administrative centre of the pro-British, Christian tribal area of Nagaland.[150]

The British administrator was Charles Pawsey a Colonial Office Deputy Commissioner or DC. His bungalow with its gardens and tennis court, which would feature significantly in the forthcoming battle, stood on the hillside at a bend in the road. Pawsey was highly respected by the Nagas and in the course of the battle any information from them about Japanese movements that was passed to him always proved reliable.

Hudson recalled that 'Whitewashed buildings gleamed amongst rich foliage, the red splash of the corrugated tin roof over the Mission Chapel and the mown precision of the tennis court contrasted with the tumbled savagery of the blue-green mountain backdrop . . . No wonder the defence of this frontier had never been taken seriously. Impenetrable jungle-covered ranges soared to the skyline in every direction, barring any passage between Burma and India. The ability of the Japanese to cross any terrain had changed all that.'

Kohima is sited on a north–south ridge. The Dimapur–Imphal road climbs to its northern end and runs along the eastern side. To the north of the ridge as the fighting developed the British gave names to features like 'Naga Village' a heavily populated area which had two distinct areas of high ground 'Treasury Hill', 'Garrison Hill', 'Jail Hill',

'FSD Hill' (Field Supply Depot), 'DIS Hill' (Detail Issue Depot) and 'Church Knoll'. To the south and west of Kohima Ridge were 'GPT Ridge' (General Purpose Transport) and the jungle-covered 'Aradura Spur'. In the course of the battle the Japanese would use their own code names for the defended locations so Garrison Hill was *Inu* 'dog' and Kuki Piquet was *Saru* 'monkey'.

Part of the U-GO plan involved sending 31 Division (the 58 Regiment, 124 Regiment, 138 Regiment and an Independent Mountain Artillery battalion) under Lt General Kotoku Sato to capture Kohima. The mission was hugely challenging and Sato so worried about the viability of U-GO that even before it had been launched he told his staff that they might all starve to death.

Sato's reservations about Mutaguchi and his ambitions were long standing. In the early 1930s the two officers had found themselves on opposite sides during factional rivalries within the Japanese Army. Sato was described by his comrades as a man of great courage, with an easy manner and open-hearted nature, with an inclination towards the unconventional.

On March 15, 31 Division with the 15 Division on its left flank began crossing the Chindwin in several places around the town of Homalin using improvised rafts and native craft.

For Lt Susumu Nishida of 11/58 Regiment the crossing was charged with drama and symbolism.

'For a moment, there was an oppressive silence. Then, in a low voice, summoning all my strength, my voice broke that silence. "Let us now bid farewell to our mother country!" My beloved sword flashed, the moon's rays slanting down on it. I was about to raise the curtain on the invasion of India.

' "Fix bayonets!" The clash of bayonets flicked from their sheaths, the blades locked on rifle muzzles. Then again silence.

' "Present ARMS!" The thunderclap of hands slapping rifles, and the single line of steel points like the crest of a wave. For a moment, there was not the slightest stir in the ranks. Eyes filled with tears.'[151]

They advanced and moved north-west on a front almost 60 miles wide along numerous jungle trails. Although the march across the mountain ridges was tough good progress was made. Excellent camouflage meant that the speed of the advance came as a surprise to British commanders who had assumed that large numbers of troops would need a substantial logistic 'tail' and this would require vehicles and so roads.

It was 58 Regiment on the left flank, under 31 Division's Infantry Group commander Major General Shigesaburo Miyazaki that had pushed ahead of 15 Division and on March 20 it clashed with men of the Indian 50 Parachute Bde.

With the prospect of going into action for the first time Lt Seisaku Kameyana of 2/58 Regiment gave his platoon a very human pep talk.

' "You see," I said to my soldiers, "keep your heads, keep cool. If you want to find just how cool you are feeling, put your hands inside your trousers and feel your penis – if it is hanging down, it is good." I tested mine, but it was shrunk up so hard I could hardly grasp it. More than thirty soldiers did the same thing, then looked at me curiously, but I kept a poker-face. I said "Well, mine's down all right. If yours is shrunk up, it's because you're scared."

'Then a young soldier said to me: "Sir, I can't find mine at all. What's happening to it?" With this everyone burst out laughing and I knew I had got the confidence of the men.'[152]

The Indian Parachute Brigade they were about to attack was composed of three battalions: 151 British Battalion, 152 Indian Battalion and 153 Gurkha Battalion under M. R. J. 'Tim' Hope Thomson and had taken up a position on the hill village of Sangshak. The battalion was covering the northern approaches to Imphal and their fight would be an epic of courage and endurance.

Captain F. G. Nields with the 153 Gurkha Parachute Battalion recalled how the big, pipe-smoking Major Lock commanding 15 Battery, 9th Indian Mountain Regiment watched the Japanese appear over the hill from the road from Ukhrul.

'He was in no hurry and waited until the whole length of the road was full of Japs before he let them have it. We saw the little white puffs bursting all along the road. Lock beamed – his only regret was that the guns had no shrapnel. He said it was the best day's shoot of his life.'[153]

Although Sangshak was not Miyazaki's objective, he decided to clear it and secure his left flank. The paratroops though lacking defence stores went into all-round defence – the now proven tactics of the 'Box'. Captain 'Dicky' Richards teamed up with Major John Ball the Brigade Machine Gun Company commander to recover some enemy dead in no-man's-land. Improvising a grapnel from a damaged radio aerial they were able – under fire – to haul in the body of a Japanese officer. On it was a map that showed the proposed routes for the 15th and 31st Divisions on Imphal and Kohima.

'We were inspired by a message from the corps commander based on the captured maps,' recalled Captain Richards, 'saying that the holding of Sangshak was vital to the main plan . . . this caused much optimism all round despite the fact that we were almost on our knees from lack of sleep alone, as well as shortage of food and water.'[154]

The battle continued for six days. The earth was only three feet deep before picks and shovels hit rock. Not only did this make it difficult to dig adequate trenches but it also meant that every time a shell or mortar bomb exploded it tended to disinter a corpse. The men were desperately short of drinking water despite heroic efforts by the RAF to deliver rations and ammunition – low cloud on the top of a hill made for a difficult drop zone and about two-thirds were estimated to have fallen in Japanese lines.

However having advanced up jungle tracks Miyazaki had been unable to bring up heavy artillery. When it became clear that 15 Division would join the battle, Hope Thompson whose men had bought valuable time received orders to withdraw.

Captain 'Dicky' Richards was visiting the Brigade HQ when a signaller hunched over his set shouted for silence.

'The signaller listened hard to the crackling set and scribbled on his pad, talking into his handset. It seemed to go on forever. Then he suddenly shouted into the microphone, "You can stuff your bloddy thoughts, General! What about reinforcements?" He was beside himself with rage as he handed over the message. It read, "FIGHT YOUR WAY OUT, GO SOUTH THEN WEST, AIR AND TRANSPORT ON THE LOOK OUT" and ended "GOOD LUCK. OUR THOUGHTS ARE WITH YOU". This had prompted the signaller's reply. Our reactions resembled a "Bateman" cartoon. For a moment we were horrified by his audacity, but seconds later broke the tension with spontaneous laughter – and that was a sound not heard at Sangshak for quite some long time.'[155]

Prior to the breakout Captain Richards recalled Swami the cook at the Brigade HQ producing a huge stew for the men.

'We were amused to see him adopting the role of a Brahmin high priest, which was hardly his status, giving dispensation to the Hindu to accept the possibility of corned beef within the cauldron, and the Muslim not to reject the infamous American-made 'soya link' sausage and gallons of rum included in the pot!'[156]

The men broke out at night carrying their wounded on makeshift stretchers.

Captain Richards made it back to British lines and learned from General Ouvry Roberts, commanding 23 Indian Division, that the brigade had saved both Kohima and Imphal from being overrun by the Japanese forward units.

'As we were taking our leave, I asked him off the record whether he had heard the British signaller's comment on his personal message . . . His reply was just an enigmatic smile.'[157]

The 50 Parachute Bde had lost 600 men and Miyazaki about 400 but his troops, who had the shortest and easiest route to Kohima, had been delayed by a week.

Meanwhile Slim, whose staff had assumed that only a force of regimental strength, about 1,000 men, could cross the rugged terrain south-east of Kohima, had now belatedly realised they were up against a division 10,000 to 15,000 men. Kohima had few fighting troops and the vital base of Dimapur, 30 miles to the north had none.

Slim moved quickly when the extent of the Japanese attack became clear.

As part of the hasty reinforcement of the Imphal front, the veteran Indian 5 Infantry Division, victors of the battle of the Admin Box, had been flown from the Arakan front. While the main body of the division went to Imphal, 161 Infantry Bde with the Indian Army 24 Mountain Artillery Regiment IA, were flown to a depth position at Dimapur. Here they reinforced the British 2 Division, 23 Long Range Penetration Bde, a force originally tasked with a role in Operation Thursday, and the Indian XXXIII Corps HQ under Lt General Montagu Stop-ford and moved to Dimapur by road and rail.

Before 161 Bde moved into the area, the only fighting troops were the newly raised Assam Regiment and Assam Rifles. In late March the Assam Regiment fought delaying actions to the east of Kohima and by April 3 Miyazaki's troops were probing Kohima. The brigade had been ordered forward to Kohima, back to Dimapur and then forward again. However only one infantry battalion, 4th Battalion The Queen's Own Royal West Kent Regiment, arrived in Kohima before the Japan-ese hooked round and cut the road west of the ridge. The West Kents were commanded by a charismatic officer Lt Colonel John Laverty a fiery Irishman, whom the soldiers had nicknamed 'Texas Dan'.

The siege began on April 6 when, in the words of Major John Winstanley, 'The 4th Royal West Kents, the Assam Rifles and odds and sods defended Kohima against an entire Jap division in a 14 day siege. The perimeter shrank and shrank until it only included the Tennis Court and Garrison Hill where the final stand took place.'[158]

The odds and sods also included 20 Mountain Battery, an engineers detachment from 2 Field Company and another from 75 Indian Field Ambulance including Lt Colonel John Young who earned the sobri-quet the 'Tactical Doctor'. Young had nothing but praise for his Indian Army orderlies who at dusk or dawn would creep into no-man's-land to recover wounded, running the risk of both hostile and friendly fire.

Early in the fighting the Japanese captured GPT Ridge and gained control of the water supply. The garrison was remorselessly shelled and mortared and slowly driven into a small area around FSD Hill and the DC's bungalow. Fortunately for the hard-pressed garrison they had artillery support from the guns of 161 Bde, now cut off 2 miles away at Jotsoma. The dressing stations were exposed to Japanese fire, and the wounded in shallow trenches were hit again by mortar fire as they waited for treatment. Young would say of the wounded 'They were the real heroes of [the] Kohima Siege. No tribute is too fine for them.' The Advanced Dressing Station received three hits – two on the same day and Young recalled, 'The shambles of this place after its second direct hit will remain always in my memory. It was a frightful task collecting medical equipment mixed in all that blood and filth – there was a head on the floor and dismembered limbs on all sides – in order to carry out our work.'[159]

Ammunition, rations and crucially water were parachuted to the garrison who were reduced to one pint a day and consequently stopped shaving. Over the battlefield hung the smell of death. Major John Nettlefield recalled that 'The place stank. The ground everywhere was ploughed up with shell-fire and human remains lay rotting as the battle raged over them . . . Men retched as they dug in . . . The stink hung in the air and permeated one's clothes and hair.'[160]

On April 8 the Japanese launched a series of attacks into the northeast region of the defences, and a day later the garrison there had been forced back out of the DC's bungalow to the other side of the tennis court. The other positions came under heavy attack and the perimeter shrank.

That night Lance Cpl John Harman a section commander of a forward platoon saw that the Japanese had set up a machine gun within 50 yards of his company. It was not possible to bring down fire from the section on the position so Harman ran forward alone, threw a grenade into the position and destroyed it. Early next morning, having ordered covering fire from a Bren gun crew he went alone, with fixed bayonet and charged another Japanese machine-gun crew who were digging in, shooting four and bayoneting one. As he walked back he was fatally wounded by a burst of machine-gun fire. In the trench his last words before he died were, 'I got the lot, it was worth it.' He was awarded a posthumous Victoria Cross.

The troops holding the area near the DC's bungalow and the tennis court came under increasingly heavy artillery and mortar fire, and had to repel frequent infantry assaults. However Major Winstanley commanding B Company had several tactical advantages.

'I had instant contact by radio with the guns, and the Japs never seemed to learn how to surprise us. They used to shout in English as they formed up, "Give up!" which gave us warning each time an attack was coming in. One would judge just the right moment to call down gun- and mortar-fire to catch them as they were launching the attack, and every time they approached us they were decimated. They were not acting intelligently and did the same old stupid thing again and again.'[161]

On April 14 there were no Japanese attacks and a day later the battered garrison heard that 2 Division, which had been in training in southern India for an anticipated amphibious landing in Burma, had arrived at Dimapur in early April. It was now fighting its way eastwards from Dimapur and had broken through Japanese road blocks.

Two days after they received this good news they were hit by the final all-out Japanese assault that captured positions on the ridge from the FSD to the Garrison Hill. The following morning further attacks were halted by massive artillery bombardments.

On April 15 the leading troops from 2 Division had relieved 161 Bde in their box at Jotsoma. Three days later men from 161 Bde broke through to Kohima. The first men to be evacuated were 300 wounded, followed by men of the support arms, the men described by Major Winstanley as 'odds and sods'. Then the men of the West Kents the British 6 Infantry Bde took over their positions. At Hospital Spur one platoon of the Royal West Kents was reduced to four men – all of whom were wounded.

However this did not mark the end of the fighting. For several more nights Miyazaki continued to try to capture Garrison Hill with heavy casualties being suffered on both sides. Elements of the British 2 Division, 161 Bde and tanks from XXXIII Corps pushed into the area north-west of Garrison Hill and forced the Japanese from their positions. The road between Dimapur and Kohima had been fully opened, and the siege was lifted.

However the Japanese did not retreat; many remained in the positions that they had captured and fought tenaciously from them for several more weeks.

When two brigades of 2 Division tried to outflank both ends of the Japanese position in Naga Village and on GPT Ridge initially it looked as if the attacks would succeed but the monsoon had broken and the steep ridges degenerated into mudslides making re-supply and reinforcement almost impossible. From May 4, 2 Division switched to concentrate on the Japanese centre along Kohima Ridge.

The Japanese who had moved from attack to defence were still a formidable enemy. Miyazaki commanded the four battalions of Left Force on the Kohima Ridge; another four battalions under Sato holding the Naga Village made up Centre Force. The much smaller Right Force held villages to the north and east.

The British had now brought up 38 3.7-inch Mountain Howitzers, 48 25-Pounders and two 5.5-inch Mediums Guns that fired big 100 lb HE shells, to support their attack on the ridge. The RAF also bombed and strafed the Japanese positions. The Japanese could oppose them with only 17 mountain guns, probably 75mm Pack Guns, for which there was very little ammunition.

However the Japanese had dug strong, well-sited bunkers and progress was slow because it seemed impossible to deploy armour on the ridge lines. Mutually supporting positions on the reverse slope of GPT Ridge covered Jail Hill on the flank and in a week of fighting Japanese machine guns in these positions inflicted heavy casualties.

It was on May 4 that Temporary Captain John Randle of 2 Battalion, The Royal Norfolk Regiment took command of a company which was leading the attack against Japanese positions on a ridge after the company commander had been severely wounded. Although wounded in the knee by a grenade splinter, he handled a very difficult situation, in the face of extremely heavy fire from the enemy: going forward, he brought in all the wounded men who were lying outside the perimeter. Although suffering from pain from his wound, he refused to be evacuated, reconnoitring enemy positions, prior to the attack by his company.

The attack opened at dawn on May 6, with Randle leading. One of the platoons reached the crest of the hill, whilst another ran into heavy machine-gun fire from a bunker. Captain Randle realised that the object must be to destroy this position, as it covered his line of communication as well as the rear of his position. Randle single-handedly charged the enemy machine-gun post, armed with a rifle and bayonet. Mortally wounded by continuous bursts of machine-gun fire he managed to reach the bunker. He then threw a grenade into the bunker, throwing himself across the embrasure in order to completely seal the blast. He was awarded a posthumous VC.[162]

This paraphrase of the Victoria Cross citation does not reflect the ghastly violence of this fighting. Sergeant Bert 'Winkie' Fitt of the Royal Norfolks saw Captain Randle attack the bunker. He watched the Captain hit at point-blank range. 'As he was going down, he threw his grenade into the bunker and sealed the entrance with his own body, so nobody could shoot from it. He killed all the occupants. I thought, "That's the end of Captain Randle." '[163]

Moments later the Sergeant found himself in a hand-to-hand struggle with a Japanese soldier.

'Before he hit the ground I had my hand around his windpipe and I literally tried to tear it out. It wouldn't come – if I could have got his windpipe out, I would have twisted it around his neck. We tossed over on the ground. I managed to get his bayonet off his rifle and finished him off with that.'[164]

On the same day SEAC issued an optimistic communiqué, 'Our troops are attacking at all points on the Kohima front. They are making satisfactory progress.' It added that patrols in the Imphal–Ukhrul area were finding 'increased evidence of the enemy's heavy casualties'.

The last position to fall was the DC's bungalow. Lee-Grant tanks of A Squadron 149 Regiment Royal Armoured Corps reached the ridge line via a track that had been bulldozed by the Royal Engineers. On May 13 a tank commanded by Sergeant J. Waterhouse reached the much fought-over tennis court. He describes the fight in his after action report.

'We next went on to the edge of the court which overlooks the DC's bungalow, and gave it quite a pasting (the bungalow). After that everything in sight was well and truly plastered. The infantry again went in and took over without a casualty . . .

'The infantry officer estimated that we ourselves had knocked out possibly forty of the enemy. I am not prepared to say that this was the full figure, but when we went down afterwards at the invitation of the infantry CO to view the shambles, as he called it, well, he was just about right.

'Altogether, quite a useful shoot.'[165]

Kohima and the ridge line features were littered with parachutes and infested with rats and buzzing with flies, everywhere half-buried human remains were visible. Major General John Grover, commander of 2 Division, who had fought in World War I at Hill 60 in Ypres, said that Kohima reminded him of 'a dirty corner of the Somme, and was worse'.

Now Allied reinforcements were arriving in strength, 114 Bde had joined 33 Bde on May 12, and the Indian 7 Division (with 161 Bde) concentrated on capturing Naga Village from the north.

Around May 15 fresh troops from XXXIII Corps began to reinforce and relieve soldiers of 2 Division and 33 and 161 Indian Bdes. Yet when on May 16 these troops launched a renewed attack on Naga Village and Aradura Spur the Japanese hung on tenaciously.

The decisive factor that clinched victory at Kohima was the Japanese lack of supplies. Since the offensive started, they had had to make do with what they carried, meagre captured stocks and rice foraged from increasingly hostile local villages. One re-supply mission was mounted, using 17 captured Jeeps to carry supplies forward up the tracks from the Chindwin, but it only brought forward artillery and anti-tank ammunition.

By the middle of May, Sato's troops were starving. He considered that Mutaguchi was ignoring his situation since throughout April he had received several confusing and contradictory orders and Fifteenth Army HQ were failing to supply his division. Sato now began pulling back his surviving troops and the British pushed forward to capture Kohima Ridge.

In an unheard-of move Sato notified Fifteenth Army on May 25 that unless he was re-supplied within the week he would withdraw. To retreat without orders or permission from a superior was without precedent in the Japanese Army. Mutaguchi threatened him with court martial but Sato replied 'Do as you please. I will bring you down with me . . . The tactical ability of the 15th Army staff lies below that of cadets.'

Finally on May 31, his troops began abandoning Naga Village and other positions north of the road, in spite of orders from Mutaguchi to hang on for a further ten days.

When, without authority, Sato finally took the step of pulling back, his men were unrecognisable as soldiers, sick, staggering, half naked, they were eating grass and slugs. Withdrawal would quickly become collapse.

As the remainder of the division began a painful retreat to the south Miyazaki's detachment fought a rearguard action and demolished bridges and culverts on the Imphal road, but were eventually driven off it and forced to retreat eastwards. By now the whole division was starving since most of the limited supplies that had been shipped across the Chindwin had been eaten by other equally hungry Japanese units. Many of 31 Division were now too weak to travel any further and 'hospitals' were set up at Ukhrul. But they were hospitals for the dying without medicines, medical staff or food.

The Kohima garrison pushed south and brushing aside Miyazaki's detachment reached Milestone 103 by June 21 – and now only 8 miles separated them from the IV Corps perimeter. At about 10.30 hours on June 22 Lance Cpl Canning of 123 Bde Intelligence Section climbed a tree to examine the ground to the north of the IV Corps's most advanced outpost. He had not looked long when his binoculars picked up the distinctive outline of a troop of Lee-Grants moving southwards down the road from Kohima with infantry riding on them firing at several enemy groups.

It was A Squadron, 149 Regiment, 3 Carabiniers. The leading troops and Stuart tanks of British 2 Division, 7 Cavalry, which had already made contact with the 1/17 Dogras, soon met 3 Carabiniers, Indian 5 Infantry Division at Milestone 109, 30 miles south of Kohima.

The siege was over.

The British and Indian forces had lost around 4,000 men, dead, missing and wounded. The Japanese had lost more than 5,000 men in the Kohima area fighting.

After ignoring orders for several weeks, Sato was relieved of command of 31 Division early in July, when the entire Imphal offensive was called off. Sato was put on the transfer list with the comment that he was 'mentally disturbed under the stress of the acute war situation'.

Slim described Sato as the most unenterprising of his opponents. Japanese historians however blame Mutaguchi, for both the flaws of the U-GO plan and the hostility between himself and Sato that led the latter to concentrate on husbanding his division rather than pushing for the prize of Dimapur.

As the Japanese withdrawal began Shizuo Maruyama a war correspondent described the collapse of the 31 Division. 'We had no ammunition, no clothes, no food, no guns . . . the men were barefoot and ragged, and threw away everything except canes to help them walk. Their eyes blazed in their lean bodies . . . all they had to keep them going was grass and water . . . At Kohima we were starved and then crushed.'[166]

In conjunction with the battle of the Admin Box and the siege of Imphal, Kohima marked the turning point of the Burma Campaign. Mountbatten described Kohima as 'probably one of the greatest battles in history . . . in effect the Battle of Burma . . . naked unparalleled heroism . . . the British/Indian Thermopylae'.[167]

John Hudson who had survived Imphal, but contracted malaria and jaundice, was on a road convoy routed through Kohima soon after the fighting ended. His was not Mountbatten's Olympian rhetoric but a front-line soldier's view.

'We passed through sad Kohima next morning and looked around like tourists. The scarred hill station was grimly different from that sunny morning the year before when I had journeyed the other way: the tragic rows of little white crosses over the graves of soldiers, the shattered trees and ravaged tennis court which no Japanese soldiers had managed to cross. This was the scene of the battle that had released us from our siege; if they had not done it we could never have done it. Oh well! They'd done it, we'd done it and now it was ended and we were the lucky ones, alive to face another day. The monument at Kohima declares:

> When you go home tell them of us and say
> For your tomorrow we gave our today.'[168]

CHAPTER 10

THE ROAD TO MANDALAY
September 16, 1944 to January 27, 1945

'Thank God they have got a place whose name we can pronounce!'
Prime Minister Winston Churchill on the capture of Mandalay

By the end of July 1944 the battles for Imphal and Kohima were over. Exhausted and starving the Japanese 15 and 31 Divisions were struggling eastwards towards the Chindwin, while to the south 33 Division hung on in the Kabaw Valley and on the Tiddim Road hoping to delay the inevitable Fourteenth Army breakout.

However the tough division now seemed almost spent.

'We were unprepared for the state of our enemy,' writes John Hudson. 'They had seemed so strong up to the last days and now, to our astonishment, we were chasing a sick and dying army . . .

'Their assaults on our fortress and the preposterously long hook round to Kohima had been more than their supply lines and fortitude could stand. Facing them on the ground, we had seen only the ferocity of their aggression, but not the human price they were paying.'[169]

Lt General Iwaichi Fujiwara who served with the Fifteenth Army at Imphal as an intelligence staff officer experienced the retreat and recalled:

'Most officers and men were suffering from a vicious circle of malaria, amoebic dysentery, beriberi and skin diseases brought on by fatigue and malnutrition. Clothing and boots were torn and broken, almost all equipment was lost, and the soldiers looked like ghosts. Moreover the change from a long offensive and death-struggle to the path of retreat slackened the fighting-spirit and threw military discipline into such disorder that the commanders of some units had difficulty in controlling their men. Scattered along the route of the retreat were countless lifeless bodies of sick soldiers who had been sent back ahead of the fitter troops, and this created a scene like that of the Inferno.'[170]

John Hudson saw this for himself when soon after the advance his Sikh Sappers came upon a Japanese soldier too sick to move and barely alive.

'He lay there in the yellow mud, gaunt, almost naked, stinking, a week's stubble on his jowls and glared at us with eyes like glass alleys waiting for us to commit an atrocity on him. After respecting their awesome invincibility for so long, looking down at our prisoners with yellow diarrhoea trickling down their trembling shanks my hatred turned to compassion. Starvation, disease, rain, jungle and the "vaulting ambition which o'erleaps itself" had brought them to this.'[171]

On August 6 Slim ordered Stopford to pursue the Japanese on three routes along the Tiddim Road to Kalemyo; through the Kabaw Valley from Tamu to Kalemyo and along the track from Tamu to Sittang on the Chindwin.

Following Kohima and Imphal Mountbatten called a press conference with the title 'Seven Months' Battle'. It was a typical and impressive *tour de force* to thank and congratulate all those who had contributed to the victory and raised the profile of the Fourteenth Army, which almost took a perverse pleasure in its ironic nickname of 'The Forgotten Army'.

Men of the 11 East African Division commanded by Major-General C. C. Fowkes drove the Japanese back to Tamu. On the road they discovered wrecked vehicles with skeletal crews still seated in position where they had died of disease and been picked clean by white ants. 'When the Japanese 15th and 31st Divisions failed to capture Imphal,' writes Frank Owen, 'they had already written their own sentence of starvation on the road back.'[172]

On August 19 the last organised units of the Japanese Fifteenth Army staggered out of Burma.

On the Tiddim Road the 5 Indian Division under Major General Warren supported by C Squadron of the Carabiniers kept up the pressure on 33 Division. In its retreat the Japanese 14 Tank Regiment abandoned thirty tanks, some still 'manned' by corpses. Among the

Type 95s and Type 97s were a few Stuarts, probably the last of those captured from 7 Armoured Brigade during the withdrawal through Burma.

Though they abandoned or killed their wounded the 33 Division still contested the Tiddim Road. It seemed as if every bend or crater was mined, booby trapped or blocked and covered by mortar and machine guns. The monsoon rain added to delays, but the bulldozers of the engineers working with 5 Indian Division cleared land slips and filled in craters and in 40 miles built 40 bridges that ranged from simple timber structures to 150-foot girder bridges. The Sappers bridged the Beltang Lui River by moonlight and opened the road to Tiddim.

To reach Tiddim involved a climb up a track known as the 'Chocolate Staircase' after the muddy terraced lengths cut into the jungle mountainside. No step in the Chocolate Staircase was longer than 150 feet and the staircase climbed 2,000 feet in just 4 miles.

The town of Tiddim was captured by men of the Dogra Regiment and Punjabi soldiers supported by a tank of C Squadron 3 Carabiniers. The crew had ascended to 8,900 feet above sea level and set a new altitude record for armoured warfare. Supported by Hurricane ground attack aircraft it had emerged through the mist with headlights blazing to pulverise the Japanese bunkers. The mountaineering ability that Fourteenth Army tank crews had demonstrated was the result of hard training and practice and the courage to take tanks along crumbling mountain roads, where sometimes half a tank track would be hanging over the void.

On November 5, Fort White at the summit of the 9,000-foot Kennedy Peak, just south of Tiddim, was taken. The fighting saw mountain gunners winching artillery up the feature and an assault on bunker defences that was supported by four squadrons of Mitchell medium bombers and Hurricane fighters.

The Chindwin was crossed at three points on December 3, 19 Indian Division 'The Dagger Division' commanded by Major General 'Pete' Rees crossed at Sittang and 11 East African Division at Mawlaik. However it was the crossing at Kalewa by 20 Indian Division that was symbolic as well as tactically important. It was here that 1 Burma

165

Corps (Burcorps) had crossed on its grim withdrawal from Burma in 1942.

When tanks of 7 Light Cavalry reached the right bank on December 2 and entered Kalewa, they found it 'empty except for a moribund Jap found in a pagoda'. Lt Harpartap Singh gave a soldier of the Bombay Grenadiers the Union Flag flying from his tank and the flag that had been flown by 11 Division when it entered Addis Ababa in Ethiopia in 1941. The Grenadier climbed to the top of the tallest pagoda and secured the flag to the pinnacle.

'To the Japanese on the other bank,' writes Bryan Perrett, 'the gesture signalled the total failure of *U-Go*. They were exactly back where they had started, and they had sustained the worst defeat in Japanese history.'[173]

Remarkably some of the Stuart tanks, abandoned by 7 Armoured Brigade in 1942, were still in place on the left bank and REME technicians were able to cannibalise them for spares.

The British and Indians were now back in strength and backed with superb equipment. Three Field Companies, 67, 76 and 361 Bengal Sappers and Miners with 322 Field Park Company under command of Lt Colonel F. Seymour Williams constructed a Bailey Pontoon Bridge across the river. At 1,153 feet it was the largest floating bridge ever erected in World War II. All the stores and equipment for the bridge had been transported 310 miles overland from the railhead at Dimapur. Work began on December 6 and it was completed in four days. Japanese artillery fired blind into what their gunners assumed was the location of the bridge and air attacks were launched, but neither closed the flow of traffic.

In addition to the bridge, amphibious DUKW[174] vehicles operated on the river ferrying stores and men. The Chindwin would become one of the supply routes for two divisions and a tank brigade as the Fourteenth Army pushed eastwards. Again the sappers were in the fore constructing simple boats using local timber. Slim would say of these river craft, 'They were not graceful craft, but they floated and they carried ten tons apiece.' The most remarkable feat of boat building were two armed escorts that mounted 40mm Bofors and 20mm Oerlikon guns. Named after Mountbatten's daughters the *Pamela* and

Una were crewed by the Royal Navy and as Frank Owen comments this was 'probably the first time that the Army has constructed warships for the Royal Navy'.

Protecting the Inland Water Transport Service, better known as the Chindwin Navy, *Pamela* and *Una* patrolled the river. When they had their first contact with a Japanese patrol, attempting to disrupt the flow of supplies, Slim signalled to Vice Admiral Sir Arthur Power, 'Our Chindwin girls have at last reached glorious womanhood' and received the reply, 'Dear me, I had no idea our girls were so fast.'

Flying above the bridge site in an RAF Stinson L-5 Sentinel liaison aircraft Mountbatten described the operation as 'Regatta Day on the Chindwin'.

In September General Heitaro Kimura, who had been Head of Ordnance Administration HQ Tokyo, was posted from the relative comfort of the Imperial capital to Rangoon to command the Burma Area Army and replace Kawabe. He found he was commanding an exhausted army on the defensive – but one still determined to fight.

By mid 1944 when it had become clear that the war in Burma had swung in favour of the Allies, SEAC began to look at larger scale operations in the theatre and draft a series of plans.

One, initially code named Plan Z, and later Operation Dracula, was an airborne and amphibious assault on the port of Rangoon.

Plan Y, later Operation Capital, was a ground offensive into Central Burma by Fourteenth Army to a line Mandalay–Pakokku. If conditions were right Fourteenth Army would have the option to exploit south to Rangoon.

Finally Plan X was the recapture of northern Burma by the NCAC, the Chinese First and Sixth Armies and Force Y, with the limited objective of clearing the Ledo Road and so freeing the overland link to China.

This plan had been put forward by Stilwell and though he would be recalled to Washington on October 19, 1944, under the new commander of NCAC General Daniel Sultan the attacks would begin on November 1.

To SEAC staff Dracula seemed the most attractive option. If Rangoon was captured it would deny the Japanese their main supply port. When it had fallen in 1942 seaborne reinforcements had greatly facilitated the Japanese invasion of Burma. If it was under British control the tenuous Japanese lines of communication through Thailand could easily be severed. From Rangoon it would be easy to launch air and ground attacks against the railway at Pegu or the bridge at Sittang and so sever the Burma Railway linking with their forces in northern Burma and western Thailand. The Japanese would then be forced to withdraw from almost all of Burma and the British would be well placed to liberate Malaya and Singapore.

On September 16, the Combined Chiefs of Staff (CCS) issued the directive to Mountbatten for the clearance of the Japanese from Burma. The CCS gave approval for Capital because it would secure air and land links with China and Dracula if it could be launched before the onset of the monsoon. In the event of the monsoon Dracula would have to be delayed until November 1945. The crossing of the Chindwin in December 1944 marked the first moves in the implementation of Capital.

However, as with the plans for earlier smaller scale amphibious operations in Burma the demands of the war in Europe and notably D-Day, took precedence in the demand for specialist craft. Landing craft were needed to support operations in Europe and after the failure of Operation Market Garden, the airborne hook around the Rhine in September 1944, they were still needed. So on October 2, Churchill agreed that Dracula could not be launched before the monsoon. This appeared to be a wise decision when the Germans launched the surprise Ardennes Offensive at the end of the year.

There were significant changes in the US command structure in Burma. In October Roosevelt had recalled Stilwell and the tough, but difficult commander relinquished his 'three hat' command. Now General Albert Wedermeyer became Chiang's adviser and General Sultan took command of the NCAC. General Raymond Wheeler became Deputy Supreme Allied Commander.

On November 12 General Sir Oliver Leese, who had arrived from commanding the British Eighth Army in Italy, took on a new post commanding Allied Land Forces South East Asia (ALFSEA).

Leese came with excellent credentials from North Africa and the

Mediterranean. He had commanded XXX Corps during the Second Battle of Alamein, the invasions of Sicily and Italy and subsequently commanded the Eighth Army in Italy in January 1944 after Montgomery departed for D-Day planning in the UK. A genial Guardsman Leese was well liked in these appointments but when he brought his former Eighth Army Staff with him Slim noted they 'had a good deal of desert sand in its shoes and was rather inclined to push Eighth Army down our throats'. Leese in turn thought Slim was 'slightly defensive about the Indian Army, the difficulties of Burma and the need to understand how to fight the Japs'.

Leese met Slim and Christison, whose XV Corps had been detached from its parent body, and though relations appeared cordial there were tensions from the outset.

Operations continued with the advance from the Chindwin on four axes. One in the north, two in the centre and a third in great secrecy in the south.

In the north 19 Division from IV Corps having established a bridgehead on December 4 drove almost due east across the Zibyu Taungdan Range through Pinlebu to the railway town on Indaw which they reached on December 16. Here they linked up with the British 36 Division and swung south along the right bank of the Irrawaddy to Shwebo.

Slim was delighted with the drive and enthusiasm of the 5-foot-tall commander of 19 Division, Major General T. W. 'Pete' Rees. 'What he lacked in inches,' Slim remarked, 'he made up in the miles he advanced and the only criticism I made to him was to point out that the best huntsman did not invariably ride ahead of the hounds!'[175] Rees, distinctive in his neatly blocked bush hat and red cravat, had served in Burma as a young officer between the wars and now despite his more elevated rank was still prepared to lead from the front – down to section level. It was inevitable that this charismatic commander would earn the nickname of the 'Pocket Napoleon'.

On December 31, 2 Division spearheading XXXIII Corps reached Kabo Weir an important source of irrigation for the rice paddies of half a million Burmese farmers. The garrison was caught off guard but reacted quickly fighting fiercely using flame-throwers, weapons not previously encountered in Burma.[176]

For Corporal Arthur Freer of B Squadron 3 Carabiniers the dash for Shwebo meant a brush with death when a sniper's bullet glanced off the turret and concussed him. Unhurt but with a bruise the 'size of an egg' he recalled how 'The next day we burst through a Jap cookhouse, smashing a huge pot of boiling rice which burst all over the tank. We were hungry and the rice smelt delicious, but we couldn't stop. By now we were out of the jungle and smashing through the Jap roadblocks.'[177]

The second axis in the centre 2 and 20 Division from XXXIII Corps under Stopford crossed the Chindwin at Kalewa, and 2 Division drove for the airfield and town of Yeu that they captured on January 3. Two days later they linked up with 19 Division and captured the key rail city of Shwebo and its airfield.

The Irrawaddy is a formidable natural obstacle and even more so when it is covered by fire. The river varies from 500 yards wide in the north where it flows through gorges to 4,000 yards where it is joined by the Chindwin. There are steep banks in the narrower stretches, while downstream the banks are lower but the river is intersected by shifting sandbanks and small islands that disappear during the monsoon months. The river normally flows at 2 miles an hour, but when swollen with monsoon rains this goes up to 6 and the river rises as much as 30 feet.

If these were not problems enough the Fourteenth Army sappers who would crew the assault boats and rafts that would ferry the troops and vehicles across the river would have to improvise from local craft and manage with a meagre supply of specialist equipment.

'Much use was made of local craft, home made rafts and flotation devices, and salvaged Japanese barges. Without proper diving equipment to raise sunken barges, the engineers improvised breathing sets from gas masks connected to a workshop air compressor by a piece of hose.' 'The lash up,' writes Graham Dunlop in *Mars & Clio*, 'was so successful that instructions for it are to be found in a subsequent Royal Engineers Training Memorandum.'[178]

An indication of the superb triumph of improvisation achieved by this crossing can be judged when it is compared with Operation Plunder, Field Marshal Montgomery's set piece crossing of the Rhine on March 23–24, 1945. To support this river crossing Landing Craft Infantry (LCI) had been brought up by road, Landing Vehicles Tracked (LVT) armoured amphibious vehicles were in position as well as DUKWs. Behind them was a full bridging train. A huge artillery and aerial bombardment preceded a night crossing by the 3 Canadian Division, 51 Highland Division and 9 US Division and at dawn landings were made by the British 6 and US 17 Airborne Divisions.

In Burma where war was still being waged on a tight budget it was 19 Division that gained the first bridgeheads across the Irrawaddy at Thabeikkyin on January 9 and with 62 Bde following on January 11 at Kyaukmyaung. From the middle of January to the end of the month the Japanese Fifteenth Army launched fanatical attacks against these bridgeheads. They threw in the 15 and 53 Divisions with artillery and even armour, taking men and equipment from the formations that had been covering the Irrawaddy bend downstream. However by early February Rees was confident that he could break out from the bridge-head and drive for Mandalay.

Meanwhile 20 Division, which had followed the north bank of the Chindwin, captured Monywa on January 14 and then drove for Myinmu on the north bank of the Irrawaddy linking up with elements of 2 Division on January 23.

To the Japanese this concentration of forces pointed only to one objective, the city of Mandalay. Mandalay was a symbolic prestige objective as the second city of Burma, but it was also the junction of rail links to Lashio and Yunnan to the east and Rangoon to the south. There were also good road links.

What Katamura did not realise was that by December 18, when the Japanese failed to hold the Chindwin and indeed began to pull back, Slim had out-thought them and changed his plans. In Operation Capital he had hoped to fight and win a decisive battle in the area between the Chindwin and Irrawaddy. Here the larger Japanese forces would be defeated by the weight of armour, artillery and crucially air power. Now he modified his plans as Extended Capital. He planned to make the Japanese believe that Mandalay was the objective so that they would concentrate their forces in its defence. They would then be outflanked and defeated which would allow Fourteenth Army mechanised forces to make the dash south to Rangoon before the onset of the monsoon.

It was Slim's plan, which he explained to Messervy and Stopford his experienced Corps commanders on December 18. They received their formal orders a day later. Slim had sent a summary of his intentions to Leese, commander ALFSEA, on December 17 and a full set arrived at his HQ three days later.

As historian Robert Lyman explains, 'Slim's decision not to involve him in the process of decision making at this most crucial of operations undoubtedly irritated Leese and did nothing to improve the already fragile relationship between the two men . . . Perhaps Slim believed that bringing Leese into the planning for Operation Extended Capital might actually jeopardise his grand design, because Leese might have wanted to cancel, change or veto any element not to his liking. It seems likely that Leese would have wanted in some way to stamp his authority on the plan, and it may have been this that Slim was keen to avoid.'[179]

Crucial to Extended Capital was the last southern axis of advance by IV Corps under the energetic Frank Messervy, who had taken command of the corps on December 8. He would make the outflanking manoeuvre to the south. In great secrecy the corps advanced almost due south along the Manipur River from Kalemyo.

The men moved at night and Lt Michael Marshall with 4/5 Royal Gurkha Rifles remembered the Gangaw Valley as hot, dry and dusty even at night.

'It was tiring for the British officers because Gurkhas have short legs and march at between two and three miles an hour, whereas the British Army marches at between three and four miles an hour. So it takes longer. By the time we had finished this march one could say that everyone was fit.'[180]

The route was so bad that tanks were sometimes unloaded to pull out their own transporters. However IV Corps emerged onto the river plain of the Irrawaddy at Tilin on January 22 and captured Pauk four days later – four days ahead of the date set in the plans. From the high ground to east of Pauk officers trained their binoculars on a silver ribbon on the horizon – the Irrawaddy. With poor roads behind them IV Corps was very dependent on aerial re-supply, with improvised airstrips and drop zones marking their route.

In London General Alanbrooke the CIGS observed presciently in his diary on January 17: 'There is no doubt that the operations there have taken quite a different turn, and there is now just a possibility of actually taking Rangoon from the north! This is due to the Japanese forces beginning to crumple up and to be demoralised. One of our difficulties arises through the fact that the transport aircraft belong to the Americans, and that the reconquest of lower Burma does not interest them at all. All they want is north Burma and the air route and pipe line and Ledo road into China. They have practically got all of these, and the rest of Burma is of small interest to them.'

Meanwhile on January 20 fighting to clear the strategic Ledo Road, the Chinese forces had only a few more miles to go. Their advance from Yunnan had reached Wanting on the border. Reopening the Burma Road was one of the objectives of Capital and a week later it was achieved as the Chinese First Army linked up with their comrades in Force Y.

General Sulton commanding NCAC had in fact pre-empted the link-up and announced that the road had been opened since January 22. His forces now began moving south towards Mandalay and Lashio by several routes.

With his usual flare for publicity Mountbatten telegraphed the British Prime Minister and the President of the United States:

'The first part of the orders I received at Quebec has been carried out. The land route to China is open.'[181]

At IV Corps HQ, Messervy's staff had examined suitable crossing points over the Irrawaddy and though Pakokku looked the best with better road links, it was also the most obvious. They selected Nyaungu 20 miles to the south. The river was only half a mile wide and unknown to the planners the town fortuitously marked the boundary between the Japanese Fifteenth and Twenty-seventh Armies. Since neither had taken measures to defend the area, it was held by units of the INA.

However before the assault river crossing the Japanese were reinforced in their belief that Mandalay was the main objective of the Irrawaddy crossings. A dummy IV Corps HQ had been established in the north through which all signal traffic to 19 Division was routed. The radio traffic included indiscreet signals, all of which were intended to give the impression that IV Corps was out on the left flank of the Fourteenth Army.

However at the end of January Japanese reconnaissance aircraft had spotted IV Corps vehicles on the road from Tilin to Pauk but as General Noburo Tanaka commanding 33 Division commented, '. . . these were not considered as part of a powerful mechanised force nor was it regarded as important by Army HQ. If the information had been repeatedly reported by our aircraft it would have received more attention, but they only reported it once and consequently it did not attract special attention.'[182]

On the assumption that the Japanese Fifteenth Army would be aware that a crossing would be attempted south of the confluence of the Chindwin and Irrawaddy, IV Corps attempted to give the idea that only a small force the 28 East African Bde was in the area. The African troops led the advance and then at Pauk on January 26 hooked south and east to the bank of the Irrawaddy at Seikpyu almost 30 miles south of the planned crossing point. This was opposite the oilfields that had been demolished in the withdrawal in 1942, it was therefore an obvious objective. Vehicles towing brushwood raised clouds of dust to simulate large numbers of vehicles and even dummy parachute drops were made east of the river. The East Africans had two tough fights with troops still on the right bank at a feature named the Springs, which added to the impression that a crossing was planned in this location. Even after bridgeheads had been formed on the east bank of the Irrawaddy the Japanese who were now effectively trapped and doomed continued to attack the Fourteenth Army.

To the north Ken Cooper with 20 Division was ordered to take a reconnaissance patrol across the Irrawaddy. As he explained to the tired soldiers in his platoon, 'When it gets dark, a couple of Navy frogmen[183] are going to swim across the Irrawaddy and place markers out for us on the far bank. The markers will be set up about two miles down-stream on the far shore to allow for the current carrying us. It means paddling like hell if we are to get anywhere near them. The idea is to test the speed of the current and get timings to assist the staff in making their plans for the big crossing.'[184]

It would be a tough, frightening patrol, but like so many of its kind brought back the fragments of intelligence that were being built up into a bigger plan.

On the night of February 12 their part in the plan came to fruition at Myinmu west of Mandalay, as 20 Division began to make second assault crossings over the Irrawaddy. By February 13, it had established a solid bridgehead despite fierce Japanese counter-attacks.

Despite the fact that the RAF and USAAF by now had air superiority the Japanese counter-attacks even included air strikes. Ken Cooper describes hearing the curious engine note of the approaching fighter bombers, 'as they came nearer, the high-powered roar sounded strangely alien yet tinny, like accelerating motorcycle engines; then we spotted the blood-red circle on the wings and fuselage . . . The sound of their rattle-trap motors clattering in a sort of mechanical rage seemed to symbolise the enemy's frustration. Here we were firmly ensconced on the southern shore of the Irrawaddy which they had sworn to defend.'[185]

Prior to the crossing Slim had visited the Border Regiment and among its ranks Lance Corporal George MacDonald Fraser heard him speak. 'Slim emerged from under the trees by the lake shore, there was no nonsense of "gather round" or jumping on boxes; he just stood with his thumb hooked in his carbine sling and talked about how we had caught the Jap off-balance and were going to annihilate him in the open; there was no exhortation or ringing clichés, no jokes or self-conscious use of barrack-room slang – when he called the Japs "bastards" it was casual and without heat. He was telling us informally what would be, in the reflective way of intimate conversation. And we believed every word – and it all came true . . .

'You knew, when he talked of smashing the Jap, that to him it meant not only arrows on a map but clearing bunkers and going in under shell-fire; that he had the head of a general with the heart of a private soldier.'[186]

The combined bridgeheads across the Irrawaddy produced what would be the widest assault river crossing of history, strung out as it was along 200 miles of the river.

For three weeks until March 5 the second bridgehead would be the scene of desperate fighting. Prisoners were very rarely taken, but from captured documents 20 Division intelligence staff identified that 13 battalions from four different divisions had been committed to destroying the bridgehead. However the division was intent on securing their hold and widening the bridgehead.

In one such small-scale operation there was a moment when Ken Cooper's platoon fighting through the burning village of Sindat 'seemed suddenly consumed with a vast black savagery. We got up whooping triumphantly, and charged through a narrow gap in the wall of flame . . . We rushed on them without pause, drunk with the intoxication of killing and destroying, our minds focused only on getting forward. When the blood lust faded seconds later there were Japanese lying all ways, some in shell craters their legs sticking out, others huddled against trees, most of them still, but a few jerking in horrible spasms, trying to get up, or turn over, or drag themselves on their hands.'[187]

Finally, with shipping now redeployed from other bridgeheads, at Ngazun a few miles west of Sagaing men of 2 Division began to make the crossing over the Irrawaddy on February 21. The Japanese resisted this landing with ferocious tenacity but by March 2 the division was over the river and ready to drive east towards Mandalay and cut it off from the south.

Just as back in 1942 Yamashita and the Twenty-fifth Army had got inside the British decision cycle, so now three years later Slim and the Fourteenth Army were out-thinking and beating the Japanese in the same way.

At 04.00 hours on Valentine's Day, 1945, the lead brigade from 7 Division commanded by Major General G. C. Evans began to push their assault boats down the muddy banks of the Irrawaddy and outboard motors roared into life. Some outboard motors broke down

– damaged by the long overland journey and the boats were carried by a swift current past Japanese machine-gun positions. These determined infantry would make the crossing confident that they had massive firepower on call. The sound of the assault boat outboard motors had been drowned out by low-flying aircraft. The boats made it to the shore and the infantry scrambled up the cliffs. A regiment of tanks lined the home bank, artillery of all calibres had registered targets and six RAF and USAAF squadrons of bombers and fighters were ready to add their considerable weight to the attack. When it was requested this fire support was awesome.

This was what the German blitzkrieg theorists called the *schwerpunkt* and in modern military terminology is the Main Effort.

What made it more effective was that Katamura and the Japanese Fifteenth Army did not realise that the whole Burma Area Army had been struck a mortal blow.

CHAPTER 11

ARAKAN – THE FINAL OFFENSIVE
September 12, 1944 to April 16, 1945

'They had to be very thoroughly slain'
Lt Colonel Peter Young, 3 Commando Brigade

'Arakan,' writes Frank Owen, 'is a corridor that leads nowhere.'[188] However this coastal area with its islands and small ports also had the airfields developed by the British before the war and now used by the IJAAF. Japanese bombers based in the Arakan had launched two air raids against Calcutta and flew missions out over the Bay of Bengal. By 1944 the IJAAF air strength had been greatly reduced, but the airfields were essential if the RAF and USAAF were to continue supplying the Fourteenth Army since the aircraft flying supplies from Imphal were now operating at their limit. Moreover possession of the Arakan airfields would allow RAF and USAAF bombers to hit Japanese supply lines from Rangoon.

Now in this final Arakan offensive the resources available to Lt General Christison's XV Corps would be a balanced tri-service force. On land he had two Indian and a West African Divisions, two brigades of a West African Division and 3 Commando Bde and 50 Indian Tank Bde.

The Commando Brigade under Brigadier Campbell Hardy was made up of two Army and two Royal Marine Commandos. While the Army Commandos had seen active service before their deployment to Burma the two Royal Marine Commandos had not.

Colonel Peter Young who was second in command, and a veteran of serious fighting in Europe as a Commando, said of Hardy,

'The greatest gift a commander can have is the gift of making his men feel that if *he* takes them to a battle they can't possibly be beaten . . . Campbell Hardy soon had the 3 Commando Brigade thinking the same way.'[189]

The 50 Indian Tank Bde commanded by Brigadier G. H. N. Todd was a balanced force of M3 Lee-Grants, Stuarts and M4 Shermans. The Shermans were crewed by the 19th (King George Vth's Own) Lancers a regiment that prided itself on its gunnery and radio communications.

In the air 224 RAF Group commanded by Air Vice-Marshal the Earl of Bandon was on call to provide close air support, while crucially Christison had the naval resources that had been missing in earlier operations. Force W commanded by Rear Admiral B. C. S. Martin had the landing craft and warships to put troops ashore and support them.

In addition to these troops Christison had the invaluable assistance of the Small Operations Group or SOG. SOG was made up of the Combined Operations Pilotage Parties (COPP) a joint Royal Navy and Army reconnaissance force that had played a key part in the beach reconnaissance at D-Day in Normandy. The COPP teams checked the high and low water depth of the *chaungs* and the viability of beaches for landing craft operations.

SOG also worked in other areas of Burma with D-Force a group of specialists in deception who, with pyrotechnics and other devices, could simulate gunfire from a major formation. Force 136, part of the Special Operations Executive (SOE) reported directly to their own SOE HQ in Delhi.

The American OSS who were not part of SOG had a 40-strong force in the country – though some cynics maintained they were actually more interested in evaluating Burma's oil resources with a view to their post-war development.

As well as these units that had come from Europe there was a long established V-Force with operatives who spoke local dialects, knew the country and had been in place since 1942. They liaised with friendly tribesmen among the Chins, Kachins, Arakanese, Lushais and particularly the Nagas who had been a completely reliable source of intelligence during the fighting at Kohima and Imphal.

On December 10 XV Corps began its offensive from the secure

base of the Maungdaw–Buthidaung Tunnels area and the Kaladan Valley. The 25 Indian Division commanded by Major General G. N. Wood had the Mayu Range as its axis, 82 West African Division commanded by Major General H. C. Stockwell reoccupied Buthidaung and advanced down the east bank of the Mayu River.

When Stockwell took command of 82 West African Division he found in his words that it was 'a rather luxury organisation'. So he said 'I picked out an RSM from the 3rd Nigeria Regiment, who had been awarded the Iron Cross fighting for the Germans in West Africa in the First World War. He stayed with me as a personal RSM for a year and a half. He advised me on the Africans and through him I could find out what they thought of their British officers. He was tremendous, I got him a DCM, and he must be about the only soldier to wear an Iron Cross and a DCM.'[190]

On the flank in the Kaladan Valley 81 West African Division under Major General Loftus-Tottenham covered the ground they had fought over before, building seven jungle airstrips for Dakotas and twelve for fighter squadrons as they advanced through the jungle.

It was on Christmas Day that 25 Division reached Foul Point on the extremity of the Mayu Peninsula and looked across to the objective of Akyab Island. Plans captured on the body of a Japanese officer indicated that the island was only lightly held.

On the basis of this intelligence the timetable was brought forward and a mixed force of Commandos and armour was tasked with the capture of the island.

However the day before the landing on January 2 an artillery observation officer flying over the island to plot targets saw no sign of the Japanese. Taking a gamble he put his light aircraft down in a paddy field and learned from the local inhabitants that the Japanese had evacuated the island.

So on January 3, 1945 when the 25 Division assault force arrived offshore they saw no naval gunfire or strikes by fighter ground attack aircraft. To Peter Young who had witnessed landings in Europe including D-Day the amphibious force was a 'strange flotilla' ranging from cruisers, destroyers, sloops and Landing Craft Infantry (LCI) to old river boats, rice barges and sampans.

The surprise of the assault force was complete when, on landing, they were greeted by General Christison. 'It was not an absolutely dry landing,' recalled Peter Young, 'but I was able to sit down on the beach, take off my boots and socks and dry my feet in peace. A gentlemanly operation.'[191]

With the capture of Akyab the first airfield had been secured.

The next objective was the Myebon Peninsula in the Arakan. The peninsula had been identified as a staging area for reinforcements, casualties and stores. It had to be neutralised before the port of Kangaw could be attacked.

The landings took place at 08.30 hours on January 12. They were preceded by a bombardment by a cruiser, eight smaller warships and a massive raid by the RAF that began at 07.45 hours. The aircraft mixed napalm with HE and then specially equipped aircraft flew low along the beachhead laying a smoke to screen the approaching landing craft.

Napalm had been recently developed in the United States and though it could be used against vehicles and combustible structures it was brutally effective against troops either in the open or dug in. When the bomb landed sticky gobs of burning napalm splashed in all directions. Even armoured vehicles were vulnerable, a hit within fifty feet of a tank would either incinerate the crews or like the inmates of a bunker starve them of oxygen.

Napalm is an incendiary mixture of 21 per cent benzene, 33 per cent standard leaded vehicle petrol and 46 per cent polystyrene. With a capacity for about 75 gallons aluminium napalm tanks were very light and since they lacked stabilising fins when they were released acquired a tumbling motion that scattered the flaming sticky fuel over a wide area.

Complete surprise was achieved at Myebon, a quantity of food, clothing and blankets captured but the receding tide created problems when a vast area of mud was exposed. However the Japanese did not put in a counter-attack and on January 13 three M4 Shermans of the 19 Lancers were landed and the tanks fought their way up the peninsula. The Commando brigade handed over to No 74 Bde having won its first battle for the loss of four killed and 38 wounded and

181

inflicted 150 casualties on the enemy – however the brigade would have harder fighting to come at Kangaw.

Fighting continued on Myebon with an attack on January 16 on two features Hill 262 and Pagoda Hill. At 11.30 hours strikes by Thunderbolts hit the hills and then men of 3/2 Gurkhas, with tanks of 19 Lancers giving fire support, assaulted the position. When the shooting, grenading and chopping were over there were 81 Japanese bodies in the positions and the Myebon Peninsula had been secured.

On New Year's Day, 3 Commando Bde was back in action now with the difficult task of capturing the inland port of Kangaw.

Peter Young writes: 'The place was a junction on the Japanese lines of communications at the point where the motorable track from Myohaung turned from the plain into the hills to follow the Kangaw Chaung and then went south to Dalet. It was a minor naval base and supply point. The 54th Japanese Division opposing the West Africans was falling back along the road through Kangaw, and the aim of the operation was to cut off and exterminate as many Japs as possible before they could reach the An Pass.'[192]

To attack Kangaw the amphibious forces would need to sail five miles along the 10-yard-wide Daingbon Chaung. It was a risk that XV Corps and the Commandos were prepared to take and it paid off.

On January 2 the operation began and bar some light small arms fire and shelling the run in went according to plan. Landings were made and by nightfall No 1 Commando had seized the tactically vital ground of Hill 170 and dug in.

That night the Japanese launched a counter-attack that was driven off and the following day men of the Hyderabad Battalion were landed.

The Commandos and Indian troops came under fire from 75mm guns that at times was very heavy as Peter Young recalled.

'One day, sitting on Hill 170, we were watching a line of Indian soldiers bringing up supplies; when some shells came down a man was hit and the rest scattered at top speed – all save one gallant soul, who knelt down beside the wounded man and amidst the shells patched up his wounds. It was done in a cool and matter-of-fact way, but in that flat exposed paddy-field it called for an iron nerve to behave as he did.

The Brigadier sent a messenger to discover his name and he was decorated for his bravery.'

At 05.45 hours on February 1 the Japanese put down a very heavy barrage and an attack went in against 4 Troop of No 1 Commando. The Japanese managed to knock out one of three M4 Shermans that had been landed and damaged another.

The dawn broke and the fighting continued all day. Lt George Knowland commanding the 24 men of 4 Troop beat off every attack while the ammunition lasted. Firing a Bren, hurling grenades he was last seen alive firing a 2-inch Mortar with the base plate braced against a tree into a mass of Japanese infantry. The first bomb killed six of the enemy.

The Commandos counter-attacked and when the fighting was over Peter Young noted that the firing had been so intense that visibility had improved as the vegetation was stripped away.

By 17.00 hours the attacks were beginning to slacken and by dawn the following day the Japanese had gone.

Young went forward and like many British soldiers was awed by the courage and determination of the adversary. Though they had attacked 'with a fanatical, brutish courage which lacked subtlety and made little use of manoeuvre . . . The determination of the Japanese could be seen from the fact that most of them had two or three wounds, any one of them fatal. They had to be very thoroughly slain . . . Their dwarf-like figures under their medieval helmets, their mongol faces, many with glasses and gold teeth, made them look like creatures from another world.'[193]

Then Young saw the Commando dead and amongst them George Knowland.

'He lay on his back, one knee slightly raised, with a peaceful smiling look on his face, his head uncovered.' Lt George Arthur Knowland, Royal Norfolk Regiment attached 1 Commando would be awarded the Victoria Cross. Out of the 24 men in his troop, 14 were casualties and six of his positions had been overrun. But 4 Troop had held on and so not only saved the Hill 170, but also the beachhead it dominated. The Commando had suffered a total of 135 killed and wounded and the Japanese about 450.

Other operations were ongoing in the Arakan.

On January 21 under supporting fire from the eight 15-inch guns of the battleship HMS *Queen Elizabeth*[194] as well as those of the cruiser HMS *Phoebe* and destroyers *Norman, Pathfinder, Raider, Rapid* and *Napier* men of the 4 and 71 Indian Infantry Brigades, 21 Indian Division landed at Kyaukpyu, on the northern tip of Ramree Island. The infantry were supported by Lee-Grants of A Squadron 146 Regiment RAC. The garrison had pulled back, blowing bridges and mining roads. The Japanese made a determined stand at the wide Yenbauk Chaung and could not be dislodged despite naval gunfire and air strikes from the 24 Grumman Hellcats operating from the Ruler Class escort carrier HMS *Ameer*.

Copying Japanese tactics Brigadier Cottrell-Hill decided on a wide outflanking movement. The tanks and infantry were finally in position after a gruelling approach march and this prised the enemy from the Yenbauk Chaung line. However they still occupied several strong points nicknamed 'Bean', 'Banana' and Point 233 south of the village of Yebadin. The fighting for these positions was hard and it was not until February 9 that the island was finally secured.

Of the 1,000 Japanese soldiers who had defended Ramree only 20 surrendered. Survivors attempting to make it to the mainland through the waterways of the mangrove swamp found their way blocked by the Royal Navy. While some Japanese were shot and killed, others drowned or in the stink of the insect-infested swamps were eaten by crocodiles. Even as this mopping up was under way, the captured airstrips were being upgraded by engineers to all-weather airfields. They would soon be ready to take the transport aircraft and fighters and bombers.

Meanwhile on January 26 Royal Marine Commandos landed on Cheduba Island, south of Ramree to find that it had been deserted. They were later reinforced by troops from 36 Indian Bde.

The fighting had bought General Sakurai and the Japanese Twenty-eighth Army time – time to construct a loop road that would allow troops to withdraw south to the town and district of An. Here they could make a stand or withdraw east from the coast through the An Pass.

If a landing was made at the port of Ruywa, Christison reckoned he could block the escape route. On February 17 an unopposed landing at Ruywa caught the Japanese by surprise – so much so that a truckload of enemy soldiers drove into Ruywa and 4,000 British soldiers. It then became a hard-fought fight for the beachhead with men and stores being safely delivered only after dark, but despite this the Royal Navy landed 18,000 troops, 14,500 tons of stores, 523 mules and 415 vehicles. The operation did not block the Japanese withdrawal, but it added to the pressure on their already depleted and harassed forces.

One of the last operations in the Arakan was the assault landing at Letpan to threaten the town of Taungup and the Taungup Pass through the mountains. The landing on April 16 by 4 Indian Brigade commanded by Brigadier J. F. R. Forman comprised 2 Green Howards, 2/7 Rajputs and 2/13 Frontier Force Rifles supported by A Squadron 146 Regiment RAC.

In the fighting for Taungup the tanks provided the infantry with invaluable support, at one stage taking on a 75mm gun that had been dug into a tunnel on a feature covering the road to the town. A duel ensued between tanks and the gun that was quickly knocked out. Major Bucknall commanding A Sqaudron commented that 'This was real pin point shooting, as the high explosive shells with delayed fuses entered and burst inside the tunnel'.

The ultimate compliment came from an infantryman, Brigadier Forman, who said that if this had been a rifle range the tank crews' shooting would have represented a 2-inch group at 100 yards.

With the airfields secured at Akyab the RAF and USAAF had been able to support ground operations from Shwebo in the north through an arc that included Mandalay and Toungoo on the Sittang. Now with the airfields at Ramree Island in Allied hands the arc increased to include Rangoon and the whole of southern Burma.

The Arakan was no longer a corridor that led nowhere – it had become the aerial highway to the liberation of Burma.

CHAPTER 12

AIR POWER

'Strike! Support! Supply! Strangle!'
Major General G. E. Stralemeyer USAAF

The Arakan was the location for the first ground attack operations of significance in Burma when on November 27, 1942 No 45 Squadron RAF equipped with Vultee Vengeance dive bombers went into action against Japanese bunkers. Their bomb load of 1,000 pounds was made up of either two 500-pound or four 250-pound bombs.

Early in 1943 it was joined by No 82 and 110 and No 8 Indian Air Force Squadrons, the dive bombers always operated with a fighter escort.

They were reinforced by No 607 and 615 Squadron with Hurricanes and it was 615 that deployed the cannon armed Mark IIC.

Pilot Officer Roger Cobley with 20 Squadron flew this mark in the Arakan in 1943. He explained that the heavily armed aircraft were 'a bit unwieldy. You couldn't do aerobatics safely. We carried high explosive or armour-piercing shells. Each gun was loaded with only 16 rounds, which you had to fire singly, not in bursts like 20mm cannons or machine guns. You had to line up very accurately on the target, and attack one at a time. We were supposed to have Spitfires as top cover, but we didn't get it to start with. But operating very low as we did, with jungle trees below, it was very difficult for Jap aircraft to see us, and in any case there weren't many about.'[195]

There might be a minimal air threat, but ground fire remained a constant danger to low-flying aircraft.

Squadron Leader George Butler of 11 Squadron RAF flying Hawker Hurricane II fighters recalled close support operations with a newly developed weapon.

186

'We carried napalm in the Hurricane's long-range tanks instead of fuel. It was very effective against the Japs, especially close to our own troops. Napalm strikes were controlled by our own troops, firing coloured smoke on to the enemy position.'[196]

By early 1943 powerful twin-enginned Bristol Beaufighters were in theatre.

Pilot Officer Harry Morrell of 211 Squadron flying Beaufighters described how the numerous pagodas, a distinctive feature of Burma, were an excellent navigation reference point for pilots.

'. . . you could see the Shwe Dagon's gold dome 40 miles off in daytime. We were highwaymen and we hit anything that moved. The big prize was a train. If there were no trains about, we attacked the stations, or the engine sheds. The Beaufighter was a formidable air-craft and had four 20mm cannon, six machine guns, eight 60-pounder high-explosive rockets or eight 25-pounder PA bombs. We always used HE on river craft.'[197]

It was 211 Squadron that introduced the powerful ground attack weapon the 25-pound and 60-pound rocket projectiles into the theatre. Mounted in two banks of rails with a total of eight rockets the 25-pound had a solid shot armour warhead while the 60-pound was HE. After 1943 the 60-pound became the standard warhead for operations in Burma.

However air combat was not entirely one-sided. Master Sergeant Satoshi Anabuki who would be the IJAAF top scoring fighter pilot with 51 victories scored 35 of these over Burma in the first five months of 1943. On October 8, 1943 he destroyed five aircraft, shooting down two Lockheed P-38s and two Consolidated B-24s and destroying a third B-24 by ramming, an action which he survived.

By December 1943 with SEAC established, at Mountbatten's request, a new command was set up by the Allied Air Forces in South East Asia; it was to be a joint RAF and USAAF command.

As Air Commander South East Asia, Air Chief Marshal Sir Richard Peirse was in command. His subordinate commanding Eastern Air Command was Major General G. E. Stratemeyer USAAF.

It was Stratemeyer who set the style for air operations in Burma with the slogan 'Strike! Support! Supply! Strangle!'

In 1944 fighters and bombers developed for combat in Europe and against superior German designs were coming into theatre. The RAF and USAAF were not only receiving modern aircraft, but with quality came quantity.

In 1944 the Vengeance dive bomber which had given sterling service was withdrawn after 18 months of almost continuous action. Despite the fact that in this period the IJAAF was still an effective force no Vengeance had been lost to air action and only a small number to ground fire.

The fall of Malaya and Burma had left the RAF and later the USAAF with few airfields within an effective range of the front-line. Phenomenal efforts by sappers and locally employed labourers were required to build airstrips and often when these were close to completion heavy rain would set the work back for weeks. However using a variety of innovative construction techniques strips were constructed and with good drainage kept operating in the monsoon. Oil was used to stabilise soil, while brick, concrete and pierced steel planking (PSP) was put down on compacted soil.

Significantly the aircraft that were arriving in theatre were modern types like the USAAF Liberator and Mitchell bombers while the RAF were taking to the air with Hurricanes, Wellingtons, and Blenheims. The arrival of the Spitfires would coincide with the virtual end of Japanese air operations – however the IJAAF could still pull surprises.

A clear Allied air strategy was developing with four main tasks that had been encapsulated in Stratemeyer's slogan.

Strike was close support against forward enemy positions and the immediate rear to prevent the movement of stores and reinforcements.

Supply was re-supply including rations, ammunition, POL (petrol, oil and lubricants), medical stores and in a country where water-borne diseases were potentially lethal – fresh drinking water.

Strangle was interdiction attacks on lines of communication, transport and depots denying the enemy vital fuel, ammunition and rations.

Finally Support was air movement including casualty evacuation and troop reinforcements who could be moved rapidly around the theatre.

The bigger USAAF bombers were ideal for interdiction, while RAF bombers and fighter ground attack aircraft hit targets within 250 miles of the front-line.

The men who would carry out these missions were the Third Tactical Air Force commanded by Air Marshal Sir J. Baldwin, the Strategic Air Force, Brigadier-General H. C. Davidson USAAF, Troop Carrier Command Brigadier-General W. D. Old and Photographic Reconnaissance Force, Group Captain S. G. Wise.

Two RAF Groups 222 and 225 were under strategic control operating over the sea and under the command of C-in-C Eastern Fleet.

The Tenth and Fourteenth US Army Air Force who flew 'Over the Hump' of the eastern Himalayas to China were under the Commanding General China-Burma-India theatre.

By mid 1944, the fighter pilots of the Third Tactical Air Force had achieved the first of their missions and enjoyed undisputed air supremacy over Burma. The last major effort by the IJAAF had been over the Arakan in February and March, when they had suffered severe losses. During the Imphal and Kohima battles, they were able to make barely half a dozen significant raids.

The effective strength of the IJAAF in Burma was now down to approximately 200 aircraft. These were divided between three commands. HQ 5 Air Division composed of two regiments with about 40 aircraft, 4 Air Brigade with three regiments and about 75 aircraft and 7 Air Brigade with five regiments and 85 aircraft.

In 1944 the first and most dramatic demonstration of Allied air superiority in Burma was the delivery, by air, of the bulk of Wingate's forces in Operation Thursday.

The USAAF force that carried them deep into the Burmese jungle was known informally as Cochran's Circus after the commanding officer, but in a gesture to Mountbatten who had just relinquished his post as Chief of Combined Operations it was designated No 1 Air Commando.

The 523-strong force assembled by Cochran and Alison deployed 348 aircraft of all types in the China, Burma, India (CBI) theatre.

It was composed of 150 CG-4A gliders, 100 L-1/L-5 liaison aircraft, 30 P-51A fighters, 25 training gliders, 13 C-47 transports, 12 UC-64 small transports and 12 B-25H bombers. In addition to these air assets No 1 Air Commando had the unique Sikorsky YR-4 helicopter.

On April 21, 1944 a YR-4 piloted by Lt Carter Harman would rescue four occupants of an L-1 light aircraft that had crashed behind Japanese lines and so make history with the first helicopter rescue in aviation history. In total the helicopters flew 23 sorties rescuing 18 men.[198]

There were other firsts: a P-51A squadron in the Air Commando became the first Mustangs to drop 1,000-pound bombs. Mustangs also went into action armed with twin triple-tube 4.5-inch rockets.

The power to strike, support and supply would be further demonstrated in the fighting in Kohima and Imphal. During operations in this theatre in the worst four months of the monsoon the Third Tactical Air Force had increased their sortie rate to 24,000, nearly six times the figure of the previous year's record.

No 221 Group who provided air cover and ground support were in a unique position of being able to fly out of the area to secure airfields in the neighbouring Surma Valley where, while crews rested, aircraft were re-armed and re-fuelled ready for the dawn patrol. At Imphal 21 squadrons including three from the Indian Air Force took part in these operations.

Hurricane IIDs of No 20 Squadron armed with two 40mm Type S anti-tank guns played a significant part in the Imphal battle when on June 12 Japanese tanks were spotted moving up. For the loss of one aircraft all the tanks were destroyed and by the end of the month the squadron had also destroyed over 500 sampans and nearly 400 bunkers.[199]

The superb American built P-47 Republic Thunderbolt appeared in mid 1944 equipping both USAAF and RAF squadrons. The Thunderbolt armed with six or eight 0.50-inch machine guns could carry up to 2,000 pounds of bombs.

In February 1945 during the crossing of the Irrawaddy and fighting around Meiktila P-47s and P-51Ds of the newly formed 2 Air Commando Group were available for the soldiers as a 'Cab Rank' of patrolling aircraft on call to attack ground targets.

Incredibly by February there was a shortage of rockets in Burma and Hurricane IV fighters that had arrived in theatre were converted to 40mm cannon armament. On February 19 13 Japanese heavy, medium and light tanks were reported in the village of Paunggadaw advancing on the Irrawaddy bridgehead. All were destroyed, largely by 40mm cannon fire but also by 60-pound rockets.

On the south bank of the Irrawaddy at the village of Alethaung, Ken Cooper watched Hurricane ground attack aircraft go into action against nine Japanese light tanks and supporting infantry.

A flight of Hurricanes swept low across the river behind us. In line astern they swooped in a shallow dive, barely skimming the line of trees in front of the gully.

A tremendous clamour broke out amongst the scrub and paddy, as the Jap tanks and infantry caught the full fury of the aircrafts' rockets and machine-guns. The enemy could not have been more surprised and dumbfounded than we were ourselves at the speed and suddenness of the attack. Again and again the aircraft saturated the area with their blasting rocket fire. Their screaming dives shocked and deafened us. Hardly had the dust settled before a second flight screamed into the attack. The howl of steel terror descended the scale in a split second: it was as if some giant hand of great power came tearing into the earth. The line of trees ahead swayed and groaned; great baulks of timber swayed and crashed to the ground. The air became choked with fine grey dust. Flurries of steel and fragments of sod and stone were tearing into the bushes and across the grass, as if driven by a high wind sucking and hurling the blast. Out ahead petrol fires blazed up in the tanks and ammunition began to explode in them.[200]

A year earlier the two USAAF squadrons and four RAF squadrons of the Troop Carrier Command were available to fly men, equipment and supplies into the airstrips at Imphal or drop them by parachute to the men in Kohima.

Patrick Davis who joined 3 Gurkhas in November 1943 compared the austere Japanese system to the Allied approach.

'Air supply gave to the 14th Army equality in mobility, along with adequate rations, sufficient artillery and ammunition for it, a splendid casualty-recovery system, and a flow of human reinforcement. The Japanese system was designed for rapid success. It disintegrated during protracted battles of attrition such as Imphal became. And what was true of individual campaigns was true of the war as a whole: Japanese industrial capacity was proving unable to sustain a long war against opponents like the United States. Though none of us knew it, the war was won before I ever came near it.'[201]

By the end of the battles of Kohima and Imphal the RAF had flown 19,000 tons of supplies and 12,000 men into Imphal, and flown out 13,000 casualties and 43,000 non-combatants.

However as Frank Owen noted parachuting stores was not an easy task:

Supply-dropping is itself an art. The aircraft must fly at a minimum height and speed during the process (which, when serving front-line troops, brings it within periodic small-arms fire of the enemy). To complete an accurate drop it must make at least eight circuits over the dropping-zone. During this half-hour the pilot must keep his heavy ship trim. Or else the parachute will get tangled in his rudder as the loads tumble out of the doorway. For the crew it means a violent and unceasing effort to haul the crates and sacks the length of the 'hold' as far as the open door, poise and push them clear. In Burma the job was complicated by the lie of the land, which placed dropping-zones in narrow valleys, jungle clearings and hollows in the hills. These sharp contours set up air turbulences, which are intensified in the monsoon: on one occasion a Dakota emerged from a cloud upside-down. When the drop took place at night, with the enemy using counterfeit signals to decoy you off course, the fun really began.[202]

By 1945 the supply operations were highly developed. As the Fourteenth Army pushed south from India through Burma it received an average 2,000 tons a day or 60,000 tons a month. On a peak day this rose to close to 4,000 tons of stores and ammunition. Tank crews even received spare tracks, pins and other spare parts to ensure they stayed running.

Aerial supply was operated by a joint Army and Air Force command. At the dispatch end were the Commander, Army-Air Transport Organisation (CAATO) and Headquarters, Combat Cargo Task Force (CCTF). CAATO under Brigadier Dawson controlled the assembly flow and delivery of stores and supplies to the rear airfield. Here CCTF under Brigadier-General Vernon Evans USAAF and Air Commodore J. D. Hardman RAF took over lifting them and either parachuting or landing the cargo for the men in the front-line.

In March 1945 aerial re-supply reached its peak when 78,250 tons of stores were delivered and 27,000 military personnel transported. However the effectiveness of these operations depended on the speedy construction of all-weather airfields. The Fourteenth Army sappers and pioneers met the challenge building 200 airfields in six months.

With the war in Europe winding down RAF squadrons with veteran fighter pilots were redeployed to Burma.

On February 19, 1945 two Spitfires of No 17 Squadron, one flown by the by RAF 'ace' Squadron Leader James 'Ginger' Lacey, were on dawn patrol when they spotted twelve Nakajima Ki-43 'Oscar' fighters.

Richard Townsend Bickers in his biography of 'Ginger' Lacey describes the agility of the fighter and the tactics employed by the pilots. 'It was a small aircraft with an amazing rate of turn. On being attacked, the "Oscar" pilot would not increase his speed, but on the contrary reduce it. Watching in his mirror, he would wait until he saw the flashes at his attacker's gun ports which indicated that he had opened fire. Even turning at this late moment, the "Oscar" could whip round fast enough to deliver a head-on attack which took its pursuer by surprise and at a lethal disadvantage.'[203]

In this attack the Japanese pilots decided to adopt the evasion, manoeuvre and counter-attack course. One however lingered a few seconds before turning – long enough for Lacey to fire a 30-second burst of cannon fire. It sent the little aircraft into a vertical dive streaming smoke and flames. The two RAF pilots did not linger for an outnumbered contest. However after Lacey and his wingman had returned to the airstrip the armourers found that his aerial victory had required exactly nine cannon rounds.

The missions of Strike and Supply had been achieved by 1944 and now the Allied air forces were providing Support for front-line soldiers and Strangling the enemy by interdicting the flow of reinforcement and supplies for the Japanese forces now enmeshed in Burma.

As part of this strangulation bombers of the Strategic Air Force hit the Siam–Burma railway. Built by Allied PoWs and conscripted civilians the 244-mile-long railway crossed 688 bridges. The greatest was the Khao Phra Bridge known as the 'Six Hundred Bridge' for the number of PoWs who died in its construction. The Japanese also built four bypass bridges as backup if a bridge was bombed, however so intense and accurate were the attacks that daily traffic was reduced to 100 tons a day.

In Europe the Germans had pioneered the use of guided bombs that were used with lethal effectiveness against Allied shipping. The United States looked at the technology and developed their own weapons that would be used against these key bridges.

The first US guided bomb was relatively crude, the VB-1 (VB for 'vertical bomb') was a 1,000-pound bomb fitted with a tail assembly containing radio-controlled movable rudders. These permitted the bombardier to attain greater accuracy by steering the bomb to the right or left (referred to as 'azimuth', hence the name 'Azon') after its release from the carrier aircraft. A bright flare was installed in the tail so the bombardier could watch the trajectory of the VB-1 as it fell earthward. The Azon was used with moderate success in the European and Mediterranean theatres and with greater success in the China-Burma-India theatre where B-24 crews knocked out 14 bridges in seven missions.

Wing Commander Lucian Ercolani with 159 Squadron RAF flew US-built Consolidated B-24 Liberators. The big four-engined bombers had a maximum range of 2,100 miles and a normal bomb load of 5,000 pounds.

'Bridges and trains themselves were the bomb targets. The Liberators were . . . the only aircraft available which could do the considerable distances involved, we had to evolve new low-level techniques . . .

'Having flown 1,000 mile plus to find our objective on the railway line, we would have to come right down on the deck and try and knock out the engines. The terrible worry in our minds was that these trains, and the lines, were crowded with our own people . . .

'We also evolved a new method for low-level bombing to knock bridges down. Bridges are, in fact, quite difficult to hit. Amongst many successes, our squadron led the flight that knocked down the famous bridge over the River Kwai. Great annoyance was caused later amongst the crews by the film when it was said that the bridge was too far away for the air force to reach!'[204]

It was destroyed in a raid on June 24, 1945.

The 1957 film *The Bridge on the River Kwai* was based on the novel by Pierre Boulle who wrote the script; it was directed by David Lean and starred Alec Guinness and William Holden. It would win seven Oscars.

In the last weeks of the war on May 1, 1945 at the key objective of Elephant Point at the mouth of the Rangoon River a US soldier, Sergeant Dave Richardson, participated in the first and only parachute operation in Burma attached to the pathfinders.

Richardson had been a copy boy for the *New York Herald Tribune* before he was drafted in 1941; in the army he would file copy for the US Army newspaper *Yank* from the Pacific and China-Burma-India theatre. He was awarded the Bronze Star for his part in the Elephant Point operation. After the war he enjoyed a distinguished career in journalism covering major news stories for *Time* and *US News and World Report*. In this article for *Yank* he described strategic and tactical air power at work.

'About mid-morning the sun broke through and an elaborate bombing schedule got under way. Lumbering B-24s of Eastern Air Command, some American and some RAF, thundered over to lay sticks of bombs on the point. Several fires were started. For three hours the Liberators bombed, with B-25s and Mosquitoes streaking in between flights to bomb and strafe . . .'

Close air support had been refined by mid 1945 and response times were very quick, as Richardson reported.

'And then the forward platoon bumped the Japs.

'The lieutenant colonel in charge of the battalion heard about it over his handie-talkie. He casually twirled his eight-inch red mustache and then gave brief orders. "Set the three-inch mortars up," he said, "and put smoke shells on those bunkers up there. We'll call for fighter support." He pointed to some high mounds that looked like pyramids about three-quarters of a mile away. The RAF air-ground radio team contacted the planes and as soon as the bunkers had been marked by smoke shells, fighters roared in to bomb and strafe. This went on for half an hour. Then the forward platoon radioed that the remaining Japs had beat it, so the battalion pushed on – a bit more cautiously now, for this was the last mile to the point.'

Air operations in the Far East had come a long way since the heroic single bomber attack by Squadron Leader King against the Japanese-held airfield at Singora, Thailand on December 9, 1941.

CHAPTER 13

VICTORY IN BURMA
February 12 to April 30, 1945

'He had the head of a general with the heart of a private soldier'
Lance Corporal George MacDonald Fraser on Field Marshal Slim

Heitaro Kimura, the 57-year-old general commanding the Burma Area Army, believed he could hold the Fourteenth Army on the line of the Irrawaddy.

He had been well served by Generals Masaki Honda and Shihachi Katamura who had skilfully withdrawn their two Armies from the Chindwin and avoided a decisive battle trapped against the Irrawaddy bend.

Kimura had three strategic objectives, to cut the Burma Road, to hold the Yenangyaung oilfields and to retain control of the rice bowl of the Irrawaddy and Sittang basin. However he was told from IGHQ Tokyo that he could expect no reinforcements.

But now to the north the two divisions of the Thirty-third Army under General Honda were under pressure from 19 Indian and 11 East African Divisions on its west flank. Honda's depleted forces were also faced by 36 British Division commanded by Major General Frank Festing which as early as August 1944 had begun to push down an axis known as the 'Railway Corridor'. This was the main line from Mogaung to Naba Junction near Katha.[205] The track allowed men and stores to be moved, however since many of the locomotives had been destroyed by Allied air attacks it fell to the resourceful men of the newly formed corps of Royal Electrical and Mechanical Engineers (REME) to build two locomotives. They were constructed from Burma Railway wagons, British engines and Japanese gearboxes. The resulting locomotives became unique 'Castle Class' engines named

'Windsor Castle' and 'Lancaster Castle'. They could pull ten loaded trucks and to the delight of their builders reach a speed of about 40 miles an hour downhill.

Festing's troops would advance on a parallel axis with the two divisions of the Chinese Sixth Army under General Liao Yueh-shang.

Honda also faced the Northern Combat Area Command (NCAC) under US Army General Dan Sultan. NCAC was composed of the Chinese First Army under General Sun Li-jen and Sixth Army under General Liao Yueh-shang with Y Force commanded by General Wei Li-Huang on the extreme east. Li-Huang who had risen from the ranks was a tough veteran of 30 years of combat and enjoyed the nickname amongst his troops of 'Hundred Victory Wei'.

In the centre the three divisions of the Fifteenth Army under General Katamura was faced by the main weight of the Fourteenth Army the XXXIII Corps. To the south the two divisions and one independent brigade of the Twenty-eighth Army commanded by General Shozo Sakurai faced 7 Indian Division with XV Corps on the coastal flank.

Kimura's forces now concentrated on the east bank of the Irrawaddy outnumbered the Allies in Burma and he was still thinking offensively. In Operation Dan he tasked the Thirty-third Army with holding the line between Lashio and the Monglong mountains but also with launching operations to cut the India–China land link in a new offensive.

In Operation Ban the Fifteenth Army was to halt the Allies on the line of the Irrawaddy. To the south the Twenty-eighth had an area of operations that reached from Yenangyaung in the north to the Irrawaddy delta and Rangoon in the south. In Operation Kan it was to hold the Allied advance through the Arakan and defend the western seaboard of Burma.

At 04.00 hours on February 14 Kimura's plans to hold the river line, or at least contain the bridgeheads, finally collapsed.

Slim's masterstroke was delivered by Major General G. C. Evans, victor of the 'Admin Box' battle and the men of the 7 Indian Division who began to cross the Irrawaddy near Nyaungu. Initially they met only slight opposition since most of the Japanese forces had been withdrawn to defend Mandalay threatened by the northern bridge-heads.

Even as they consolidated their hold and shipped across armour and artillery Kimura still looked north. When on February 10, tanks and infantry from 19 Division began moving south it seemed clear that Mandalay was the objective so the Japanese concentrated their forces in the area and moved up over 60 guns.

The build-up of the IV Corps's bridgehead continued including the heavy armoured punch of the 255 Tank Brigade, and on February 20 it began to break out and advance towards Meiktila.

The brigade included the Humber armoured cars of 16 Light Cavalry the first armoured regiment to be commanded by an Indian officer, Lt Colonel J. N. Chaudhuri. After Independence Chaudhuri eventually became the Chief of Staff, Indian Army. His old regiment 16 Light Cavalry is the senior Indian Cavalry regiment tracing their descent back to 3 Cavalry raised in 1776.

On February 24, 17 Indian Division took Taungtha and two days later Mablaing fell and at 14.00 hours the undefended airfield at Thabuktong was captured by armoured cars of the Royal Deccan Horse. Sappers immediately set to work making the airfield operational and the following day 17 Division's third brigade the air-portable trained 99 Bde was flown in.

Four days later IV Corps began its attack on Meiktila in strength. It was here that British and Indian tank crews encountered human anti-tank mines.

Lt Colonel Miles Smeeton commanding Probyn's Horse watched Japanese soldiers leap from cover holding demolition charges which they attempted to detonate against the tanks.

'In harvest time I had seen a rabbit, shaken out of a corn stock, turn suddenly on its pursuers . . . I couldn't have been more surprised than I was at the sudden appearance of these Japanese soldiers, with their anguished look of determination and despair, pitting their puny strength against such tremendous force. Their desperate courage was something . . . we saw with amazement, admiration, and pity too.'[206]

At one point a series of holes dug on the likely approach route for tanks were spotted. In each one a Japanese soldier crouched holding a

250kg aerial bomb between his knees, with the fused nose uppermost. When a tank was within range the soldier would strike the fuse with a brick. Under orders to destroy a tank and knowing they were doomed the soldiers waited patiently – so patiently that a British Colonel who had spotted the unusual pattern of holes dismounted, and covered by his tanks' guns walked forward to shoot each soldier in the head.

The loss of Meiktila would be critical to the Japanese since it was a vital communications centre, serving all the forces around Mandalay and to the north.

On March 1 Slim accompanied by Messervy visited Cowan's HQ outside Meiktila. Having satisfied himself that the operation was proceeding well, he and Messervy went forward to watch the battle and talk to many subordinate commanders on the way. The outcome of the Burma campaign might have been changed dramatically when the Army and Corps Commanders found themselves with the leading troops and in the line of fire of the supporting tanks.

'Nevertheless,' writes Geoffrey Evans, 'the effect on the soldiers of seeing the Army Commander in the forefront was rousing and, although one of the party was wounded, the two senior officers returned unscathed.'[207]

On March 2 Second Lt Hidetaro Kotani a supply officer at Meiktila found himself a front-line platoon commander.

'The enemy tanks blazed away at us with guns and machine guns. We started to hurl grenades, jumping up on the tanks and trying to open the turrets and throw grenades inside, but many of us were cut down by gunfire . . .

'Those of our men who had survived, seemed to have been knocked flat by the battle. Their morale was low, and because they had no anti-tank weapons they were overcome by a feeling of terror . . .

'When all the skill and will to fight of a human being comes face to face with an enormous machine, whatever the differences between them, the result is the same.'[208]

By March 3 Meiktila had been secured by IV Corps in a three-pronged attack that saw 63 and 48 Brigades hit the city from the west while the tanks of 255 Tank Bde hooked round to cut the roads to the east of the city. The main route for supplies to the bulk of the Japanese forces in Burma was therefore cut, and they were compelled to turn away from the fighting further north, and to try to clear their lines of communication. At the same time they were still obliged to hold off XXXIII Corps to the north.

Within a day the Japanese began a series of counter-attacks against IV Corps lines of communication and when the small town of Taungtha was retaken 17 Indian Division was almost cut off in Meiktila. However the division could rely on air re-supply and did so for the next three weeks.

To the north, while XXXIII Corps continued to attract the main Japanese forces 20 Division under Major General Douglas Gracey, which had crossed the Irrawaddy near Ngazun on February 24, punched south and east cutting road and rail links from Meiktila to Mandalay. General Nicholson's 2 Division drove east towards Ava south of Mandalay.

By March 9, in converging attacks on three axes 19 Indian Division had reached the northern outskirts of Mandalay. To the east 62 Indian Bde had been detached to capture Maymo which fell on March 14 and with it rail links to the east and Japanese troops fighting in China. In a night climb and dawn assault on March 11 the pagoda-studded Mandalay Hill to the north of the city was captured by men of the Gurkhas and Royal Berkshires. Rees had refused to order bomber missions against the historic religious site but now the Japanese hung on and fighter ground attack aircraft raked the area with machine-gun fire. When the Japanese barricaded themselves in a tunnel beneath the great Reception Hall drums of petrol were rolled in followed by grenades. Rees as always close to the action directed the battle from a terrace amongst the pagodas, he was so close that an officer was killed by a sniper as he spoke to the General.

The fighting around Meiktila was still very fierce, as the Japanese continued to bring troops from the Mandalay area, in a desperate attempt to free their communications. On March 12 the airstrip and railway station of Myotha, south-west of Mandalay, fell to 20 Indian Division.

Two days later 19 Indian Division were still fighting in Mandalay but had captured much of the city in bitter house-to-house fighting.

To the soldiers the conduct of the population was a source of amazement – as rounds cracked overhead and explosions shook the air, old men puffed their pipes and women washed clothes or prepared food. The population that before the war had stood at 400,000 had shrunk to 7,000 but these stalwarts hardly bothered to look up when circling Dakotas dropped 50,000 gallons of fuel, 500,000 cigarettes and 90,000 ration packs to the troops below.

The Japanese stepped up their efforts against Meiktila, but could make no significant progress against 17 Indian Division.

On March 17 the Chinese Sixth Army took Hswipaw on the Burma Road, 50 miles south-west of Lashio as the Chinese First Army was still trying to advance along the road from Lashio clearing Japanese road blocks.

The 1 Queen's Own Highlanders, part of British 2 Division took the moated fort at Ava on the bend of the Irrawaddy only a few miles south of Mandalay.

General Honda now realised that the fight for Meiktila was critical and took personal command. With men from 18 and 49 Division as well as two regiments from 33 and 53 Divisions under his command the 56-year-old general created a new force *Kesshōgun* or 'The Army of the Decisive Battle'.

In a brutal army Honda was renowned for his kindness to his men, even to private soldiers with whom he was happy to share filthy stories – probably as a morale booster. He was an academic soldier who, though he enjoyed sake and was attractive to women, did not gamble and conducted his personal life and career with 'studied correctness'. Following the surrender in Burma he became a PoW and remained with his troops until he was repatriated to Japan in 1947. He died on July 17, 1964 aged 75.

By mid March the weight of the RAF and USAAF firepower and the strength of the 17 Division and its armour had worn down the Japanese.

On March 19, 19 Indian Division completed the capture of Mandalay. Fort Dufferin held by the Japanese 60 Regiment was amongst the most stubbornly defended positions. It was here that the fighting took on the character of a medieval siege. The fort was a massive moated stronghold with ramparts one and a quarter miles long, a 200-foot-wide moat and massive brick-built ramparts 30 feet high. Gunners from 19 Division brought up a 5.5-inch Medium Gun and at a range of 500 yards fired 50 shells over open sights at the walls – the only effect was to make deep impressions in the brickwork. Rees called a conference and it was agreed that air strikes would be the only way to breach the walls. Three squadrons of B-25 Mitchells from 12 Bombardment Group USAAF would bomb a 200-foot-wide strip inside the north wall. Then 42 Squadron RAF with Hurribombers would strafe the ramparts to neutralise any surviving AA guns. Finally two squadrons of Thunderbolt fighter bombers from 910 Wing RAF would make as many breaches in the northern wall as possible and widen any existing gaps.

In a devastating demonstration of air power bombers and fighters ripped into Fort Dufferin. Two Thunderbolts put their complete bombload a total of 4,000 pounds into the wall blasting a 50-foot-gap in the rampart.

Under this onslaught the Japanese 60 Regiment had had enough and withdrew during the night.

Captain Frederick Rowley of 5 Battalion 10 Baluch Regiment took a patrol into the fort. 'We were going along gingerly, when we heard and saw a figure about fifty yards away. As it got closer, it didn't look like a Japanese. I shouted a challenge, and he turned out to be an American from Shwebo who had just driven his jeep to look for souvenirs. He said, "The gates were open, I came in. I'm on leave, I'm on holiday." '[209]

The XXXIII Corps soldiers discovered that the fort had been used as a prison and found 346 civilians including several French and Irish Roman Catholic missionaries who had been interned.

On March 21 Slim arrived and accompanied by Air Vice-Marshal S. F. Vincent commanding 221 Group and five generals took the salute from a simple platform in the centre of the fort. The Union Flag was hoisted and three cheers called for the King Emperor. A photographer with some of the rare colour film captured images of Slim, the parade and British and Indian soldiers amongst the pagodas.

It was reported that Mountbatten was bitterly disappointed to have missed the public relations opportunity of this historic occasion.

On March 22 the river port of Myingyun fell to 33 Bde pushing north along the left bank of the Irrawaddy. As soon as it was secure work began urgently on restoring the quays and rebuilding bridges. Wrecked railway locomotives and rolling stock were repaired along with the metre-gauge track to Meiktila.

By March 28 Honda realised that he could not retake Meiktila, and XXXIII Corps had been making important gains to the north along the south bank of the Irrawaddy cutting the Japanese Twenty-eighth Army's withdrawal routes in the Arakan. The main thrust south down the Sittang had become the responsibility of IV Corps. As overall commander in Burma Kimura decided that with his main communications cut, withdrawal towards Rangoon and Malaya was his only option.

Captain John Scollen an Air Observation Post (AOP) pilot with the Royal Artillery recalled that at the end of the fighting for Meiktila 'almost every building . . . was gutted by fire or shattered by blast, and to drive through it when we first took it was a sickening experience. Jap dead lay by the roadsides and in the ruined houses, and there hung about the place the dreadful stench of death that overcomes one with horror and remains in the memory like a nightmare.'[210]

On March 31 with the capture of Kyaukme north-east of Mandalay by British 36 Division and units of the Chinese Sixth Army the Burma Road from Mandalay to Lashio was now clear. The 36 Division were sent to relieve 19 Indian Division in Mandalay.

The capture of Yindaw south of Meiktila on April 6 by 17 Indian Division which had hooked round Pyawbwe to the west blocked Honda's retreat and virtually destroyed what was left of the Thirty-third Army which now consisted of about 8,000 men.

The Fourteenth Army had suffered 10,500 casualties in the battle for the Irrawaddy and 7,000 sick had been evacuated. At Meiktila alone Japanese battle casualties in 18 and 49 Divisions were over 8,000 with the latter losing all but three of its 48 guns.

By April 8 the Fourteenth Army had regrouped following the

victories at Mandalay and Meiktila and were ready for a rapid armoured and mechanised advance to finish the campaign in Burma.

It was on that day that the 7/10 Baluchis were tasked with the capture of Point 900 a prominent hill feature about 3 miles west of the town of Pyawbwe on the Sittang. They were supported by tanks from an Indian cavalry regiment, whose crews reported, before they pulled back, that they thought the Japanese troops seemed willing to surrender. The men on Point 900 did indeed seem unusually passive but as John Randle's company closed in, the enemy opened fire killing a sepoy.

'This was one dead sepoy too many for B Company who dropped any idea of taking prisoners and simply went fighting mad . . . they were in a blood lust, the only time I have ever seen men in one, and a terrible and awesome thing it was to witness. They were baying in high-pitched screams, with their lips drawn back over their teeth which gave them a ghastly wolflike insane grin. I found myself both exhilarated and appalled by this sheer animal lust to kill. In about ten minutes of grenade work, tommy and Bren-gun fire and the bayonet the whole Japanese company was wiped out, with no prisoners taken.'[211]

On April 10 the railway junction at Thazi, east of Meiktila, was captured by IV Corps and two days later the corps started its drive down in the Sittang Valley. To the west of Meiktila, 7 Indian Division from XXXIII Corps took Kyaukpaduang.

Five days later 20 Indian Division leading XXXIII Corps' advance captured Taungdwingyi. Now Stopford sent part of the corps westward to capture Magwe and Myingyun on the Irrawaddy which fell on April 19, meanwhile the corps drove south towards Thayetmyo and the river port of Prome. On the same day in the Sittang Valley, Pyinmana fell to 5 Indian Division which now led the IV Corps's advance.

Next day tanks of 5 Indian Division almost captured General Honda who was forced to escape on foot as the rains that preceded the full monsoon, known as the Mango Rains, began to fall.

By April 21 the IV Corps's advance in the Sittang Valley was beginning to pull ahead of the parallel efforts in the Irrawaddy Valley.

Yedash was taken by 5 Indian Division while in the rear, the airfields around Pyinmana which had been captured a day earlier, were being cleared to be put into Allied service.

In the Irrawaddy Valley, after four days of fierce fighting the battered oil fields of Yenangyaung fell to formations of XXXIII Corps, mopping up in the rear of the main advance.

Despite these spectacular successes, Slim was uneasy.

The monsoon, which was rapidly approaching, could slow operations and allow the Japanese time to recover their balance. Fourteenth Army's road and air supply lines, already stretched by the rapid advance, would be badly restricted by monsoon rains.

Messervy and several of his commanders believed that there was a chance of beating the monsoon and capturing Rangoon at the beginning of May. There was the added impetus for the capture since it was feared that the Japanese might defend Rangoon to the last man exacting a huge price in civilian as well as military casualties.

As a precaution in mid April, Slim asked for Operation Dracula to be reinstated and launched in early May before the monsoon broke. As a preliminary move, IV Corps was tasked with the capture of Toungoo and its airfields, to ensure land-based air cover for Dracula. On April 22 Toungoo was captured by 5 Infantry Division, three days ahead of the date scheduled in the operational orders. IV Corps was following their commander's instructions: 'Speed is all important and risks must be accepted to obtain it. Every day is precious.'

Three days later Salin on the west bank of the Irrawaddy was captured in a joint attack by 114 Bde and 89 Bde while the main thrust of the XXXIII Corps advance was towards Allanmyo. The spectacular progress of 5 Indian Division in the Sittang Valley continued with the capture of Perwegen.

After four days of fighting the wrecked and rusting oil derricks of Yenangyaung were captured by XXXIII Corps on April 25.

On April 28 Allanmyo fell to XXXIII Corps. The remaining Japanese forces in this area had become very disorganised by attacks on two axes down the river valleys. In the Sittang Valley, 17 Indian Division had now taken over the lead and after capturing Nyaunglebim, attacked near Payagi.

In Germany the last desperate fighting was taking place in the rubble of Berlin and before the week was out the war in Europe would be over. In Burma the fighting continued with no apparent conclusion in sight.

CHAPTER 14

DEATH ON THE SITTANG
May 1 to August 27, 1945

'54 Division here! Help, for God's sake, don't let us go!'
The shouts of Japanese soldiers caught in the flooded Sittang

On May 1, preceded by solemn music, a Radio Hamburg announcer told what remained of the Third Reich that Nazi Germany's leader Adolf Hitler and his propaganda minister Dr Josef Göbbels were dead. World War II in Europe was over, but it was still being fought with grim ferocity in the Far East and Pacific.

Attacks by Indian 17 Division in the Sittang Valley in Burma had nearly reached Pegu to the north-east of Rangoon. If the critical rail link town fell, the route eastwards from Rangoon would be cut.

In Rangoon General Heitaro Kimura commanding Burma Area Army had his HQ and staff but no fighting formations in the city.

As 17 Division and the tanks of 255 Armoured Bde approached Pegu, Japanese rear-area troops, including anti-aircraft gun crews, airfield construction battalions, 13 Naval Guard Force, training staff from NCO schools along with civilian technicians were hastily formed into an ad hoc formation called KAN-I Force.

Commanded by Major General Hideji Matsui it had the formal designation 105 Independent Mixed Bde. Believing that they were buying time for an effective defence of the city to be built up, this scratch force held Pegu and Payagi for several days blocking the IV Corps drive south. If Pegu had fallen the overland route from Rangoon across the Sittang would have been cut.

Before he committed KAN-I Force, Kimura had already decided to evacuate Rangoon and withdraw to Moulmein in southern Burma. Many of the troops not in KAN-I Force boarded a convoy of eleven ships. They were intercepted by a flotilla of five Royal Navy destroyers and nine were sunk.

In a move that was regarded as shameful by his brother officers Kimura flew out of Rangoon, while his staff along with Subhas Chandra Bose and Ba Maw escaped by road.

When word of the evacuation reached Matsui, he was furious. By now KAN-I Force had been driven into the hills west of Pegu and so were unable to reach the city or escape to Moulmein. Matsui received orders to continue to wage guerrilla warfare. He attempted to move fit PoWs under his control towards the Sittang but on April 30 ordered that those who were unfit should be released when Fourteenth Army forces were encountered.

Meanwhile the forces tasked for Operation Dracula were on their way. Since SEAC had assembled ships, men and aircraft for Operation Roger the amphibious assault on the Japanese-held Thai island of Phuket all that was necessary was to re-assign them to Dracula.

They were the Indian 26 Infantry Division commanded by Major General Henry Chambers part of the experienced Indian XV Corps, under General Christison. Between April 27 and 30 the division with its supporting arms sailed in six convoys from Akyab and Ramree islands in the Arakan.

Overhead 224 Group RAF, under Air Vice Marshal the Earl of Bandon covered the landings from the airfields around Toungoo and Ramree.

On May 1 twelve squadrons of B-24 Liberators bombed known Japanese defences south of Rangoon.

Now, in the only parachute operation of the war in Burma, 2/3 Gurkha Parachute Battalion with a team from Force 136 and a Royal Air Force forward control team jumped into a DZ at Elephant Point at the mouth of the Rangoon River.

The Force 136 team were probably inserted to make contact with the Burma National Army (BNA), particularly the Karen battalion in Rangoon.

Although from August 1943 Burma had been nominally self-governing, in reality it was under Japanese military occupation. Japanese attitudes turned the majority population against them and the exploitation of the country disenchanted the BNA. In 1943 the BNA had contacted other Burmese political groups including the Communists who a year earlier had taken to the hills. The groups coalesced into the Anti-Fascist Organisation (AFO) under Thakin Soe. Through the Communists and the Arakan Defence Army, a Japanese-sponsored force, the Burmese were eventually able to make indirect contact with agents of Force 136.

At the end of 1944 the AFO told the Allies that they were prepared to launch a national uprising spearheaded by the BNA. Some senior British officers were not happy about supporting a formerly hostile force that had sided with the Japanese. However true to their word the first BNA attacks were launched early in 1945 in central Burma.

In late March 1945 the bulk of the BNA paraded in Rangoon, ostensibly prior to joining the Japanese forces in the fighting in Central Burma. It was a *ruse de guerre* and on March 27 the BNA announced that they had switched sides and declared war on the Japanese.

Grouped in ten regional commands they went into action across the country seizing control of the administration of most major towns. Those units close to the Irrawaddy and the Fourteenth Army asked for weapons and equipment. Many senior British officers and some prominent Civil Affairs officials in SEAC HQ distrusted Aung San and some even urged that he be tried for the murder in 1942 of a Burmese Indian and for his pre-war contacts with the Japanese.

However Force 136 issued Aung San and his associates with safe passes, and they met Slim on May 15. Thakin Soe and Aung San hoped that the BNA would be accepted as Allied forces and the AFO would be acknowledged as the provisional government of Burma. Slim refused to accept the AFO as a government and insisted that once the fighting was over the BNA should be disarmed by British forces. In return for recognition as a political movement and promises that the officers and men of the BNA would be incorporated into the new Burma Army the AFO agreed to the disarmament. Renamed the Patriotic Burmese Forces, the BNA assisted in driving the Japanese out of southern Burma.

SEAC's co-operation with the BNA was pragmatic. With the draw-down of forces in South East Asia, and the challenge of India's

looming independence SEAC did not want to become entangled in a
difficult counter-insurgency campaign in Burma particularly as the
Indian Army could no longer be counted on to impose British colonial
rule. Though the British withdrew gracefully from Burma an insurgency broke out two years later, when Aung San and other political
leaders were assassinated, it was reported, on the orders of U Saw a
pro-Japanese Burmese politician. The death of this charismatic leader
then triggered a full-blown civil war in 1949.

However back in May 1945 the war was on and writing for the July
1945 issue of *Yank* Sergeant Dave Richardson who jumped with the
pathfinders left a vivid personal account of the operation.

Rangoon, Burma

The jumpmaster groped through the darkened C-47 to rouse you
an hour before dawn. You opened your eyes as he offered you a
cigarette and said, 'One hour to go.' He did it as matter-of-factly as
though he were an ATC steward on the Calcutta–New Delhi run.
Yet in a little while he would slap you out the door and you would
take part in the paratroop operation that paved the way for the
capture of Rangoon.

You were going to jump with the Pathfinders – 17 British Signals
men and 20 Gurkhas who were to land 45 minutes ahead of the
main body of paratroopers. They would prepare the way. Some
would direct the other planes in by radio, others would mark out the
drop zone with colored panels and smoke bombs. Still others would
reconnoiter the vicinity of the drop to learn where the nearest Japs
were . . .

Then the jump bell rang. The jumpmaster shoved out three large
parapacks, which were snapped away by the howling wind. The
Number One man stepped to the door. He was a sandy-haired old
sergeant who had told you he had made 49 jumps and was returning
to Blighty in a few weeks.

The bell rang again. The jumpmaster yelled 'Go!' and slammed
the sergeant's back. The sergeant kicked out his right leg, hollering
'Number One' and spun down and off into space. You shuffled
forward in line, grasping the static line in your left hand, as man

after man stepped to the door, yelled his number and kicked off.

'. . . Number Five, Number Six, Number Seven . . .'

Your number was Ten in the 20-man stick. Your heart was pounding hard and your lips quivered. You felt weak and unsteady as you kept your eyes fixed to the parachuted back of the Number Nine man.

'. . . Number Eight, Number Nine . . .'

In an instant you were facing the open door, sliding your static line down the cable . . . You got to the door, hollered 'Number Ten' and kicked your right leg out into the howling wind as the jump-master slammed your back . . .

Then the little hunk of cord attaching the static line to the top of the chute snapped. The silk bellowed out. You were yanked up and, in a flash, sitting still. The chute was open . . . One moment you were watching it come up and the next – cu-rump – you were lying in the grass . . .

One of the British officers had taken the Gurkhas on a reconnaissance patrol of nearby villages. Soon one of his men appeared across the open paddy fields, trotting toward you. He handed you a message to deliver to the CP. As you carried it over, you read it.

'Tawkai Village unoccupied by Jap,' it said. 'Villagers say no enemy between here and Elephant Point, but enemy dug in at point.'

Getting back to your position, you unfolded your map and went over the parachute battalion's mission, as outlined in the previous day's briefing. The outfit was to land on D-minus-one about 25 miles south of Rangoon and then clear all Japs from Elephant Point, at the entrance to the Rangoon River. This would allow the seaborne invasion of Rangoon to pass up the river on D-Day.

You were now six miles from the point and there was estimated to be between a company and a battalion of Japs manning shore defenses there. That meant the paratroopers would have to work fast in getting to and taking their objective. If it wasn't taken by sundown, the Japs could hold it all night and give a pasting to the landing craft at dawn.

Nearby, one of the Pathfinders let out a shout. 'Here they come!'

212

he said. 'Look at 'em – what a bloomin' armada!' In the distance the sky was dotted with little specks that came nearer with an increasing drone. Now you could make out the C-47s of the Combat Cargo Task Force – 40 of them, flying in threes, one group behind another like a parade. British and American fighters scooted back and forth on all sides of the C-47s. Light bombers buzzed the thatched-roof villages and clumps of brush, looking hungrily for targets. On the ground the Pathfinders lit smoke bombs to give wind direction.

Now the C-47s were overhead. Craning your neck, you saw little black objects spill out of their doors, plummet down and then blossom chutes. You looked closely to see which were men and which equipment. The way you spotted the men was by their dangling limbs . . .

The paratroops had fanned out in skirmish lines, plodding through ankle-deep mud across the broad paddy fields towards Elephant Point. The point and flank platoons carried orange umbrellas to mark the advance for the supporting fighter-bombers.

By mid-afternoon, one and one-half miles from the point, they passed through burned and wrecked villages that had been hit by the Liberator raids. The inhabitants, some terrified and shaken, streamed back. They told the paratroops that Japanese were coming in the direction of the Gurkhas. However although there were Japanese anti-aircraft emplacements none of them appeared to have been used recently.

The Gurkhas discovered that the bunkers, now overgrown with grass, had been built some time ago but they were obvious because there was no other high ground in the vicinity. Near them Richardson noted were freshly dug foxholes. He watched as a stolid-faced Gurkha flattened the ends of the splayed split pins in his 36 Grenades ready for quick use.

The forward company, which you were travelling with now, got to a series of bunkers only 600 yards from the point when a sniper's bullet whined overhead. More shots followed. Everyone ducked for cover. A Gurkha grabbed your arm and pointed. There, in plain

213

view 200 yards away, were some figures walking among beached landing barges and bunkers. A Gurkha Bren gunner opened up. The figures started running. The whole company began shooting. Once more the three-inch mortar was brought up and the fighters dove in. For some reason the Japs refused to take cover; they kept running from barge to bunker across open ground.

'Must be bomb-happy,' said a captain. 'In three months at Imphal and Kohima last year I only saw two Japs who exposed themselves.'

Dave Richardson watched, as covered by fire, the Gurkhas began to run and squirm up to the position.

But before they could get to within 100 yards of them, the Japs disappeared. The place we had seen them was north of Elephant Point. The company commander put his glasses on the point for a few moments, then decided to slip his company south of the Japs to get to the point while another company occupied them with plenty of firing.

You moved the last 600 yards with ready rifle as the company skirted bomb craters, peered into bunkers and frisked bushes. Before you knew it, you were walking up to a Jap radar tower and realizing that the water 30 yards on the other side of it was the Rangoon River.

You had reached the objective – but the fighting was not over.

The point, like the previous villages, was a maze of bomb craters. It contained little besides the radar tower, two shrapnel-shattered bungalows, a few gun emplacements and a half-dozen bunkers. 'I reckon,' said a Britisher, 'that the Jap threw all his radar equipment and shore-defense guns in the drink.'

Then the Japs started firing again. There was *Nambu*[212] fire this time, crackling in short bursts. And again the Japs started coming out into the open. Other paratroop companies moved up and filtered into positions between the point and the Japs. The firing increased on both sides. A flame-thrower was brought up to silence the machine gun in one of the bunkers, but the ground was too open to get it near enough. A British officer and two Gurkhas crawled up

214

with grenades. When within 10 yards of the *Nambu* they popped to their feet to attack the slit it was firing from. The officer was killed and one of the Gurkhas wounded. They had succeeded, however, in forcing the Japs out, and a heavy Vickers machine gun caught them as they ran out the back.

Snipers' bullets were pinging all over the place. A big steel landing barge on the beach 200 yards inshore seemed to be the Japs CP, so mortar fire was put on it. Just then a flight of C-47s with fighter escort started circling to drop supplies to the rear company. The air-ground radio team borrowed the fighters to thoroughly strafe the Jap barge until it was aflame from stem to stern. It burned brightly all night.

'Looks like it's going to be a nice quiet evening,' grinned a sergeant. There were Japs on three sides of the perimeter, with the river on the other side. You had wondered why there had been no Japs on the point, but now you began to feel uneasily that it had been a trap. The firing finally tapered off to scattered shots now and then, but everyone expected a counter-attack during the night.

Richardson confessed that he was too tired to dig in and curled up in his ground sheet in a bomb crater. The expected Japanese counter-attack did not materialise that night.

The Gurkhas suffered thirty casualties in their part in Operation Dracula, some caused by inaccurate Allied bombing.

With Elephant Point secured, minesweepers cleared a passage up the river, and landing craft carrying 26 Indian Division began the run in the early hours of May 2.

From the shore Dave Richardson watched the invasion force arrive on May 3. 'Suddenly a shout went up. Everyone ran to the crest of a sand dune and looked. It was the D-Day convoy. The landing craft chugged up the channel and swung past a buoy 300 yards offshore. The paratroopers hollered 'Good luck,' and some of the men on the boats waved back.'[213]

When the ramps went down the troops went ashore to encounter no Japanese resistance.

Offshore Vice Admiral H. T. C. Walker commanded a formidable

Task Force 63 with two 15-inch battleships, *Queen Elizabeth* and the Free French *Richelieu*, two escort carriers, as well as four cruisers (one from the Royal Netherlands Navy) and six destroyers.

Meanwhile Wing Commander A. E. Saunders the pilot of an RAF Mosquito of 110 Squadron flying over the city of Rangoon saw no sign of the Japanese, but noticed a message painted on the roof of the city jail. It read, *Japs gone. Extract digit.* He landed at the bomb-damaged Mingaladon airfield, but blew out a tyre. Undaunted he walked to the jail and found 1,000 former PoWs who informed him of the Japanese evacuation. He then went to the docks, commandeered a sampan and sailed down the river to meet the landing craft carrying 26 Indian Division.

The Japanese had in fact left on April 29 and Wing Commander 'Bill' Hudson a PoW in Rangoon found that they had left a note.

Gentlemen,

Bravely you have come here opening prison gate. We have gone keeping your prisoner safely with Nipponese knightship. Afterwards we may meet again at the front somewhere. Then let us fight bravely each other. (We had kept the gate's keys in the gate room.)

Nipponese Army[214]

Rangoon was taken without any resistance though contingents of the INA had, on orders of Subhas Chandra Bose, remained in the city to keep order.

Further north, Prome on the Irrawaddy was taken by XXXIII Corps.

Since looting and lawlessness had broken out in Rangoon the British were joyfully welcomed, both as liberators and a force that could bring law and order and humanitarian assistance.

Reconnaissance troops from 26 Division moved out from the port along the main roads. On May 6, at Hlegu 28 miles north-east of Rangoon, they met the leading troops of 17 Division, pushing their way through monsoon rains from Pegu. On the same day the Rangoon River was opened for shipping and two days later supply ships berthed at Rangoon.

Mopping-up operations continued as far as the monsoon permitted, but British attention was now directed to Operation Zipper the amphibious landings on the west coast of Malaya.

On May 7 Leese replaced Slim as commander of Fourteenth Army, on the grounds that he thought Slim was tired after the long campaign, and that Christison with his experience of the Arakan and Operation Dracula was better suited to command the Army in a major amphibious operation. Leese explained that Slim would take command of Twelfth Army to be formed on May 28, a force that would carry out the final clearance of Burma.

Slim regarded this as tantamount to being sacked and therefore resigned. Mountbatten intervened, but decisions were being taken at higher levels in London.

On May 17 General Sir Alanbrooke Chief of the Imperial General Staff confided to his diary: '. . . Back to WO (War Office) for interview with Auk (General Auchinleck C-in-C India) about appointment of Slim to Burma Command. Leese is going quite wild and doing mad things, prepared a fair rap on the knuckles for him!'

The outcome was that Stopford would take command of the Twelfth Army, Christison temporary command of the Fourteenth Army until General Sir Miles Dempsey, who had been appointed to the command of the Fourteenth Army, arrived from Europe. However perhaps the most unusual promotion was for Slim who was then on well-deserved leave in Britain. When he returned to theatre he would become C-in-C ALFSEA replacing Leese who had been ordered back to Britain.

On June 14 a victory parade was held in Rangoon to celebrate the recapture of the city and liberation of Burma.

To the north trapped in the Pegu Yomas range in central Burma between June and August 1945 30,000 men of the Twenty-eighth Army under General Sakurai attempted to break out of their hiding places hoping to join forces with Honda's Thirty-third Army on the Thai border.[215]

The northern flank was protected by troops of a division under command of General Miyazaki, the man who had led the abortive assault on Kohima. Between July 3 and 11 Honda launched attacks

217

against Waw in the south in an attempt to distract the 7 Division as the breakout took place further to the north.

Sakurai made it across the Sittang on July 28 but behind him desperate men and some women attempted to reach safety.

'As an example of military stupidity,' wrote an observer, 'it must rival the Charge of the Light Brigade and in the same way it has an epic quality.'

Well dug in along the line of the road, railway and swollen River Sittang were 19 Division in the north, 7 Division in the south and by a grim twist of fate 17 Division the men who had fought at the Sittang Bridge were in the centre. Patrols of tanks and armoured cars and aircraft covered the gaps between the positions.

Casualty figures for what became known as the 'Battle of the Break-out' are imprecise for the Japanese – between 10,000 and 17,000 along with 1,400 prisoners while about 6,000 reached the east bank of the Sittang. The Fourteenth Army losses were 97.

'They started to cross the tarmac Toungoo–Pegu road in a steady stream and make straight for the river bank as fast as they could. The slaughter was terrific . . . Heavy concentrations of artillery were firing almost day and night. On the river bank fighter aircraft kept up an almost continuous daylight patrol.'

The Japanese struggled towards the river that was now in flood and had burst its banks. In some places the fugitives were confronted by 'a vast lake, not marked on any map, but which stretched for miles . . . It was no lake, just the result of the Sittang overflowing and obliterating the banks between patches of land. It wasn't deep, therefore, and they put together banana stalks . . . for buoyancy and pushed these little "rafts" ahead of them as they swam through the water. They had finished off the last of their food before they began. For five days they swam, resting every fifty yards, and snatching what sleep they could at night in the branches of submerged trees. They did not dare to leave their mouths open for fear of water leeches, and to save themselves falling in the river as they slept, they strapped themselves to branches with their gaiters (puttees).'[216]

'Elsewhere the river raged past chest high, whirling corpses and frantic figures shouting "54 Division here! Help, for God's sake, don't let us go!" '[217]

On August 6, thousands of miles to the east the USAAF B-29 bomber *Enola Gay* commanded by Colonel Paul Tibbets flew high over the Japanese city of Hiroshima. The bomb bays opened and a single bomb descended – the world's first atomic bomb. In seconds 80,000 men, women and children were dead, a further 10,000 were later reported missing and 37,000 seriously injured.

Three days later the B-29 *Bock's Car* dropped a second atomic bomb on the city of Nagasaki killing 35,000 with 5,000 missing and 6,000 severely injured. On the same day three Army Groups of battle-hardened Soviet troops, veterans of the war in Europe, invaded Manchuria. It was an uneven contest – the Soviet forces outnumbered the Japanese by three to two, in guns by five to one, tanks in the same proportion and aircraft by two to one.

In a blitzkrieg that lasted only a few days Japan's prized colony on the Asian mainland was no more. It was the final blow and on August 10 Japan accepted the Allied surrender terms drafted at the Potsdam Conference.

On August 27 in Rangoon a Japanese delegation signed a pre-liminary agreement ordering local Japanese commanders in Burma to assist and obey instructions from British commanders.

The fighting was over, but in the first weeks of a world now officially at peace, the brown swirling waters of the Sittang continued to carry Japanese alive and dead down to the sea. Three years and six months after the demolition of the Sittang Railway Bridge, the pain had come full circle.

219

APPENDIX 1

It would be easy to characterise the Press Conference held by Mountbatten in August 1944 as a piece of self-publicity. In fact closer scrutiny shows that it was a bold attempt not only to ensure that the servicemen and women in the theatre were not ignored as the fighting in Europe reached a new intensity, but a thorough summation of the operations and roles of the commanders in the theatre.

Admiral Lord Louis Mountbatten's Address to the Press, August 1944

SEVEN MONTHS' BATTLE

My object in this Press conference is to try to put before the Press of the world that every effort has been and is continuing to be put into the South East Asia campaign; that the Burma battle front is a single unified front: that my plans are made in close consultation with my deputy, General Joseph Stilwell, and, we carry them out with a common end in view.

Please therefore look upon Burma as one big Allied effort. British, American and Chinese with the help of the Dutch and the other nations that are with us. It is going extraordinarily well as an Allied effort. We do not want a lot of limelight, in fact we do not want any, but I go round and talk to the men in the Command and what worries them is that their wives, their mothers, their daughters their sweethearts and their sisters don't seem to know that the war they are fighting is important and worth while, which it most assuredly is.

The South East Asia Command is a long way off: it is apt to be overshadowed in Europe by the climax of the war against Germany and in the Pacific by the advances of Admiral Nimitz and General MacArthur. Therefore a major effort by Allied forces, doing their duty in inhospitable places, has been somewhat crowded out and the forces have not received their proportion of credit. My purpose this afternoon is to put their achievements before you.

Enemy-held territory in the South East Asia theatre extends 2,500 miles southwards from the north of Burma. The front on which we are at present fighting in Burma alone extends some 700 miles and is second only in length to the Russian Front. It is the hard land crust which protects the Japanese conquests in China and Indo-China. It is Japan's land route to India and, more important, the Allies' land route to China. Both offensively and defensively Japan has strained and is straining every nerve to hold Burma.

In my appreciation of the achievements of the forces of South East Asia Command it must be borne in mind that the Japanese are fighting from interior lines. They control Burma's rivers, railways and roads, and since they are a rice-eating army they live off the fat of the land. We, on the other hand, are fighting from the most difficult lines of communication imaginable.

Before 1943 there were no roads into Burma from the north; while the lower reaches of the Brahmaputra River are unbridgeable. Assam is, in fact a logistical nightmare. Moreover advancing as we are from the west, we are fighting against the grain of the country, for its steep jungle-clad mountains and swift flowing rivers, all running north-south, constitute a barrier instead of a route between India and China.

In 1943 the imagination of the world was captured by a small force of British and Indian troops, under Brigadier Wingate, which made the first experiment in long range penetration and proved that we could outfight the Japanese in a kind of war which he had made his own and under conditions which were to his advantage. It was a harbinger of bigger things, but in itself, of course, the experiment was on a small scale.

At Quebec, the British and American Governments decided that the time had come to form an Allied operational command to take over the British Command from GHQ India and include the American Command in Burma and India and be responsible for land, sea and air operations against Japan in South East Asia.

In view of my original association with Combined Operations a lot of people, myself included, jumped to the conclusion that large scale amphibious operations in South East Asia would at once be the order of the day. It need now be no secret that all the landing ships and craft originally allotted had to be withdrawn for more urgent operations in the west, and, in fact, carried the troops that assaulted the Anzio beaches, and have subsequently been taking part in the invasion of France. The order to us in Burma was to carry on with what we had left.

Our plans had to be recast on a less ambitious scale but there was one thing we could do and that was to drive the Japanese out of the north-east corner of Burma, to improve our communications with China, and thus increase the supplies which are so badly needed to keep our Chinese Allies in the war, and to enable General Chennault to continue his effective operations with the US 14th Air Force from China.

A concerted plan was therefore made for the whole of the Burma Front to enable the forces in the north-east to advance. General Stilwell, Deputy Supreme Allied Commander and the Commanding General of the American forces in the China, Burma and India theatre, with great gallantry himself commanded the forces on the Ledo front.

General Stilwell had under his command those Chinese forces which he had originally withdrawn from Burma into India and which had since been augmented. These forces are a good example of Allied collaboration, being equipped and trained by the US and paid and fed by the English. 'Merrill's Marauders', of the American Rangers contributed valiantly to the successful advance of this force down the Hukawng valley to Myitkyina and Mogaung.

An advance in Burma is a different affair from an advance in France or Russia, since it has largely to be carried out along the single axis of your supply line and a relatively small force can thus stop the advance of a much larger force, however resolutely led. It thus became of the utmost importance that the overall plans for Burma should prevent Japanese reinforcements being able to bar the progress of the Chinese-American forces.

There were two ways in which the Fourteenth Army could most materially help the advance of the Ledo forces. Firstly by cutting the communications of the veteran Japanese 18th Division who were facing the Ledo front, and, secondly, by engaging the greater number of other Japanese Divisions elsewhere in Burma.

The first task, that of cutting the Japanese 18th Division's L of C, was given to General Wingate's Long Range Penetration forces which included a West African Brigade, and were flown into Burma by Colonel Cochran's Air Commandos, aided by British and American transport squadrons. The second task would have proved a more serious problem if it had not been that the Japanese plan was no less than an advance into India through Chittagong on the Arakan front and through Dimapur on the Imphal front.

This began when the advance of 15th Indian Corps was held by a Japanese encircling movement which cut off their Administrative troops and also the Headquarters of the 7th Indian Division. On February 23rd, after a heroic 17 days' battle, the encircled troops of 7th Division, aided by the rest of 15 Corps, inflicted our first medium scale land defeat on the Japanese.

The importance of the battle of the 7th Division 'Administrative Box' was twofold. First it was a victory of morale by men who refused to withdraw when their L of C were cut; the hitherto successful tactics of outflanking and infiltration were thus defeated. The second factor was the exploitation of air supply by American and British transport aircraft which enabled our forces in the Admin Box to be fully supplied throughout the siege.

On the 16 March three complete Japanese Divisions advanced across the River Chindwin and attacked all along the Manipur front with the avowed object of capturing the Imphal Plain and cutting the main rail L of C to General Stilwell's forces, and the Chinese Command, and subsequently, of invading India. Their radio and propaganda never ceased to boast that they were 'Marching on Delhi'. Further Japanese forces were moved up in support, but British and Indian forces were rushed to the defence of air, rail and road communications.

Although the enemy cut the main supply road from Dimapur to Imphal British and American air transport aircraft continued to supply the beleaguered garrisons by air; 33rd Indian Corps was moved in from Reserve and the British 2nd Division led the spearhead of the attack to clear the road. This Corps so severely battered the Japanese 31st Division that the remnants were forced to retire in disorder. Meanwhile 4th Indian Corps from Imphal were attacking to the south and eventually a major victory was secured over the whole Japanese force.

In point of numbers engaged this must have been one of the greatest land battles fought between the Japanese and British forces and I am glad to say the Japanese have now been flung out of India.

The Fourteenth Army's exploits under the leadership of Lieut-General Sir William Slim and the overall command of General Sir George Giffard, were deservedly praised by Mr Churchill in Parliament.

Meanwhile American and Chinese forces by a great feat of arms, crossed the Naun Hykit Pass and descended with complete surprise on the airfield at Myitkyina, thus enabling American and Chinese reinforcements to be flown in, in addition Long Range Penetration forces, of whom Maj-General Lentaigne assumed command when Wingate met his death in an air crash in the jungle, entered Mogaung from the south and were soon joined by the Chinese forces from the north.

It will thus be seen that the capture of Myitkyina and Mogaung was the result of a series of closely coordinated operations on the part of British, American, Chinese and West African troops. The 3rd Indian Division, as Long Range Penetration groups came to be known, now came under General Stilwell's command, on this section of the front. The death of Wingate was a great disaster. He was killed at the moment of triumph and fulfilment.

All these impressive results have not been secured without heavy casualties. Allied forces in 1944 have suffered 10,000 killed: 2,000 missing and 27,000 wounded, but these have been amply avenged by the killing of no fewer than 50,000 Japanese.

Even more deadly and persistent in inflicting casualties is the mosquito. Malaria has conquered empires and can cripple armies. In the British campaign in the Arakan in 1943 it inflicted a particularly heavy toll. The zeal and skill of American and British medical services have succeeded this year in reducing the ravages of malaria by no less than 40 per cent; particularly effective has been the development of advance treatment centres which have virtually perfected a lightning cure. More than 90 per cent of the patients report fit for duty after three weeks. All the same, since the beginning of the year Allied forces have suffered close on a quarter of a million casualties in Burma from sickness, mostly malaria and dysentery.

Parallel with the developments on land we have gained a major victory in the air. In December special measures were taken to co-ordinate the Allied air operations under Air Chief Marshal Sir Richard Peirse through Eastern Air Command, which is under the direction of Maj-General Stratemeyer USAAF, who is also Second-in-Command of all Allied Air Forces in South East Asia. We have practically swept the Japanese air force from the Burma skies. Between the formation of South East Asia Command in November 1943, and the middle of August 1944, American and British forces operating in Burma destroyed or damaged more than 700 Japanese aircraft with a further 100 'probables'. These simple statistics mean that the Japanese air force in Burma is greatly depleted and rarely ventures out either for attack or defence.

I mentioned air supply earlier. Since May alone we have carried by air just on 70,000 tons and 93,000 men, including 25,500 casualties.

These figures exclude the great air supply with China and have been accomplished under the worst flying conditions possible.

By sea also we have not been idle. The Eastern Fleet under Admiral Sir James Somerville, now succeeded by Admiral Sir Bruce Fraser, had been increasing their pressure to see whether they could entice the Japanese fleet into action or else to contain part of them in the Malacca Straits and thus keep them from interfering with the American operations in the Pacific. Our fleet's first move was an air strike from the sea in April on Sabang which proved highly successful and left the Allied Eastern Fleet unscathed. Their next move took them further afield and with the aid of a US aircraft carrier, which had also been in the first Sabang operations, they made a very successful strike on Sourabaya, followed by a strike against the Andaman Islands.

In the knowledge that we had complete command of the Indian Ocean and the Japanese had reduced their air defences to a low level we decided not only to strike from the air but to ride in and bombard with all types of surface craft from battleships to cruisers and destroyers. Sabang was again selected as a target of strategic importance to the Japanese.

The Royal Navy has received valuable help from the Royal Indian Navy and various American and Dutch naval units. The RIN has helped to maintain the bases for the Eastern Fleet to operate from and provided a very valuable addition to convoy escorts.

I should like to take this opportunity of paying a tribute to the Government of India and the India Command. The importance of India as a base from which operations are launched in South East Asia cannot be over-emphasised.

I would like to stress in particular the personal help and support I have received from Lord Wavell and General Auchinleck also from my deputy, General Stilwell, whose long experience of the east has been of signal assistance to me in our common task.

I am glad to have had this opportunity of endeavouring to explain the significance of the 1944 Burma campaign. I am proud of the gallant fighting which has taken place on all fronts and I hope that my statement may make the people who read it proud of the achievements of their own countrymen and grateful to their Allies who helped them in these achievements.

APPENDIX 2

British Malaya Command
February 1942

Malaya Command Lt Gen A. E. Percival
Singapore Fortress Maj Gen F. K. Simmons — Southern Area
    1 Malaya Inf Bde Brig G. G. R. Williams
    2 Malaya Inf Bde Brig F. H. Fraser
    Straits Settlements Volunteer Bde Col Grimwood

Command Reserve — Reserve Area
    12 Indian Inf Bde Brig A. C. M. Paris

8 Australian Div Maj Gen H. G. Bennett — Western Area
    22 Australian Inf Bde Brig H. B. Taylor
    27 Australian Inf Bde Brig D. S. Maxwell
    44 Indian Inf Bde Brig G. C. Ballentine

3 Indian Corps Lt Gen Sir Lewis Heath — Northern Area
    11 Indian Div Maj Gen B. W. Key
    28 Indian Inf Bde Brig W. R. Selby
    55 (British) Inf Bde Brig C. L. B. Duke
    8 Indian Inf Bde Brig W. A. Trott — (Div Reserve)
    18 (British) Div Maj Gen M. B. Beckwith Smith
    54 (British) Inf Bde Brig E. K. W. Backhouse
    55 (British) Inf Bde Brig J. B. Coates
    15 Indian Inf Bde Brig J. B. Coates — (Corps Reserve)

Japanese Twenty-fifth Army
February 1942

Twenty-fifth Army Lt Gen T. Yamashita

5 Div Maj Gen T. Matsui
   11 Inf Rgt
   41 Inf Rgt
   21 Inf Bde Maj Gen E. Sugiura
   21 Inf Rgt
   42 Inf Rgt

18 Div Lt Gen R. Mutaguchi
   23 Inf Bde Maj Gen H. Takuma
   55 Inf Rgt
   56 Inf Rgt
   35 Inf Bde Maj Gen K. Kawaguchi
   114 Inf Rgt (less one coy)
   (124 Inf Rgt)

Imperial Guards Division Lt Gen T. Nishimura
   3 Guards Inf Rgt (less 2 Bns)
   4 Guards Inf Rgt
   5 Guards Inf Rgt

77 Indian Infantry Brigade (Chindits) February 1943

NORTHERN (No 2) GROUP
Brigade HQ Brig O. C. Wingate
Group HQ Lt Col S. A. Cooke
   No 3 Column Maj J. M. Calvert
   No 4 Column Maj R. B. G. Bromhead
   No 5 Column Maj B. E. Fergusson
   No 7 Column Maj K. D. Gilkes
   No 8 Column Maj W. P. Scott
   2 Burma Rifles Lt Col L. G. Wheeler
Independent Mission Capt D. C. Herring

SOUTHERN (No 1) GROUP
Group HQ Lt Col L. A. Alexander
   No 1 Column Maj G. Dunlop

No 2 Column Maj A. Emmett
142 Commando Company Maj J. B. Jeffries

Allied Land Forces in South East Asia
December 1943

South East Asia Command Vice Adm Lord Louis Mountbatten   Delhi

Eleventh Army Group Gen Sir George Giffard   Delhi
Fourteenth Army Lt Gen W. J. Slim   Calcutta (later Comilla)
15 Corps Lt Gen A. F. P. Christison   Arakan
    5 Indian Div
    7 Indian Div
    81 West African Div (less 3 W. A. Bde)
4 Corps Lt Gen G. A. P. Scoones   Imphal
    17 Indian Div
    20 Indian Div
    23 Indian Div
Northern Combat Area Command Lt Gen J. W. Stilwell   Ledo
    22 Chinese Div
    30 Chinese Div
    38 Chinese Div
Army Reserve
    26 Indian Div
    254 Indian Tank Bde
Ceylon Army Lt Gen H. E. de R. Wetherall   Colombo
    11 East African Div
    99 Indian Infantry Bde
    Mobile Naval Base Defence Organisation, Royal Marines
33 Corps Lt Gen M. G. N. Stopford   India
    2 (British) Div
    36 Indian Div
    19 Indian Div
    25 Indian Div
    50 Indian Tank Bde
50 Indian Parachute Bde   India

Special Forces Maj Gen O. C. Wingate India
   77 Indian Bde
   111 Indian Bde
   14 (British) Bde
   16 (British) Bde
   23 (British) Bde
   3 West African Bde
3 Commando Bde

Japanese Land Forces, Burma
January 1944

Southern Area Army F. M. Count H. Terauchi
Burma Army Lt Gen M. Kawabe
   18 Div Hukawng Valley area
   56 Div Salween front
   24 Independent Mixed Bde Tenasserim
Fifteenth Army Lt Gen R. Mutaguchi
   15 Div Arriving Chindwin front
   31 Div Chindwin front
   33 Div Chindwin front
   1 Div Indian National Army Chindwin front
Twenty-eighth Army Lt Gen S. Sakurai
   2 Div Arriving South Arakan
   54 Div Northern Arakan
   55 Div Northern Arakan

Japanese Land Forces, Burma
January 1945

Southern Area Army F. M. Count H. Terauchi
   Burma Area Army Lt Gen H. Kimura
   Thirty-third Army Lt Gen M. Honda Northern Sector
   18 Div
   56 Div
   Fifteenth Army Lt Gen S. Katamura Central Sector

15 Div	North of Mandalay
31 Div	Mandalay area
33 Div	Mandalay to Pakokku area
53 Div	In reserve Kyaukse area
1 Div Indian National Army	Pakokku area
Twenty-eighth Army Lt Gen S. Sakurai	Southern Sector
54 Div	
55 Div	
24 Independent Mixed Bde	
Area Army Reserve	
2 Div	
49 Div	

The Indian National Army

1 Div Mohammed Zaman Kiyani
   1 Guerrilla Rgt, or Subhas Brigade Col Shah Nawaz Khan
Three infantry battalions
   2 Guerrilla Rgt, or Gandhi Brigade Col Inayat Kiani
Two infantry battalions
   3 Guerrilla Rgt, or Azad Brigade Col Gulzara Singh
Three battalions
   4 Guerrilla Rgt, or Nehru Brigade Lt Col G. S. Dhillon

2 Div
Aziz Ahmed
Formed after U-GO had begun it drew recruits from an earlier INA formation.
1 Inf Rgt merged with the 5 Guerrilla Rgt to form the 2 Inf Rgt Col Prem Sahgal
It had a large number of Malay and Burmese civilian volunteers and was well armed and equipped.
   5 Guerrilla Rgt

3 Div
Composed chiefly of local volunteers in Malaya and Singapore it was

disbanded before Japan surrendered. There was also a motor transport division, but it had limited capability or resources.

The Rani of Jhansi Regiment
  Lakshmi Sahgal
  A force of Malay and Burmese female volunteers

ACKNOWLEDGEMENTS

We Gave Our Today is not the work of a single writer. As with all books it has been the product of a team: Ian Drury who proposed the idea and title, Alan Samson of Weidenfeld & Nicolson who took it on, and Keith Lowe who as editor gave the final book its shape and cohesion.

However without the quotes from vivid first-hand accounts of John Randle in *Battle Tales from Burma* and John Hudson in *Sunset in the East* it would have been dry history. I would like to thank Pen & Sword Books Ltd for permission to use these quotes.

Writer and historian Max Arthur teamed with the Imperial War Museum Sound Archives to produce the superb *Forgotten Voices of the Second World War*. In previous books veterans from World War I to the Falklands have talked frankly to Max about their experience of war in all its raw intensity. I am grateful to him and the Imperial War Museum for permission to use quotations from *Forgotten Voices of the Second World War*.

Ted Nevill of Cody Images has provided many of the photographs that have helped to give a sense of the terrain of Burma and the men on both sides who fought there. I am grateful to fellow Royal British Legion battlefield guide Colonel Mike Bradley for permission to use his photograph of the grave of Lt George Knowland VC.

My thanks also go to the many friends who have taken the time to share their ideas and insights with me about Burma and its place in World War II.

Finally thanks to my wife who has provided love and support from the beginning to the completion of *We Gave Our Today*.

NOTES

The Man

[1] *A Child at Arms*, Patrick Davis, Hutchinson & Co, 1970

[2] *Images of War*, Marshall Cavendish, 1990

[3] *Echoes from Forgotten Wars*, R. McKie, William Collins, 1980

[4] http://www.burmastar.org.uk/slim.htm

[5] Recruited from the mountainous kingdom of Nepal to the north of India, Gurkhas would serve the crown on the North West Frontier and in World War I 100,000 fought in France and the Middle East. At Gallipoli they were the only troops to reach the ridgeline that overlooked the straits. It was only in World War I that Gurkhas became eligible for the Victoria Cross.

In all, 26 Victoria Crosses have been awarded to Gurkha Regiments for acts of extreme bravery in the face of the enemy. Some 6,500 Gurkhas have been decorated for bravery, 45,000 have been killed in action and 150,000 seriously wounded.

[6] In *An Improvised War* Michael Glover says of the Essex 'even the best troops can panic and the unfortunate Essex, ill-led, ill-trained and subjected to the horrors of unopposed bombing on their first contact with war, can only be regarded as unfortunate. They were withdrawn from the line, retrained, reorganised and in time became a worthy battalion.'

[7] http://www.burmastar.org.uk/slim.htm

[8] *The Campaign in Burma*, Lt Col Frank Owen OBE, HMSO, 1946. The heavily illustrated paperback prepared for South East Asia Command (SEAC) by the Central Office of Information had seven maps and 93 photographs and was the first history of the war in Burma. Colonel Owen OBE had a readable style that included some subtle biblical and literary references and a good mix of anecdote and human interest alongside the key facts of the campaign. With many of the senior officers alive and vigorous he had to temper the detail and accuracy of his record with discretion, but it still stands the test of history. The cover photograph of an unshaven cigarette-smoking British Bren gunner wearing a battered bush hat encapsulates the tough no-nonsense efficiency of the Fourteenth Army.

[9] *Four Samurai – A Quartet of Japanese Army Commanders in the Second World War*, Arthur Swinson, Hutchinson, 1968

[10] File 99, Auchinleck Papers

[11] *Defeat into Victory*, Field Marshal Sir William Slim, Cassell and Co, 1956
[12] Ibid.

Chapter 1: Rising Sun

[13] *Images of War*, issue 9, Volume 1, Marshall Cavendish
[14] *Japan at War an Oral History*
[15] Ibid.
[16] *Spearhead General*, Henry Maule, Odhams Press, 1961
[17] Tsuji, M., *Singapore 1941–42: The Japanese Version of the Malayan Campaign of World War II*, Sydney, NSW, 1960 quoted in *World War II Jungle Warfare Tactics*, Dr Stephen Bull, Osprey Publishing, 2007
[18] British Pamphlet 'Japanese in Battle' quoted in *Soldiers of the Sun*, Meirion and Susie Harries, William Heinemann, 1991
[19] *Spearhead General*

Chapter 2: Disaster and Defeat

[20] http://www.bbc.co.uk/history/worldwars/wwtwo/battleships_02.shtml
[21] *Images of War*
[22] Thailand had signed a military alliance with Japan on December 21, 1941 and as part of this agreement three infantry and one cavalry division with armoured reconnaissance troops would cross into Burma's Shan States on May 10, 1942 to attack elements of the Chinese Ninety-third Army. The Thai forces captured the town of Kengtung the main objective on May 27. Renewed offensives in June and November drove the Chinese further back into Yunnan. Though the operational boundary between the Japanese and Thai forces was the Salween River the Karenni States, south of the Shan States and the homeland of the Karens, was specifically retained under Japanese control. In 1945 the Shan States were abandoned and reoccupied by the Chinese.
[23] *Grim Glory*, Gilbert Mant, Currawong, Sydney, 1942 rev. edn 1955
[24] Charles Anderson was born in Cape Town, South Africa on February 12, 1897. He was awarded the Military Cross in World War I while serving with the King's African Rifles in East Africa. In 1934 he emigrated to Australia and bought a farm near Crowther, New South Wales.

Between the wars he served in the Citizen Military Forces (a volunteer militia similar to the British Territorial Army or US National Guard) and then on July 1, 1940 enlisted in the AIF. He was appointed second in command of 2/19 Battalion when it was formed in late July 1940. The AIF left for Malaya in February 1941 and Anderson was promoted to command of 2/19 on August 1, 1941.

When Singapore fell on February 15, 1942 he became a prisoner along with about 15,000 Australian soldiers. For his leadership and bravery at Muar River he was awarded the Victoria Cross and would be the only Australian unit commander to be so honoured in World War II.

After the war he returned to farming and between 1949 and 1961 was involved in state politics. He retired to Canberra. Charles Anderson VC died on Remembrance

Day, November 11, 1988 and was buried with full military honours in Canberra six days later.

[25] The prickly commander of 2 ('Konoe') Imperial Guards Division, Lt Gen. Takuma Nishimura, was forcibly retired from the Japanese Army in 1942. He had demanded that the Imperial Guards have an equal share in the attack on Singapore but was regarded as petulant and uncooperative by Yamashita. Following the fall of Singapore he organised a memorial service for his dead a day before the official Twenty-fifth Army ceremony. When the Commander-in-Chief Southern Army Count Terauchi was informed of his attitude he refused to grant the Imperial Guards Division the Emperor's Victory Citation which was a supreme disgrace.

In 1945 Nishimura was brought back to Singapore, tried by a British military court in relation to the Sook Ching massacre of Chinese civilians in 1942 and the murder of Allied prisoners at the Muar River. Nishimura received a life sentence, of which he served four years. As he was returning to Japan, Australian Military Police boarded his ship at Hong Kong, removed him and charged him in relation to the Park Sulong massacre. Nishimura was taken to Manus Island, New Guinea, evidence was presented to an Australian military court stating that Nishimura had ordered the shootings at Parit Sulong and the destruction of bodies. He was convicted and hanged on June 11, 1951.

[26] Tsuji, M., *Singapore 1941–42: The Japanese Version of the Malayan Campaign of World War II*, Sydney, NSW, 1960

[27] *Images of War*

[28] *War Diaries 1939–1945*, Field Marshal Lord Alanbrooke, Weidenfeld & Nicolson, 2001

[29] Some days later the Japanese went to Changi jail and demanded that the officer who had carried the Union Flag should surrender it. 'You cannot have it. It does not exist. I burned it that same night on the ramparts of Fort Canning looking towards England and home.' It was an honourable explanation entirely understandable to the Japanese. In fact the flag remained hidden in the jail and during the next three years was used for funerals for men who had died in captivity. On September 12, 1945, the day that Singapore was formally liberated, the Union Flag was raised over the city.

[30] *Life on a Square-Wheeled Bike*, George Sprod, Kangaroo, Sydney, 1983

[31] *Singapore 1941–42: The Japanese Version of the Malayan Campaign of World War II*

[32] BBC broadcast February 15, 1942 quoted in *the Daily Telegraph Record of the Second World War*, Sidgwick & Jackson, 1989

[33] *The War in the Far East 1941–1945*, Basil Collier, William Heinemann, 1969

[34] *Soldiers of the Sun*, Meirion and Susie Harries, William Heinemann, 1991

Chapter 3: Out of Burma

[35] The West African soldiers who fought in Burma were loyal members of the Burma Star Association even into the 21st Century, much to the delight and surprise of British soldiers posted to Sierra Leone.

[36] In *Slim as a Military Commander* Geoffrey Evans points out that the Burma Army consisted of six battalions of the Burma Frontier Force composed of Indians not Burmans and effectively an armed police force. Half of the strength of the Burma

Rifles had been raised since the outbreak of war. The Burma Army was actually drawn from four different races – Chins, Kachins, Karens and Burmans. All spoke a different language, only after emergency commissioned officers had been posted from the big industrial firms in Burma were they led by British officers who spoke their language. As Masters observes the Burmese troops had family in the country and Evans notes, 'there were many desertions during the fighting by men who returned to their homes to protect their families and this naturally brought about an unreliability which had a very adverse effect on operations.' Those men of the Burma Rifles who remained with the Fourteenth Army were a major asset with their local knowledge and command of linguistic skills.

[37] http://www.mgtrust.org/afr2.htm

[38] Masters, John, *The Road Past Mandalay*, Michael Joseph, 1961

[39] The responsibility placed on a British officer in the British Indian Army was considerably greater than that within the British Army in the UK. Within an infantry battalion there were only about 12 British officers – the Commanding Officer (CO), his Second in Command, Adjutant, Quartermaster, the four Rifle Company Commanders, Signals Officer, Motor Transport Officer and two Company Officers in the Rifle Companies and an Indian Medical Service, Medical Officer. However the CO could rely on his Subedar Major a rank that carried greater responsibilities than those of a British Regimental Sergeant Major. The Subedar Major was an Indian officer who had reached the top of the parallel promotion structure open to Indian soldiers. He would advise the CO on a multitude of subjects including religion, promotions and morale and attitudes in the battalion.

[40] British Military Intelligence was not able to establish the exact organisation and strength of the Indian National Army (INA) since its records held in Rangoon, by the Azad Hind Government the political arm, were destroyed in 1945.

There were three divisions, though the lightly armed 1 Division was the only force to play a significant role. 'The two divisions in Burma were a military joke,' writes Jon Latimer in *Burma The Forgotten War*, 'amounting to only around 6,000 men. In the "March on Delhi" they were employed as decoys, trying to persuade Indian troops facing the Japanese to defect, much to the latter's amusement.'

[41] The 1905 Japanese 6.5mm Arisaka Rifle Type 38 was a development of the earlier Type 30 rifle designed by Colonel Arisaka and was often referred to by the Japanese as the Arisaka Sampachi (or Sampachi Shiki Hoheiju).

Snipers used two types of bolt action rifle, the 6.5mm Arisaka Type 97 fitted with a x 2.5 scope or the 7.7mm Arisaka Type 99 with a x 4 scope. In the early years of the war men armed with the Type 97 fired a special 'smokeless and flashless' ammunition – because the rifle had a long 31-inch barrel the flash and smoke from the 30 grain nitro-cellulose reduced charge round was eliminated.

Writing of these snipers in *Sniper Rifles of Two World Wars* William Tatum IV comments that though 'the Japanese sniper was not the best sniper in the war . . . he certainly worked hard at the job, and few Japanese snipers were taken alive. He was very patient and had plenty of fine physical endurance. He had one other strong point, he was not afraid to die.'

[42] *Soldiers of the Sun*

[43] *The Campaign in Burma*

[44] TM-E 30–480 Handbook on Japanese Military Forces, United States Government Printing Office, Washington, 1944

[45] *Forgotten Voices of the Second World War*, Max Arthur, Ebury Press, 2004

[46] *Sunset in the East*

[47] *The Little Men*, K. W. Cooper, Robert Hale, 1973

[48] Ibid.

[49] *Forgotten Voices of the Second World War*

[50] Aung San was born in 1915 Natmauk in Magwe in Central Burma, his father U Pha was a well-to-do lawyer and a Communist and along with his mother was active in independence politics. It was a long tradition, his great-uncle Bo Min Yaung had fought the British annexation in 1886. As a student Aung San was politically active and eventually on a British wanted list. On the run in China in 1940 he was recruited by the Japanese who saw the opportunity to use his nationalist ideals for their own ends. Eventually Aung San became disenchanted with the Japanese and switched allegiance to the British near the close of the war.

He married in 1942 and his youngest daughter the Nobel Peace Prize laureate Aung San Suu Kyi leader of the Burmese pro-democracy party, the National League for Democracy (NLD) continues the family tradition with her opposition to the current military regime.

[51] Born on October 25, 1893 in Teignmouth in England John, George 'Jackie' Smyth, later Brigadier Sir John 1st Baronet, was a 21-year-old Lieutenant in 15 Ludhiana Sikhs on May 18, 1915 near Richebourg L'Aouve in France in World War I, commanding a ten-man fighting patrol. He and his men had lugged a box containing a total of 96 grenades (then known as bombs) to within 20 yards of the German trenches. While under heavy small arms and artillery fire Smyth had to swim a stream to get the grenades in position for an attack. Two other patrols had failed in the attempt and eight of his men were either killed or wounded in this operation. For his bravery in this patrol Smyth was awarded the Victoria Cross.

He was already ill and exhausted following the Sittang disaster when Wavell relieved him of his command on February 29.

After World War II Smyth went into politics but also established a reputation as an author, playwright, journalist and broadcaster. He died at Marylebone, London on April 26, 1983.

[52] Bryan Perrett in *Tank Tracks to Rangoon* writes of this ballad that it 'places the city in a highly debatable geographic context, as the administrative capital of Burma is many hundreds of miles from the sea, and the prospects of seeing flying fish, old flotillas of British Ironclads, or the possibility of watching the dawn rise over China, "cross the bay", suggests that the poet was under unusual strain'.

[53] *Forgotten Voices of the Second World War*

[54] *The Campaign in Burma*

[55] *Diary of Lt D. H. West* quoted in *Burma the Forgotten War*

[56] *The Campaign in Burma*

[57] The four-man M3A1 Stuart Mk III deployed by 7 Armoured Brigade had two inches of armour protection and was armed with a 37mm M6 gun, three 0.30-inch

machine guns. The 14ft 10-inch long tank was powered by a Continental W-670, 7-cylinder, radial, petrol engine that gave an impressive top speed of 36 mph and range of 70 miles. By now the vehicle was becoming obsolescent in the European theatre but would give sterling service in Burma against Japanese armour and infantry.

[58] *Battle Tales from Burma*, John Randle, Pen & Sword, 2004

[59] *Tank Tracks to Rangoon The Story of British Armour in Burma*, Bryan Perrett, Robert Hale, 1978

[60] The little 37mm Type 97 anti-tank gun was a modified copy of the German 3.7cm Pak 35/36 and could penetrate 38mm of armour at 400 yards.

[61] *Defeat into Victory*

[62] Ibid.

[63] The division commanded by General Sun-li-jen enjoyed the reputation of being one of the best in the Chinese Army. As Bryan Perrett notes in *Tank Tracks to Rangoon*, 'In spite of being entirely deficient in artillery, tanks, transport and indeed any heavy equipment, they were considered to be a very brave and valuable fighting force, and what they lacked in skill they made up for in guts. Their officers made a point of being conspicuous in action, with the result that their casualties were high amongst the commissioned ranks. Morale and discipline were excellent, and they regarded evacuation through wounds or sickness to be a form of disgrace.'

[64] On September 2, 1945 both Wainwright and Percival stood behind MacArthur to witness the final Japanese surrender aboard the USS *Missouri* in Tokyo Bay.

Much to MacArthur's annoyance Wainwright was awarded the Medal of Honor for his heroic defence and stoicism as a PoW. In contrast Percival was largely ignored by the British military and political establishment.

[65] *Slim as a Military Commander*, Geoffrey Evans, B. T. Batsford, 1969

[66] *Defeat into Victory*

[67] *Slim, Master of War*, Robert Lyman, Robinson, 2004

Chapter 4: The First Arakan Offensive

[68] *Forgotten Voices of the Second World War*

[69] Ibid.

[70] The division was made up of 47, 55, 88, and 123 Indian Bdes to which were added later 4, 23, 36 and 71 Indian Bdes and 6 British Bde that was borrowed from 2 British Division.

[71] *The Campaign in Burma*

[72] The 17-ton Valentine had a crew of three and was armed with a 2pdr gun and one 7.92mm (0.31in) Besa machine gun. Armour protection ranged from 0.32in to 2.56in. It was 19ft 4in long, 8ft 8in wide and 7ft 6in high. The engine was either a 6-cylinder diesel or petrol that produced a top speed of 14.9 mph and range of 90 miles. This was the only time that gun-armed Valentines were used in Burma, though armoured bridgelayers were employed later in the campaign.

[73] *The Campaign in Burma*

[74] Along with Cavendish his Brigade Major and Operations Officer were captured though Captain W. D. Rees the Brigade Intelligence Officer, who was wounded, survived by feigning death. Tragically Cavendish was killed by British artillery fire,

though reports circulated at the time that he had been murdered. These were fuelled by the discovery of his socks on the corpse of a Japanese soldier killed in an ambush.
[75] *Forgotten Voices of the Second World War.*

In World War II Gurkha recruits were issued with mass-produced Indian government kukris but nearly all soldiers brought back their own from their first home leave.

Ordinary kukri blades vary in quality. Superior ones are forged from railway track or car springs. The scabbards are made of wood covered in leather, with a metal cap protecting the point. Two pockets on the back hold a blunt steel for sharpening the blade or striking sparks from flint (the chakmak) and a little knife (the karda) is used for skinning small game or as a penknife, some also have a small purse for the flint.

Most handles are made of wood, often walnut. They are secured to the blade either by rivets through a two-piece hilt or by the tang inserted through a one-piece grip and riveted over the cap.

Though the notch (kaura) in the blade near the hilt may act as a check to excessive blood on the hilt, and be used to catch and neutralise an enemy blade, it is essentially a Hindu religious and phallic symbol.

A story circulated in Burma that Slim early in his command of Fourteenth Army had encouraged constant patrolling by all forward units. Gurkhas returning from a successful fighting patrol presented themselves before their General, proudly opened a large basket, produced three gory Japanese heads, and then politely offered him the freshly caught fish which filled the rest of the basket.
[76] *The Campaign in Burma*

Chapter 5: Chindits

[77] Born in India on March 6, 1913 James Michael Calvert would win a bar to his DSO and the nickname 'Mad Mike' for his personal courage. He died in the Royal Star and Garter Home in Richmond on November 26, 1998, at the age of 85.

He had a varied and distinguished military career during and immediately after World War II. At the end of the war 'private armies' like the SAS and Army Commandos were disbanded so when the Communist insurgency broke out in Malaya there were virtually no units in the British Army with experience of unconventional warfare.

With his experience and background Calvert was sent to evaluate the problem. His analysis proposed that the insurgency could be defeated by 'a man with a plan and the power to carry it out'; this proved critical and General Sir Gerald Templer was sent to Malaya in February 1952, with substantial military and civil powers.

A further suggestion from Calvert was that a force be created within the British Army that could live and move in the jungle, like the guerrillas. This was accepted and Calvert, who had commanded the SAS in Europe at the close of World War II, was given the task of setting up a unit known as Malayan Scouts. It would operate in deep jungle areas not already covered by other security forces. As a 'Special Forces' formation drawn from volunteers within the armed forces the Malayan Scouts contained both good and bad – there was no selection process and the bad men gave the good a poor reputation. However the Scouts would lay the foundations for the resurrection of the Special Air Service and the formation of 22 SAS Regiment.

241

[78] *Beyond the Chindwin*, Bernard Fergusson, Collins, 1945

[79] *The Campaign in Burma*

[80] *Forgotten Voices of the Second World War*

[81] *Central Asian Revue*, June 1944

[82] *Beyond the Chindwin*

[83] Each man carried about 72 pounds on his back. This load consisted of seven days' rations, a rifle and bayonet, a dah or kukri (machete or Gurkha knife), three 36 Grenades, ground sheet, spare shirt and trousers, four pairs of socks, balaclava helmet (knitted head cover) jack knife, rubber-soled sports shoes, housewife (clothing repair kit), toggle rope, canvas life jacket, mess tin, ration bags, water bottle and a chagal (canvas water carrier) besides any items of personal kit.

[84] Memorial Gate Trust http://www.mgtrust.org/ind2.htm

[85] *Beyond the Chindwin*

[86] The aerial re-supply workhorse in Burma was the superb Douglas DC-3 Dakota that had begun life before the war as a commercial airliner manufactured at the Douglas plant at Santa Monica in California.

The United States Army Air Force (USAAF) designated it C-47 and called it the Skytrain, while the RAF who operated over 1,200 of the aircraft called it the Dakota. During the first Chindit expedition an RAF Dakota landed in a clearing to evacuate casualties – it would be a pointer to the future. Fitted with folding bench seats it was used as a troop transport carrying 28 fully armed soldiers while with a reinforced floor and wider doors it was used for 2.6 tons of cargo, a representative load being two Jeeps, a 6-Pounder anti-tank gun, or 14 freight baskets. The Dakota had a span of 95 feet, was powered by two 1200 hp Pratt and Whitney 'Twin Wasp' R-1830 engines and had a top speed of 230 mph. Total production reached 10,123 aircraft.

[87] Born in 1888 in Saga prefecture, Japan, Mutaguchi was a tough seasoned professional who had entered the Army in December 1910 and as a regimental commander was involved in the 'Marco Polo Bridge Incident' in China in 1937. In April 1939 he was promoted to Lt General and command of 18 Division in China. For the invasion of Malaya the division was initially split with 13,000 men being detached and assigned to Twenty-fifth Army with the HQ and two regiments remaining in China. The Takuma Detachment and Koba Regiment landed at Kota Bharu on December 8, 1941. The main body of the division landed at Singora on January 23, 1942 and five days later the division was reunited at Kluang.

For the attack on Singapore it was given the right flank. Leading from the front Mutaguchi was wounded in the left shoulder after crossing Singapore Strait. His division combined with the 5th for a night attack on Bukit Timah heights on February 10–11, 1942.

Powerfully built, shaven headed and with a neat moustache, in 1943 Mutaguchi's star was in the ascendant. Before the war his sympathies had been with the Kodo-Ha 'Imperial Way' faction of the army who were fanatically loyal to the Emperor. He agreed with the aims of the young Kodo-Ha officers who were executed for rebellion on February 26, 1936.

His ability to act quickly and personal bravery meant that his subordinates respected but did not like him. He was ruthless, during operation U-GO the attack on the

British Fourteenth Army in India he would sack three divisional commanders one of whom – Kotoku Sato – had become so angry with his bullying and irrational manner that he refused a direct order.

Though he was a deep believer in the Samurai code of Bushido he clearly did not accept any responsibility for the terrible suffering and losses he would inflict on the troops under his command or his failure. Suicide as the ultimate apology was not considered. He was transferred to General Staff HQ Tokyo and retired in December 1944 to become Director of the Junior Course at the Military Academy until the surrender in August 1945. At this juncture, when other senior Japanese could not face the shame of defeat and took their own lives, Mutaguchi, a man who was known to enjoy favourable newspaper coverage and the private pleasures of alcohol and women, accepted the new order and lived on – dying at the age of 76 on August 2, 1966.

[88] *The Campaign in Burma*

[89] Leonard Marsland Gander was a prolific correspondent for the *Daily Telegraph* who would cover the war from the Battle of France in 1940 to the London Victory Parade in June 1946. Though the world has shrunk with air travel and satellite communications modern reporters will feel a kindred sympathy with him when he noted, 'My relations with the *Daily Telegraph* office were peculiar. Skelton, the assistant editor in charge of news, usually had no idea where I was and equipped apparently with a penny atlas sent impossible demands when he did not know. I was now ordered to Rangoon. His cable ran, "Agree Calcutta and Lashio [China] *en route* for Rangoon, but want you Colombo earliest." '

Ruefully Gander later noted, 'After nearly five months of travel by sea, air, gharry, taxi and my two feet I had achieved virtually nothing.'

[90] *The Campaign in Burma*
[91] *Spearhead General*
[92] *The Campaign in Burma*
[93] *Wingate in Peace and War*, Derek Tulloch, Macdonald and Company, 1972
[94] *Eagle against the Sun*, Ronald H. Spector, Viking, 1984

Chapter 6: Chindits and Marauders

[95] Cochran was a skilled and daring pilot who at the age of 33 had the unusual distinction of becoming the hero in a comic strip series in a US newspaper entitled 'Flip Corkran's Adventures'.

[96] *Forgotten Voices of the Second World War*

[97] By June 1944 the IJAAF in Burma comprising 4, 5 and 12 Air Divisions had a strength of 161 aircraft compared to the 1,500 RAF and USAAF aircraft in theatre.

[98] Born in 1903, Merrill had joined the army as a private soldier at the age of 18. He passed the entrance examination for the officers' academy at West Point six times before the authorities were willing to overlook his short-sightedness and accept him as a candidate. He was commissioned into the US Cavalry in 1929. Merrill had been in Rangoon at the start of World War II and served in Burma as Chief of Staff to General Stilwell. Merrill had previously served as military attaché in Tokyo before the war, spoke Japanese and had familiarised himself with Japanese tactics and military philosophy. During operations in Burma Merrill suffered two heart attacks and was

temporarily evacuated with command passing to his second in command. Following Stilwell's posting back to the United States Merrill was promoted to Deputy US Commander in the Burma-Indian theatre and later became Chief of Staff of the US 10th Army in the Pacific. He died in 1950.

[99] *Reports of General MacArthur: Japanese Operations*, Vol. 2, Part 2

[100] *Eagle against the Sun*

[101] Ibid.

[102] In *The Little Men*, Ken Cooper with the Border Regiment recalled American K-Rations on which he and his fellow soldiers had subsisted for months. 'They came in wax packets containing small tins (about one and a half inches in diameter) of pork and beans, jam, bacon and egg and similar mixtures. Included in each container were two Camel or Lucky Strike cigarettes and a couple of matches. The wax wrappers would burn like a miniature camp fire, long enough to heat up a mug of water for making tea.'

[103] The Ledo Road ran from Ledo in Assam south into the Hukawng Valley, then to Kamaing and Bhamo and then east to Wanting in China terminating at Kunming. It was intended to replace the Burma Road as a land link to China. Under the direction of General Stilwell work on this remarkable engineering project began in October 1943 but was delayed until Myitkyina had fallen and it was only completed on January 27, 1945. A projected oil pipeline, planned to run alongside the road was never completed.

[104] Lt Col Charles N. Hunter, *Galahad*, San Antonio, 1963 quoted in *Eagle against the Sun*

[105] As the infantry section automatic weapon the Bren gun would become a World War II VC winner, when a corporal or soldier would use it to lethal effect against the enemy at close range. The gun was initially built at the Royal Small Arms Factory at Enfield Lock, London and was based on the ZB 26 an LMG design from the Czechoslovakian Brno small arms factory. The two factory names were combined to produce the name Bren and an iconic light machine gun that soldiered from World War II and in 7.62mm NATO calibre right to the First Gulf War in 1991. The Bren was an air-cooled gas-operated gun that fired a .303-inch round from a 30-round box magazine. It had a slow rate of fire around 500 rpm, but was very accurate with sights set out to 2,000 yards and light – it weighed only 22.12 pounds and was 45.5 inches long. The gun could be fired from the hip which made it ideal in the attack. The Bren was easy to strip and experienced gunners could change magazines or barrels in less than five seconds. Brens were also made in Australia, Canada and India during the course of the war.

[106] He survived the war and in 2007 aged 84 living in Nepal and suffering from diabetes, high blood pressure, heart problems, asthma, poor eyesight and hearing difficulties, applied for indefinite leave to enter Britain in order to receive proper medical support.

British Embassy officials in Nepal turned down the application on the grounds that they were 'not satisfied . . . your application meets the requirements' because you 'failed to demonstrate strong ties with the UK'.

After a massive campaign by the British public and supporters across the world, the British government eventually bowed to the weight of public pressure and on June 1, 2007 allowed Tul Bahadar Pun the right to live in Britain.

[107] *The Campaign in Burma*

[108] The 5307th did receive a tribute of sorts when the Raoul Walsh film *Objective Burma!* starring Errol Flynn was released in 1945. Flynn played the part of a US officer commanding an airborne unit modelled on Merrill's Marauders. He stormed through the jungle killing Japanese in droves. In Britain the film enraged the public so much that it was withdrawn after just one week since it implied that the victory in Burma had been entirely the work of US forces. '*Objective Burma!* was only screened in the UK in 1953 – preceded by an apology to the veterans of the Fourteenth Army.

[109] *Forgotten Voices of the Second World War*

Chapter 7: Arakan – The First Victory

[110] The main armament of the M3 was an M2 75mm gun mounted in the right side of the hull that could penetrate 2.36 inches of armour sloped at 30 degrees at a range of 547 yards but had only limited traverse, 30 degrees in azimuth and 29 degrees in elevation. The 37mm gun in the turret was fully rotatable by hand, a 360-degree sweep taking 20 seconds. At Imphal John Hudson recalled that 'General Grant [*sic*] tanks had rotary engines and our special treat was to stand with arms outstretched behind the open steel doors as the driver ran them at fast tick-over to blow warm air through our wet clothing and dry us out'.

[111] The M4 Sherman had a crew of five and was armed with one 75mm gun, one 0.5-inch and two 0.30-inch machine guns. The rugged and reliable Wright R-975-C1, radial, 9-cylinder engine produced a top speed of 24 mph and a range of 100 miles. Maximum armour protection of 2.45 inches was thin by European standards but sufficient against Japanese anti-tank guns.

[112] Of Messervy, an Indian Army cavalry officer, Slim would write in *Defeat into Victory*: 'He had had his ups and downs as a divisional commander in the Middle East, but I welcomed him as an offensively minded leader, steadied by experience and misfortune in a hard school.' Messervy would more than repay Slim's confidence.

[113] WO 208/3750 quoted in *Soldiers of the Sun*

[114] *The Campaign in Burma*

[115] Ibid.

[116] Ibid.

[117] Ibid.

[118] A bizarre example of the rigid adherence to orders by the Japanese at the Admin Box was what Messervy called the 'Ascot car park'. This was a large number of vehicles within the perimeter that were in full view of the Japanese and 100 large trucks carrying pontoons that were outside in no-man's-land. None of these vehicles was fired on by the Japanese who were under strict instructions to capture them intact so that they could be used to drive westwards in a victorious advance into India. Afterwards Messervy described how 'I decided to thin out the Ascot car park and stick some more of my motor transport into No Man's Land, an even more complete safety zone!'

[119] *The Forgotten War*

[120] After the Partition into India and Pakistan Nand Singh joined in the Indian Army and was killed in fighting between India and Pakistan in 1947. He was posthumously awarded the Maha Vir Chakra (MVC) the new nation's highest award for gallantry. He would become the only holder of the VC and MVC and the only VC of World War II to be killed in a subsequent conflict.

[121] *The Campaign in Burma*

[122] WO 208/1401 quoted in *Soldiers of the Sun*

[123] At the 1995 VE Day Celebrations in Hyde Park Singh met the Prime Minister John Major and complained about the paltry £168 annual pension paid to Indian VC holders. 'I don't think the prime minister speaks Hindi,' Singh said after the meeting, 'but when I talked to him he just said yes to everything.'

He had won a significant victory for himself and the then nine surviving Indian VC holders: after the meeting their pensions were raised to £1,300 a year.

[124] 'It must be remembered', writes John Randle in *Battle Tales from Burma*, 'that to the Indian soldier his "izzat", his personal honour, was the mainspring of his moral motivation. A man convicted of desertion would be forever disgraced in his village and his community. It had to be driven home that battle discipline, even wounds or death, were preferable to loss of "izzat".'

Chapter 8: Imphal

[125] *Sunset in the East*, John Hudson, Leo Cooper, 2002

[126] *Defeat into Victory*

[127] *Sunset in the East*

[128] *Forgotten Voices of the Second World War*

[129] Ibid.

[130] About half the 61,000 were British, slightly fewer than a quarter Australian and the rest were Dutch. The total also included about 700 Americans.

[131] *Battle Tales from Burma*

[132] *Images of War*

[133] Born on January 23, 1897 and reported killed in an air crash on August 18, 1945 the Indian nationalist leader Subhas Chandra Bose who adopted the title 'Netaji' or 'Respected Leader' remains one of the more controversial figures in modern Indian history.

Highly intelligent, a graduate of Fitzwilliam College, Cambridge, England he was elected president of the Indian National Congress for two consecutive terms but resigned because he advocated violent resistance to British rule in India. He believed that Mahatma Gandhi's tactics of non-violence would never secure India's independence.

Bose was a powerful and charismatic speaker and produced what today would be known as memorable sound bites: 'Give me your blood and I will give you your freedom' resonated with many Indians, as did 'If people slap you once, slap them twice'.

He established his own party, the All India Forward Bloc demanding full and immediate independence of India from British rule. Inevitably he fell foul of the authorities and was imprisoned eleven times.

To him World War II was an opportunity to exploit British weakness. He fled India in disguise and travelled via Afghanistan and the USSR, to Nazi Germany. Hitler showed little interest in Indian independence, Bose became disillusioned and in 1943 decided to leave Germany where from 1941 he had been living with his Austrian wife Schenkl. He travelled by the submarine U-180 via the Cape of Good Hope to link up with the Japanese submarine I29 off South Africa and thence on to Imperial Japan where he met the War Minister Hideki Tojo.

Though he had helped raise a force of Indian troops from PoWs in Germany to assist the Wehrmacht, the numbers were not large, and it was more of a token force. Now with Japanese financial, political, diplomatic and military support he was closer to realising his dream. The Indian National Army formed from Indian PoWs and plantation workers from Malaya and Singapore would spearhead the attack to liberate India within the political structure of Azad Hind 'Free India' movement.

[134] *The Faraway War*, Richard J. Aldrich, Doubleday, 2005

[135] Powered by two 2,000 hp Pratt & Whitney R-2800–51 Double Wasp radial engines the Curtiss C-46 Commando, like the Dakota, was originally a commercial aircraft. It had a range of 1,200 miles and maximum speed of 269 mph. Crucially it could carry 54 troops or 50,675 pounds of cargo.

[136] *History of the Second World War*, Purnell & Sons

[137] A rumour had circulated amongst American personnel in Burma that the injury was the result of a punch thrown by the irascible General 'Vinegar Joe' Stilwell – it was actually caused by a bamboo splinter.

[138] The plans for the role of the INA in U-GO that were agreed by Bose and Kawabe envisaged the INA having its own sector and operating at battalion strength. In fact when the HA-GO and U-GO offensives were launched the main unit involved was Subhas Brigade or 1 Guerrilla Regiment that consisted of three infantry battalions, commanded by Col Shah Nawaz Khan. It covered the Japanese flanks against attacks by Chin and Kachin guerrillas during the Chindwin River crossing and advance into the Naga Hills. However, by the time the 1st Guerrilla Regiment left Tamu, U-GO was stalled and the INA troops were redirected to Kohima to beef up the attack. They arrived too late as the 31 Division was beginning to withdraw. Now they were starving, soaked by the monsoon and under attack by the RAF and USAAF as well as local Naga guerrillas. While some of the INA joined the hopeless retreat of Fifteenth Army others decided that surrender was a wiser course.

[139] *Sunset in the East*

[140] *The Little Men*

[141] *Images of War*. It is difficult to place exactly where this action took place, however it amply illustrates the hazardous nature of the fighting and increasingly exotic and improvised character of the weapons employed.

[142] According to the Harrieses in *Soldiers of the Sun* the grenade was called a *chibi-dan* or tich bomb. 'The bomb was a thick glass sphere the size of a baseball, containing prussic acid in liquid form; this turned to gas when the glass shattered against the tank's armour, and streams of white smoke were drawn in through the aperture, asphyxiating the crew.'

In *Tank Tracks to Rangoon* Bryan Perrett has an account of an attack on a 7

Armoured Brigade Stuart earlier in the war during the withdrawal through Burma. Lt John Parry of the 7th Hussars describes how a Japanese soldier on a road block attacked Troop Sergeant Campbell's tank and threw a phial into the turret. Apparently this phial contained some form of knock-out gas which immediately overcame the crew inside the turret, Campbell, who was unaffected as his head was outside the turret, acted with great presence of mind, and slid into the driving compartment, sitting on the unconscious driver. He managed to manoeuvre the tank out of trouble and then scrambled back into the turret and operated his guns on the enemy position.' These attacks with chemical grenades were local and not sanctioned, since the Japanese High Command were aware that extensive use of chemical weapons would trigger a massive Allied retaliation.

[143] *Battle Tales from Burma.* John Randle adds that in the 1990s the All Burma Veteran Association of Japan (ABVAJ) received permission from the Indian government to erect a memorial to the 190,000 Japanese killed in the Burma campaign. The site chosen was Red Hill and a Service of Reconciliation held there with ABVAJ and the (British) Burma Campaign Fellowship Group in 2001.

[144] *Soldiers of the Sun*

[145] *Forgotten Voices of the Second World War*

[146] L. Allen, *Burma The Longest War 1941–45*, Phoenix Press, 2000

[147] *Images of War*

[148] Richard Aldrich, *The Faraway War*, Doubleday, 2005

[149] *The Campaign in Burma*

Chapter 9: Kohima

[150] Though pre-war psychological warfare operations by Japanese intelligence officers had built up internal resistance to the British and Dutch by fostering nationalism in their colonies, their efforts with the Nagas were a failure. Speaking in English a Japanese officer addressed a group of Nagas. 'Before the war, the East people was thought for animal by our enemies English and USA. Now we treat for a dear friend by Nippon, and build a happy countries by their own hands . . . India has many guns, balls, swords tanks and motor cars which is presented by Nippon. You can strike English by your own hands . . . To capture a happy India please you will give me much rices, grains, cows, pigs, hens, eggs and so on. Rice is equal to a hard hammer knocks down our enemies.'

[151] *The War Years 1939–1945 Eyewitness Accounts*, Marshall Cavendish, 1994

[152] *Kohima*, Arthur Swinson, Cassell, 1960

[153] *Forgotten Voices of the Second World War*

[154] Ibid.

[155] Ibid.

[156] Ibid.

[157] Ibid.

[158] Ibid.

[159] *The Campaign in Burma*

[160] *Kohima*, A. Swinson, Cassell, 1960

[161] *Forgotten Voices of the Second World War*

[162] Randle's brother-in-law Flying Officer Leslie Manser VC had won a posthumous VC over Belgium on the night of May 31, 1942 when following flak damage he ensured that the crew had parachuted to safety before the aircraft went out of control and crashed.

[163] *Forgotten Voices of the Second World War*

[164] Ibid.

[165] *Tank Tracks to Rangoon*

[166] *History of the Second World War*, Purnell & Sons

[167] *The Campaign in Burma*

[168] *Sunset in the East*

Chapter 10: The Road to Mandalay

[169] *Sunset in the East*

[170] *History of the Second World War*, Purnell & Sons

[171] *Sunset in the East*

[172] *The Campaign in Burma*

[173] *Tank Tracks to Rangoon*

[174] Developed from the GMC 6 × 6 2.5-ton truck chassis the DUKW, universally known as the 'Duck', was the brainchild of an American ocean-racing yacht designer. The US Army was initially resistant to the concept of an amphibious truck, but the rescue by a prototype DUKW of the crew of a Coast Guard cutter during a storm off the US east coast convinced them of its utility. Over 21,000 would be built before the end of the war.

With a crew of two the DUKW weighed 14,880 lb was 37 ft long and had a road speed of 50 mph and water speed of 6 mph. Its ability to transit smoothly from water to land carrying a useful cargo ensured that from 1942 onwards it would become a key vehicle in the amphibious operations in Europe and the Far East.

[175] *Defeat into Victory*

[176] These were either Model 93 or 100, weapons that had a range of 25 to 30 yards with bursts of 10 to 12 seconds. The tanks held 3.25 gallons of fuel that was pressurised by a nitrogen tank.

[177] *Forgotten Voices of the Second World War*

[178] *Mars & Clio*, Autumn 2007, The British Commission for Military History

[179] *Slim, Master of War*

[180] *Forgotten Voices of the Second World War*

[181] *The Campaign in Burma*

[182] *History of the Second World War*, Purnell & Sons

[183] These would probably have been men from COPP, Combined Operations Pilotage Parties – experienced swimmers and canoeists with excellent navigational skills.

[184] *The Little Men*

[185] Ibid.

[186] *Quartered Safe Out Here*, G. M. Fraser, HarperCollins, 1992. George MacDonald Fraser would enjoy a distinguished career as an author and scriptwriter and after the war made his name with his *Flashman* series of carefully researched and racy historical

novels. In Burma serving with 9 Section, B Company, 9 Battalion The Border Regiment he was busted from Lance Corporal to Private three times for minor offences, one of them losing a tea urn.
[187] *The Little Men*

Chapter 11: Arakan – The Final Offensive
[188] *The Campaign in Burma*
[189] *Storm from the Sea*, Lt Col Peter Young, William Kimber, 1958
[190] *Forgotten Voices of the Second World War.*

General Sir Hugh Charles Stockwell would serve with distinction in the British Army after World War II. In November 1956, following its illegal nationalisation by the Egyptians, he would command the landing force in the ill-fated Operation Musketeer, the Anglo-French airborne and amphibious assault to recapture the Suez Canal.
[191] *Storm from the Sea*
[192] Ibid.
[193] Ibid.
[194] Launched in 1913 HMS *Queen Elizabeth* was a veteran of the Gallipoli landings in World War I. She had survived an audacious attack by Italian frogmen in Alexandria harbour in December 1941 and after an overhaul and refit in the United States sailed for the Far East. In addition to fire support in Burma as part of a naval task force she also shelled Japanese installations in the Dutch East Indies.

Chapter 12: Air Power
[195] *Forgotten Voices of the Second World War*
[196] Ibid.
[197] Ibid.
[198] Designed by the talented Igor Sikorsky the Sikorsky experimental XR-4 helicopter made its first flight at Stratford, Connecticut on January 14, 1942. The production YR-4 was powered by a 189 hp Warner R-550–1 radial piston engine, had a maximum speed of 75 mph and range of 130 miles. Its use by the Air Commando was in effect an operational trial of a new aircraft type in the very testing conditions of the Burma theatre.
[199] Tanks captured at Imphal were the subject of a weapons trial with Hurricane IICs and IIDs. The IIDs fired 128 rounds gaining 33 hits while the quad 20mm cannon armed IICs of No 11 Squadron fired 680 rounds and gained only 19 hits.
[200] *The Little Men*
[201] *A Child at Arms*
[202] *The Campaign in Burma*
[203] *Ginger Lacey Fighter Pilot*, Richard Townsend Bickers, Robert Hale, 1962
[204] *Forgotten Voices of the Second World War*

Chapter 13: Victory in Burma
[205] Not a man to be overawed by Stilwell, General Festing was reported to have stuck his head into the tent that Stilwell used as his austere NCAC headquarters and said

cheerfully, 'Festing reporting for duty, sir. Any orders?' To which 'Vinegar' Joe without raising his eyes from the situation map replied 'Take Taungyi'.

[206] *A Change of Jungles*, M. Smeeton, Rupert Hart-Davis, 1962

[207] *Slim as a Military Commander*, Geoffrey Evans, B. T. Batsford, 1969

[208] *Images of War*

[209] *Forgotten Voices of the Second World War*

[210] *Images of War*

[211] *Battle Tales from Burma*

Chapter 14: Death on the Sittang

[212] Commonly known by the Allies as the Nambu, the Type 11 LMG was designed by the prolific General Kijiro Nambu, entered service in 1922 and was known by the Japanese as the *Taisho 11 nen Kikanju*. It was the standard Japanese Army LMG in 1941 though it was replaced by the Type 96 and 99 later in the war. It drew on Hotchkiss principles but had an unusual feed mechanism in the shape of a hopper. Up to 30 rounds in standard five round clips could be dropped into it, however the complex mechanism could not handle the powerful rifle rounds, so to operate it required its own lower powered 6.5mm ammunition. The gun was capable of automatic fire only, firing at 500 rpm.

[213] Sergeant Dave Richardson, *Yank*, July 1945

[214] *The Faraway War*

[215] Honda was assisted in his own escape from encirclement by the redoubtable but insubordinate Colonel Tsuji who last appeared in the successful campaign in Malaya. The Japanese intelligence officer left a note for the British: 'Sorry to cause you so much trouble. This spot is where Lt Gen Honda was. Try harder next time. Sayonara.'

[216] J. Bowen, *Undercover in the Jungle*, William Kimber, 1978, quoted in *Soldiers of the Sun*

[217] *Soldiers of the Sun*

251

BIBLIOGRAPHY

Alanbrooke, Field Marshal Lord, *War Diaries 1939–1945*, Weidenfeld & Nicolson, 2001

Aldrich, Richard J., *The Faraway War*, Doubleday, 2005

Allen, L., *Burma The Longest War 1941–45*, Phoenix Press, 2000

Arthur, Max, *Forgotten Voices of the Second World War*, Ebury Press, 2004

Barber, Noel, *Sinister Twilight: The Fall of Singapore*, Collins, 1968

Bevan, Nicholas (editor), *Images of War*, Marshall Cavendish, 1988

Bickers, Richard Townsend, *Ginger Lacey Fighter Pilot*, Robert Hale, 1962

Bull, Dr Stephen, *World War II Jungle Warfare Tactics*, Osprey Elite, 2007

Calvert, Michael, *Prisoners of Hope*, Jonathan Cape, 1952

Cooper, K. W., *The Little Men*, Robert Hale, 1973

Cross, J. P., *Jungle Warfare Experiences and Encounters*, Arms and Armour Press, 1989

Davis, Patrick, *A Child at Arms*, Hutchinson & Co, 1970

Dennis, Peter, Grey, Jeffrey, Morris, Ewan, Prior, Robin with Connor, John, *The Oxford Companion to Australian Military History*, Oxford University Press, 1995

Elphick, Peter & Smith, Michael, *Odd Man Out, the Story of the Singapore Traitor*, Trafalgar Square, 1994

Evans, Geoffrey, *Slim as a Military Commander*, B.T. Batsford, 1969

Fergusson, Bernard, *Beyond the Chindwin*, Collins, 1945

The Wild Green Earth, Collins, 1946

Fraser, George MacDonald, *Quartered Safe Out Here*, HarperCollins, 1992

Fuller, Richard, *Shōkan Hirohito's Samurai*, Arms and Armour, 1992

Gates Memorial Trust (The), http://www.mgtrust.org/afr2.htm

Glover, Michael, *An Improvised War The Abyssinian Campaign of 1940–1941*, Leo Cooper, 1987

Harries, Meirion and Susie, *Soldiers of the Sun*, William Heinemann, 1991

Haruko Taya Cook & Theodore F. Cook, *Japan at War an Oral History*, The New Press, 1992

Hudson, John, *Sunset in the East*, Leo Cooper, 2002

Kirby, Major-General S. W., *The War against Japan*, Vols I to IV, HMSO, 1955

Latimer, Jon, *Burma the Forgotten War*, John Murray, 2004

Lyman, Robert, *Slim, Master of War*, Constable & Robinson, 2004

Mant, Gilbert, *Grim Glory*, Currawong, 1942, rev. edn 1955

Masters, John, *Bugles and a Tiger: A Personal Adventure*, Michael Joseph, 1956
The Road past Mandalay, Michael Joseph, 1961

Maule, Henry, *Spearhead General*, Odhams Press, 1961

McKie, R., *Echoes from Forgotten Wars*, William Collins, 1980

Messenger, Charles, *World War Two Chronological Atlas*, Bloomsbury, 1989

Montgomery-Massingberg, Hugh (editor), the *Daily Telegraph Record of the Second World War*, Sidgwick & Jackson, 1989

Owen, Lt Colonel Frank, *The Campaign in Burma*, HMSO, 1946

Percival, Arthur Ernest, *The War in Malaya*, London, Eyre & Spottiswoode, 1949

Perrett, Bryan, *Tank Tracks to Rangoon*, Robert Hale, 1978

Pitt, Barrie, *History of the Second World War*, Purnell & Sons, 1966

Randle, John, *Battle Tales from Burma*, Pen & Sword, 2004

Shores, Christopher, *Ground Attack Aircraft of World War II*, Macdonald and Janes, 1977

Slim, Field Marshal Sir William, *Defeat into Victory*, Cassell & Co Ltd, 1956

Smeeton, M., *A Change of Jungles*, Rupert Hart-Davis, 1962

Smyth, J., *Milestones*, Sidgwick & Jackson, 1979

Spector, Ronald H., *Eagle against the Sun*, Viking, 1984

Stilwell, J., *The Stilwell Papers*, ed. T. H. White, Macdonald, 1949

Swinson, Arthur, *Kohima*, Cassell, 1960
Four Samurai – A Quartet of Japanese Army Commanders in the Second World War, Hutchinson, 1968

TM-E 30–480 *Handbook on Japanese Military Forces*, US Government Printing Office, Washington, 1944

Tsuji, M., *Singapore 1941–42: The Japanese Version of the Malayan Campaign of World War II*, Sydney, NSW, 1960

Tulloch, Derek, *Wingate in Peace and War*, Macdonald and Co, 1972

INDEX

Ghana 54–5
Gideon Force 93
Gilkes, Major K. D. 98
Gokteik viaduct 97–8
Goppe Pass 118–19
Gracey, Major-General Douglas 137, 201
Great Britain 21, 62–3
Greater Asia Co-Prosperity Sphere 16, 20
Grover, Major General John 159–60
guided bombs 194

Hackney, Lt Ben 42–3
Haile Selassie 93
Haiphong 20
Hanaya, Lt General Tadashi 117, 118
Hanoi 20
Hardman, Air Commodore J. D. 193
Hardy, Brigadier Campbell 178–9
Harman, Lt Carter 190
Harman, Lance Corporal John 156
Harries, Meiron and Susie 53, 118, 145
Harumichi, Nogi 22
Hawker Hurricane MkIIC 186–7
Heath, Lt General Lewis 28
helicopters 189–90
Himalayas, the 189
Hiroshima, atomic bomb dropped on 219
Hobson, Lt Colonel Pat 119
Homalin 135
Homma, General Masaharu 37
Honda, General Masaki 197, 202, 204, 205, 217–18
Hong Kong, fall of 23–4
Hope Thomson, M. R. J. 152, 153
Horner, Lt Sam 60
Hsian 51
Hswipaw 202
Hudson, Wing Commander 'Bill' 216
Hudson, Lieutenant John 55–6, 60, 128, 129, 138–9, 141, 150, 162, 163, 164
Hugh-Jones, Brigadier N. 70, 72
Hutton, Lt General Tom 66, 67, 73

Iida, General Shojiro 63, 130, 132
Imperial Defence College 9
Imperial Japanese Army Air Force 178, 187, 189
 III Air Group 32, 43
 III Air Division 27
 5 Air Division 64
 22 Air Flotilla 34–5
Imperial Japanese Navy 18, 27, 77
Imphal offensive
 terrain 128
 communications 128–9
 Japanese planning and preparations 130–6
 supplies 133–4, 138
 aerial resupply 133, 139, 192
 objectives 135
 British forces 136–7
 Japanese assault 137–40
 aerial reinforcement 139–40
 the defence 140–3
 armoured action 140–1
 air support 142, 190
 Japanese attacks come to halt 143–5
 Japanese collapse 145–8
 assessment 147–8
 Mountbatten on 223
Indaw 106
Indian Independence League 22–3
Indian National Army (INA) 56–7, 124–5, 134–5, 174, 216, 232–3
Indian Nationalists 64
Indo China 20
Inland Water Transport Service 167
Iran 13
Iraq 12–14
Irrawaddy River 31–2, 61, 77, 78, 79, 97, 110, 170–1, 173, 197–9
Irrawaddy River assault crossing 173–7, 190
Irwin, General Noel 84–5, 90
Italy 10–11, 17
Ito, Major 146–7
Iwaichi, Major Fujiwara 22–3